AN ALTERNATIVE VISION

The Socialist Party in the 1930's

AN ALTERNATIVE VISION

The Socialist Party in the 1930's

Frank A. Warren

INDIANA UNIVERSITY PRESS

Bloomington & London

To Joyce

Published in Canada by Fitzhenry & Whiteside Limited,
Don Mills, Ontario

Manufactured in the United States of America

Library of Congress Cataloging in Publication Data

Warren, Frank A
  An alternative vision.

—Bibliography: p. 195
  1. Socialist Party (U. S.)   I. Title.
JK2391.S6W37 1974   329′.81   74-181
ISBN 0-253-30520-9

Contents

v
HISTORY

vi   Contents

Acknowledgments

During the researching and writing of this book, there was much to be discouraged about in the United States; the politics of the present constantly impinged upon my more scholarly activities. That the work is completed is due in large part to those people who encouraged me to believe that "lost causes" had their own interest and that the perspective I brought to the lost cause of the Socialist Party during the 1930's made a valuable addition to the understanding of our radical past. I hope that I have not disappointed them.

The members of my original undergraduate seminar in American Socialism first encouraged me to think that I had something useful to say. The members—Maddy Heller, Rhea Margulies, Lew Smoley, Sam Kagan, Peter Weissman, Laura Oren, Arthur Hascup, Mike Goldstein, Sharon Rosenhause—all contributed research, ideas, and inspiration. Students too numerous to mention in subsequent classes, both graduate and undergraduate, also have made similar contributions. An article that furnished the basic perspective for the book was solicited by Professor Daniel Walden of Pennsylvania State University for a special issue of the *Journal of Human Relations*. Later, the issue was printed as a paperback entitled *The Ambiguous Legacy*. The response of Professor Walden and a number of other scholars to the article encouraged me to develop my arguments further. A summer grant from the American Philosophical Society and two research grants from the City University of New York provided me with the opportunity to pursue the necessary research. A number of librarians have been very kind to me. I wish to mention, in particular, Mrs. Dorothy Swanson of the Tamiment Library, New York University, and Mr. Paul Rugin and Miss Jean R. McNiece of the Manuscript Division of the New York Public Library. Their gracious help in fulfilling my requests was constant over a period of several years. The librarians at the William B. Perkins Collection at Duke University were also extremely generous in their aid. Mr. Evan W. Thomas kindly granted me permission to use his late father's papers. For the typing of the manuscript, I am especially grateful to Mrs. Thelma Daub, Mrs. Catherine O'Looney, and Mrs. Ruth Estwick.

I am deeply indebted to Miss Lilian Bombach, Mr. Stephen Freiband, and Mr. Grant Morrison, who aided me with research in the periodical literature. To George Kirschner, especially, I owe a deep debt. Not only did he help me greatly in my research in the Norman Thomas Papers, but in long discussions he enlightened me with the wisdom gained from his years as an activist. There will be, I am sure, many judgments and analyses in the book with which George will disagree, but I have learned from him as I hope he has learned from me. To my colleagues and friends, Michael Wreszin, Solomon Resnik, and Raymond Franklin, I owe a special note of thanks. Mike read the book in manuscript and made many useful comments. Sol and Ray have encouraged me along the way. Again, I am certain that there will be opinions throughout the book with which they will strongly disagree. But I want them to know in print that the many enlightening discussions and the varieties of causes that we have participated in over the past several years have contributed to my education as a radical, even if that education has meant, at times, defining the limits of my radicalism. Perhaps in some way that education has contributed to this book.

Finally, there are my most personal debts. My parents—over seventy and still peace activists—continue to inspire me. My children—Victoria, Catherine, and Charlotte—far from being the burdens and causes for delay that many scholars either write or joke about, have brought only pleasure and joy. For so many, many things, the book is dedicated to my wife, Joyce.

Introduction

"For Socialists . . . the challenge is not to be freer than the worst, but to be really free." These words, written in 1935 by Devere Allen, chief author of the controversial 1934 Declaration of Principles and a leading Socialist and advisor to Norman Thomas, seem peculiarly old-fashioned today. In an age where politics, despite the rebirth of radicalism in the 1960's, is still defined not simply as the art of the possible, but as the art of the immediately possible, such vague utopian sentiments with their overtones of historical optimism can hardly be said to characterize the political scene. Though few Socialists today would support, as a theoretical proposition, the principle of the "lesser evil," that is exactly what the majority of the Socialist Party today does in practice. The optimistic spirit behind Allen's remark, a spirit which gave it concrete meaning in terms of politics, has disappeared. Norman Thomas, who constantly accented the essential meaninglessness of the Democratic-Republican alternatives in the 1930's, endorsed John F. Kennedy, a far less radical president than Roosevelt, in 1960. And the main body of the Socialist Party for all intents and purposes lined up behind Lyndon B. Johnson in 1964, and clearly supported Hubert Humphrey in 1968, thereby taking a position that in the eyes of the party in the 1930's would have been considered class-collaborationism *par excellence.* Circumstances change, and the issue of presidential endorsement is only one measure of radicalism. Yet the distance between opposing both old parties and endorsing Democratic presidential candidates measures symbolically the vast chasm that separates the radical hopes of the 1930's from the precarious politics of Socialists today. If a faith in the direction of history and in the possibility of being "really free" symbolizes the drama of Socialism in the thirties, it is the image of Sisyphus that most characterizes Socialist assumptions today—whether those assumptions are the reformism that operates within the official Socialist Party or the more intransigent socialism that characterizes many outside of it.[1]

It might be expected that post-World War II historians and political commentators with a vague sympathy for the Left would have bemoaned this loss of optimistic élan. Perhaps there are some Socialists and a few liberals working toward a liberal-radical synthesis who have been so inclined. But historians who have directly or indirectly addressed themselves during the years following World War II to the history of Socialism have more or less calmly accepted this diminishing élan as part of the growth of wisdom. David Shannon in his history of the American Socialist Party criticized the Socialist Party of the thirties for failing to deal with the practical day-to-day problems of building grass-roots support, and though his book is generally sympathetic to the party, it does not serve as a defense against the criticisms of Socialist ideology that can be found in Daniel Bell's *Marxian Socialism in America* and *The End of Ideology* or in Arthur M. Schlesinger, Jr.'s *The Vital Center*. In fact, in so far as Shannon faults Socialism largely for its failure to concentrate on the immediately practical, it can be said that he reinforces the general critique by Schlesinger and Bell.

Schlesinger, writing in 1949, was anxious to reinvigorate the postwar politics of something he labeled the "democratic left"; Bell, in *The End of Ideology* (1960), was analyzing the decline of a period in history which spanned the period from the early nineteenth century to the mid-twentieth. Neither was writing a history of American Socialism in the thirties, but a view of Socialism in this decade emerged from their writings. This picture is one of a Socialism that was overly optimistic concerning man and history, rigidly and dogmatically wedded to ideology, and ineffectual in its diagnosis and analysis of politics. In contrast to this excess of ideology, Bell and Schlesinger applauded a politics of limited objectives and compromise. Schlesinger wrote optimistically of the rediscovery of "the tradition of a reasonable responsibility about politics and a moderate pessimism about man." And Bell wrote that "one ultimately comes to admire the 'practical politics' of Theodore Roosevelt and his scorn for the intransigents, like Godkin and Villard, who, refusing to yield to expediency, could never put through their reforms." In short, the loss of faith in the possibility of being "really free" and an adherence to the "lesser-evil" politics of being "freer than the worst" marked the beginning of political insight.[2]

And now Norman Thomas has arrived historically—to be judged by the tenets of historical realism and practical politics. Thomas's earlier biographers, Harry Fleischman and Murray Seidler, wrote sympathetically and compassionately, though even they were quick to criticize the heady radicalism of the Militants of the early 1930's, a radicalism they believed Thomas tolerated too leniently. But in Bernard Johnpoll's recent biography, *Pacifist's Progress,* Thomas has been subjected to an extended historical critique from a point of view closely related to Bell's theoretical assumptions about the ways and means of politics. As everyone's radical, however, Norman Thomas can not be dismissed in a simplistic and one-sided manner, and Johnpoll must, and does, give credit to his dedication, his goals, his ideals, his sincerity. He was, in short, a "success as a human being." But he was, Johnpoll claims, a failure as a politician. This startling bit of news resulted from Thomas's puristic "search for absolute ideals," when, as we all know, politics is the "art of the possible." Unwilling to compromise, leaning too heavily on youth's adulation, unable to comprehend the workingman's bread-and-butter aspirations, irre-

sponsible in not trying to mediate the serious internal party differences of the 1930's, Norman Thomas was, in this view, one of the
main reasons for the decline of Socialism and the Socialist Party.[3]

This book approaches the Socialist Party of the 1930's from a
perspective that would restrict neither politics in general nor
Socialist politics in particular to as narrow a framework as the
"ultra-realism" of Bell, Schlesinger, and Johnpoll. It does not
provide a definitive history of the Socialist Party in the 1930's—
that task is still open and necessary. Nor is it even general "party"
history in a traditional sense, though it does touch on many of the
issues that a traditional history would include. Rather, it is an
analysis of some of the problems the Socialist Party faced in the
1930's, a defense of the Party during those years, and a critique of
the major interpreters of American socialism and radicalism. Its
chief targets are, as may already be obvious, Daniel Bell's works
on radicalism, the pragmatic liberal politics represented by Arthur
M. Schlesinger, Jr., and Bernard Johnpoll's recent evaluation of
Norman Thomas. The criticism of the points of view presented
by these men and their works (which criticism does not imply that
the books are without value) is part of the defense of Socialism:
a critique of pragmatic liberal politics is conjoined with a defense
of the ideological Socialist politics of the 1930's. In defending
Socialist politics, however, I hope that I do not do so uncritically.
There were many questions the Socialists did not answer; many
problems for radicals they failed to meet; many developments of
American capitalism they did not confront. But it is the thrust of
the politics that I find meaningful. It gave them, as I argue in this
book, *an angle of vision* which permitted them to analyze and
evaluate many events which, if it did not solve the practical problem
of party building or movement building, kept alive, in hard times,
a resistance to oppression and an intransigence against the forces of
state and industry that can overwhelm us.

With the rebirth of radicalism in the 1960's, the critique of
the liberal "art of the possible" might seem superfluous in some
quarters. Indeed there is something quixotic about setting out to

defend a brand of radicalism that has been rejected by its own party and by many, if not most, of the elements in that amorphous movement called "the New Left." The Socialist Party, in its headlong rush to embrace the center of the Democratic Party, has found its own politics of the thirties fundamentally in error; the New Left, in its struggle to find new forms of radicalism, has found little that is relevant in the Socialist politics of the thirties. Both, I believe, are wrong. But my purpose is not to write a corrective to the present-day Left's sins of commission and omission. It will be enough if this book makes a small dent in the values of the historical profession. For despite many attacks on the theoretical framework of politics as the "art of the possible," and despite overwhelming evidence of its failures in practice, the historical profession continues, for the most part, its stolid defense of this limited conception of politics. History suggests, to many historians, the limited, the complex, the contingent. And so perhaps it should. But if these are not to become the acquiescent, the adjusted, the paralyzed, other values must be asserted. I hope this book will contribute toward doing so. As for the non-historians whose path this book should happen to cross: for the older, it may recall old issues forgotten, but perhaps now necessary to recall if any new start is to be made; for the young, it may teach them something about the history of radicalism, its difficulties and dilemmas, and perhaps that there exists a posture between a kind of nihilistic "worse-the-better" philosophy and the pragmatic acquiescence into practical liberalism. That many have already learned this is only to the good. That some have not; that some have perceived it, but have been unable to translate this perception into meaningful action; that others have perceived it and, perceiving the tremendous chasm between individual actions and what must be done, have retreated into apolitical solutions—this is part of the tragedy of our time.

PART ONE

The Socialist Party and the "Realist" Critique

I

The Realist Critique Examined

BY 1928, Socialist Party membership, which had numbered over 100,000 before World War I, was reduced to less than 8,000. Norman Thomas's first presidential candidacy in 1928 brought some new interest in the Party. The 1929 depression quickened economic discontent, and in 1930 the Socialist Party, with Clarence Senior as a new and active national secretary, began to show signs of growth. Membership rose from 9,500 in 1929 to almost 17,000 in 1932. But the superficial signs of growth could not hide the increasing divisions in the Party that were caused by the emergence of Norman Thomas and the "progressive" Socialists and left-wing Militants who challenged Morris Hillquit's leadership of the Socialist Party. The challenge to Hillquit failed at the 1932 convention, but the issues that divided the factions were barely set aside for the 1932 presidential campaign.

The left-wing Militants' sympathy for Russia, their critique of a parliamentary road to power, their demand for a more activist trade-union policy led them into a showdown struggle with the Old Guard leadership, which had passed to James Oneal and Algernon Lee after Hillquit's death in 1933. The struggle reached an intense peak at the 1934 Socialist Party Convention in Detroit. At the Convention, Norman Thomas, the progressives, the Militants, and the Wisconsin Socialists led by Mayor Daniel Hoan of Milwaukee were able to pass a new Declaration of Principles. The Declaration of Principles manifested too much sympathy for Russia and too great an emphasis on a nonelectoral seizure of power for the Old Guard to accept it readily. For the next two years a constant struggle for control of the Party took place. Party membership, which had grown as high as 20,000 in 1934, began to decline. By 1936, when the Old Guard split from the Socialist Party to form the Social Democratic Federation, the membership had declined to less than 12,000. The withdrawal of the Old Guard did not bring calm to the Party. The Trotskyists, who had joined the Socialist Party in 1936, were forced out the next year, and for the remainder of the 1930's the left-wing Clarity group struggled with former Militants like Jack Altman and Paul Porter for control of party policy. Norman Thomas, who had received over 800,000 votes for president in 1932, could only obtain 187,000 in 1936—a figure only 12,000 more than he received when he ran for mayor of New York in 1929. By 1937 the membership was down to 6,500—the lowest it had ever been. And in 1940, with the Party badly split over the war issue, Thomas was to receive fewer than 19,000 votes.[1]

The record is hardly auspicious. In the midst of a severe depression, a radical party that declined in influence and power as the decade progressed; a party beset by internal feuding throughout the decade; a party that was consistently critical during the 1930's of the popularly-supported New Deal—it is not surprising that such a party would receive its share of criticism in the post-World War II period. The decline of all forms of left-wing radicalism after World War II, the emergence of the Cold War, and the seeming viability of liberal capitalism all contributed to what I have labeled the "realistic" critique of the Socialist Party of the 1930's. It is my contention that, when examined, this critique tells us more about the values of its spokesmen than about the failures of the Socialist Party.

The critique of the Socialist Party in the 1930's by Daniel Bell, Arthur M. Schlesinger, Jr., and Bernard Johnpoll derives from a framework of "realism." The word realism is used here not in a philosophical sense, but to describe the approach to politics that has prized limited results and has disparaged those critics and parties who have demanded more fundamental societal change as impractical and unworldly. This "realistic" critique of Socialism, the Socialist Party, and Norman Thomas covers many bases. But central to its vision is their failure to appreciate the kind of "pragmatic give-and-take" politics that might bring tangible, if limited, reforms. It first becomes necessary, then, to explore the adequacy of this vision.

Pietism, Pragmatism, and Politics

In *The End of Ideology,* Daniel Bell writes that, within the frame of societal rewards, privileges, obligations, and duties, "ethics deals with the *ought* of distribution. . . . Politics is the concrete *mode* of distribution, involving a power struggle between organized groups to determine the allocation of privilege." He then praises Max Weber's distinction between politics as an "ethic of responsibility" and politics as an "ethic of conscience." The former, he says, "is the pragmatic view which seeks reconciliation as its goal. The latter creates 'true believers' who burn with pure, unquenchable flame and can accept no compromise with faith." From this analysis, Bell concludes that rather than work toward pragmatic compromise, the Socialists tended to wander off toward a chiliasm that would overthrow the entire system and usher in the eternal reign of glory. In *The Vital Center,* Schlesinger, in a much less sophisticated way, draws a similar dichotomy between the "vital center" of liberal reform and the utopian seekers for absolute perfection. More recently, in *A Thousand Days,* Schlesinger has repeated his stark categories:

> From the start of the republic American progressivism had had two strains, related but distinct. The pragmatic strain accepted, without wholly approving, the given structure of society and aimed to change it by action from within. The

utopian strain rejected the given structure of society, root and branch, and aimed to change it by exhortation and example from without. The one sprang from the philosophy of Locke and Hume; its early exemplars were Franklin and Jefferson. The other sprang from the religion of the millenarians; its early exemplars were George Fox and, in a secularized version, Robert Owen. The one regarded history as a continuity, in which mankind progressed from the intolerable to the faintly bearable. The other regarded history as an alternation of catastrophe and salvation, in which a new turn of the road must somehow bring humanity to a new heaven and a new earth. The one was practical and valued results. The other was prophetic and valued revelations. The one believed in piecemeal improvements, the other in total solutions.

And when one examines Johnpoll's catalogue of Norman Thomas's sins, one discovers that, in many ways, it too is a restatement, with more historical data, of Bell's and Schlesinger's categories. Weber's ethic of responsibility and Schlesinger's belief in "piecemeal improvements" becomes "the art of the possible," a mode of operation in which, according to Johnpoll, Thomas did not excel. Weber's ethic of conscience and Schlesinger's belief in total solutions becomes the search for absolute ideals, a pursuit in which Thomas, the exemplar of the Social Gospeler, was, according to Johnpoll, most at home—to the detriment of the building of Socialism and the Socialist Party.[2]

One need hardly deny the chiliastic overtones in much Socialist literature, or the "idealism" of Norman Thomas, to recognize that this neat dichotomy, while perceptive in theory, has been used to load the dice against Socialist politics and in favor of the Theodore Roosevelt tradition of "practical politics." What must be tentatively explored here is not so much American Socialism, which, as indeed Bell recognizes, had its pragmatic moments along with its chiliastic fevers, but American politics itself to see whether such a stark dichotomy can be drawn.[3]

In a provocative essay, William McLoughlin has argued that the American character is as much pietistic (a quality close to

Bell's definition of chiliasm) as pragmatic. In particular, he has
written of American politics:

> Now it may be argued that regardless of campaign slogans
> the American two . . . party system is essentially a compro-
> mise system. . . . It might even be argued that the doctrinaire
> politics of the multi-party systems of Europe are more morally
> rigid than American politics. But the weight of these argu-
> ments is really the other way around. Doctrinaire political
> parties are immoral by American pietistic standards because
> they insist that all politicians and party members vote not as
> their consciences tell them but as their party line tells them.
> American political parties, while resting upon compromise
> between the pietistic extremes of right and left, are neverthe-
> less dedicated to the belief that the compromise itself is the
> only right and just course toward the millennium.

Without asserting that McLoughlin's analysis holds static for all
American history (there have been periods when pietism was more
prevalent than in others), it becomes necessary to recognize that
American politics has also sought a millennium; the Socialists have
not been the only seekers after perfection. Thus, Andrew Jackson
slew the "hydra-headed monster" to restore Arcadia, and Theodore
Roosevelt, in a flourish that would have embarrassed the "moral
figure" of Norman Thomas, stood at Armageddon and battled for
the Lord. Even Franklin Roosevelt defined the New Deal in terms
of a "crusade." It might be suggested that these remarks miss the
point, that all politicians use moral rhetoric, and that the main
thrust of American politics has been toward a compromising tradition. But this would be truly to miss the point: American politicians have been able to compromise only because they have been
able to persuade themselves that the road of compromise was the
road to the promised land. Their very millennialism has made compromisers out of them; they have been pragmatic because they
have been pietistic.[4]

At this point, a question intrudes: what have these pietistic tendencies in American politics to do with Socialism in the 1930's?
Simply this: Socialism's inability to command support from the

American populace is only superficially explained by contrasting
its ideological approach with American pragmatism. More important was the fact that Socialism's version of millennialism had
to compete with the American consensus version, and it was rejected for the latter not so much because it was millennial *per se*
as because its millennialism ran counter to the American tradition
of millennialism. For American millennialism, at best and at worst,
has been individualistic (resting on the individual conscience),
moralistic (inclining toward ethical judgments), and open-ended
(in the sense that Utopia remained undefinable—although occasionally it might be confused with the American forest). Socialist
millennialism in the 1930's was social (rooting itself, in theory, in
the working class), historical (inclining toward the acceptance of
the imperatives of history), and while it was not closed-ended,
Utopia was more nearly definable—as Socialism.

In the confrontation of millennial traditions, the former, buttressed by a longer tradition in the United States, won out. Its
victory, however, should not be interpreted as a victory of pragmatic realism over abstract millennialism; it was the victory of one
abstraction over a different abstraction. If this is understood, it is
possible to explore the question of whether American politics has
ever been really pragmatic at all. Thus far, the term pragmatism
has been used in its everyday sense to imply a politics that deals
with immediate tangible issues and handles them in as expeditious
a way as possible, without breaking the essential good feelings of
American consensus. But this definition, common as it may be, is
somewhat different from John Dewey's concept of problem solving,
which meant not just tidying things over without ruffling the
feathers of one's political opponents, but a root solving of the
problem at hand. In urging that all one's weapons be brought to
bear on the problem, Dewey did not overlook the role of ideology,
though he may have preferred the term "theory." The "experi-
mental method," he wrote, "is not just messing around nor doing a
little of this and a little of that in the hope things will improve. Just
as in the physical sciences, it implies a coherent body of ideas, a

theory that gives direction to effort." Dewey believed, then, that theory could enlighten action; it was not antithetical to pragmatism. It was because theory was important for Dewey that he rejected the New Deal version of pragmatic politics. In *The Politics of Upheaval,* Schlesinger recognizes this in his analysis of Dewey's relation to the New Deal. But he mistakenly sees Dewey's hostility to the New Deal as a puzzle, a puzzle that Schlesinger can only unravel by attributing to Dewey a new-found stringency. Dewey, according to Schlesinger, would fit "social policy to the require- ments of ideology." In short, for Schlesinger, Dewey, like all ideologists, had become an abstractionist. He is led to this con- clusion only because his own definition of experimentalism must see Dewey's insistence on the need for a "coherent body of ideas" and his rejection of "trial-and-error pragmatism" as a variety of absolute ideology.[5]

Schlesinger's definition of pragmatism—just this nontheoretical approach—has won out. It is for this reason that American politics has been labeled "pragmatic." But if there is another tradition of pragmatism, a tradition that combines theory and ideology with experiment, a tradition of which Dewey was a major proponent, a tradition that insisted on searching for the roots of social problems, then it is questionable whether American politics can be labeled "pragmatic" in any but the most narrow sense. And this narrow sense can make no special claim to an ability to solve problems— the supposed purpose of pragmatism. As David Potter (who ac- cepted the pragmatic nature of American politics) said, we have "overleaped" problems rather than "solved" them. Socialism did confront the American version of pragmatic politics, but the nature of that confrontation has been distorted. For it was the Socialists who offered the root solutions in the Dewey tradition of pragma- tism; American politics offered superficial remedies and resolu- tions of interest that appear pragmatic because they were passed. Indeed, the Socialists failed because they took politics too seriously; they mistakenly assumed that the American people were ready for a sustained commitment to and participation in politics. The

American people, however, with their strange combination of millennialism and practicality, threw the "devil" out in 1932 and were satisfied with expedient resolutions of problems.[6]

Norman Thomas and the Socialist Party

And the latter-day saint, Norman Thomas, crushed by the onslaught of this supposed American practicality, floundering, to use Sombart's metaphor, on the "reefs of roast beef"—what are said to be the roots of his failure? Why, just that: he did not compromise—either within his own party or with the American populace's enchantment with Franklin D. Roosevelt. More will be said later about the relations between the Socialist Party, Thomas, and the New Deal, but it is necessary here to briefly make one point about the issue of whether Thomas should have compromised with the New Deal. According to Johnpoll, if Debs or Hillquit or Berger had been at the helm of the Socialist Party in the 1930's, he would "likely . . . have accepted the reality of the situation and worked out a compromise which would have saved the party and its political existence—even if only as a wing of a labor-progressive coalition in the Democratic Party. But it was under Thomas's leadership that the party faced the New Deal, and it was his inability to effect a compromise by which the party could have accepted the new realities that helped lead to its demise." Now, there is not one iota of evidence that Debs would ever have made peace with a liberal reform administration like Roosevelt's. Possibly Hillquit might have; certainly his followers in the Old Guard chose to function this way through the American Labor Party. Yet, it is also possible that their move in this direction came partly because Hillquit's death in 1933 deprived them of their most prominent leader. And, again, Berger might have; the leader of the Wisconsin Socialists, Dan Hoan, finally took the Wisconsin Socialist Party into the Wisconsin Farmer-Labor Federation, although originally the move was not made as part of a pro-New Deal strategy. But in the case of neither the Old Guard and the American Labor Party nor the Wisconsin Socialists and the Wisconsin Farmer-Labor Progressive Federation was the particular party, or fraction of the party, saved. Andrew Biemiller, a former Socialist, was ultimately elected to Congress from Wisconsin, but he was elected as a *former* Socialist. And as the New York Old Guard turned to support the New Deal, increasingly less was heard of socialism or socialist education, or anything that might have suggested that the socialist ideal was still relevant, a fact that the former editor of *The New Leader,* James Oneal, himself a hostile critic of Thomas and an ardent supporter of Roosevelt, complained of in letters to his former associates from his retirement in California. And today, when the Socialist Party has chosen to function in exactly the fashion that Johnpoll believes politically wise, when it has chosen to assume that the prime responsibility of the Socialist Party is to function as a force within the Democratic Party, its influence and relevance to the American political scene are in no way commensurate with the arguments it presents for its course as "realistic." It is bad enough that the Socialist Party should be in the hands of the Paul Feldmans and Tom Millsteins with their meager social vision, but that the strategy that these leaders have opted for should have accomplished so little in terms of any tangible results suggests that Johnpoll's historical critique of Thomas in the 1930's would likely have failed its own "pragmatic" test, as the Socialist Party's strategy today has clearly done.[7]

But it is not simply Thomas's unwillingness to compromise with the New Deal that concerns Johnpoll. It is his refusal to moderate the bitter internal dispute that absorbed the time and energy of the Socialist Party from the late 1920's till the final break in 1936. Thomas, writes Johnpoll, "eliminated himself as a potential healer of party wounds" by associating himself with the Militants. There is very little evidence for Johnpoll's assumption that the history of the Party might have been different if Thomas had attempted conciliation, even if that conciliation had been successful. Thomas had more in common with the Militants than with the Old Guard, and felt, rightly or wrongly, that a Socialist Party dominated—or even held back—by the Old Guard was doomed to failure. But according to Johnpoll, the proper role of the responsible political leader is to conciliate and moderate and compromise differences.[8]

To accept Johnpoll's premise, for the sake of argument, that it is the role of the political leader to moderate differences requires that there be something to compromise. It is not necessary to demonstrate that the Old Guard and the Militants were opposed on *all* issues to see that basic, irreconcilable issues divided the two groups. For what could Thomas have compromised? The Old Guard was convinced that the 1934 Declaration of Principles was an open declaration in favor of armed insurrection; Thomas believed it was a necessary statement to indicate that Socialists would not lie down in the face of fascism. The Old Guard believed that the anti-war sections of the Declaration of Principles placed the party under the threat of legal prosecution for advocating unlawful actions to oppose war; again Thomas believed that a strong statement was necessary to put capitalism on warning that if it engaged in imperialist war there would be opposition. The Old Guard believed that a united front with the Communists was immoral and would be disastrous for the Socialists, that even limited united action on specific causes should be banned, and even that exploratory discussions about a united front were going too far. Thomas opposed a united front on a general level, including any joint actions in political contests, but he thought that carefully planned united action on specific cases could, and should, take place. And he believed that it was worth while to conduct exploratory talks, even though he felt that they would likely lead to nothing. The Old Guard felt that the Socialists' invitation to unaffiliated radicals and the Party's acceptance of former Communists, Lovestoneites, and Trotskyists was turning the party away from democratic socialism and over to Communism. Thomas, though he disagreed with the ideology of these anti-Stalinist Communists, was willing to try to work with a party that included them, if they were willing to accept party discipline and not try to take over the Party. The Old Guard considered the Revolutionary Policy Committee, a far-left group within the Socialist Party, a Communist and anarchist group that had no place in a democratic socialist party. Thomas disagreed with the "romantic revolutionaries" in the Revolutionary Policy Committee (as he also disagreed with the "romantic parliamentarians" of the Old Guard), but still felt it was useful to try to salvage some of the enthusiasm and dedication that went into the Revolutionary Policy Committee by permitting its members to remain in the Party if, again, they followed party policy and party discipline.[9]

All of this is not to say that Thomas was necessarily right on these—and other—issues dividing him from the Old Guard and placing him closer to the Militants. The question here is not correctness, but rather what, in the last analysis, was there really to compromise? If one seriously believed that permitting the Revolutionary Policy Committee members to function within the Socialist Party was turning the Party into a Bolshevik Party and if Thomas, for all his disagreements with the Revolutionary Policy Committee, did not see such catastrophic consequences, where lay the area for conciliation? If one were firmly convinced that the 1935 Browder-Thomas Madison Square Garden debate on the possibilities of a united front between Communists and Socialists was itself a united-front action, how could Thomas—who believed basically that it was a way to explore the problem and the differences, as well as a very useful way to get the Socialist case, as distinct from the Communist case, before a large audience—how could he moderate the Old Guard hostility? By refusing to participate in the debate? Unless Thomas was prepared to accept the Old Guard position, in practice, on these issues, whatever his personal beliefs, there seems little that he could have done to reconcile the conflict. This is not to say that Thomas always led his side and formulated his policies in the best manner; he could be incredibly self-righteous when he was engaged in normal political infighting and this self-righteousness was bound to exacerbate existing ideological debates. But even without the unnecessary exacerbation, the fundamental ideological and tactical disputes would have remained. Of course, if one's conception of a political leader is of a man with no ideas, with no policy, with no politics, as simply a technical coordinator among groups in a party with ideas and policy, then perhaps Thomas may have seriously erred in taking sides. But what kind of *socialist* leader would Thomas have been if he had not had strong commitments and policy positions of his own? Yes, Thomas sided with the Militants, though he made a number of overtures and attempts—far more than some of his Militant friends wished—to conciliate the conflict. Without him, the split would probably have occurred two years earlier. Yet, in the last analysis, Thomas did use his prestige and power on one side in a vicious internal party fight, though his correspondence never reveals the kind of personal backbiting and petty vindictiveness that the Old Guard correspondence does.[10]

One cannot understand the course Thomas chose if one does not accept the existence of serious ideological differences between the Militants and the Old Guard. His letters certainly do not support the kind of amateur psychological interpretation that sees Thomas as being flattered into his support by the adulation and admiration of the younger Militants. Thomas's correspondence with young Militants like Paul Porter, Andrew Biemiller, and Amicus Most is filled with serious discussions of tactics and conceptions about what a Socialist Party should be and how it should act. This is not to deny that Thomas was above the personal flattery of the young; no doubt he was susceptible to it. But to focus on this aspect leads one away from the serious ideological and tactical differences separating Thomas and the Militants from the Old Guard. This "psychological" focus is typical of the approach which refuses to consider that men could differ seriously over ideological questions. At one point, Johnpoll writes: "The Militant-Old Guard confrontation in the Socialist Party, which began in 1930, was more a struggle between generations than between ideologies. The ideological content of the struggle did not develop until the disagreement was almost two years old, and the issues over which the fight developed had little connection with objective reality." Elsewhere, he writes: "Ideological disagreement was merely a facade, for the real struggle was over power within the party. Thomas perceived this fact early, but he believed that only the Old Guard was interested in personal ad-

vantage. He ignored the fact that there was also considerable interest in power—for its own sake—in the left-wing factions as
well."[11]

No doubt there was a generational problem: the Militants who
flocked into the party in the late 1920's and early 1930's, and who
aligned themselves with Norman Thomas, were younger than the
Old Guard leaders, and they were impatient. And there was a
power drive. One cannot understand the Old Guard's actions unless one recognizes its intense desire to maintain its place in the
party hierarchy; the drives of the young were a threat to the power
of the New York Old Guard. And clearly one would falsely idealize the Militants if one failed to recognize that their ambitions
were not always selfless. But if the question of power was always
present, and if a generational conflict existed, so too did serious
ideas and concerns, and they deserve to be taken seriously in
themselves. Generational differences, after all, are usually about
something; power conflicts usually, at least, start out about something. Indeed, ideology and power should not be separated as alternative motives for conflict; they are usually interwoven. So, too,
are debates over tactics and principles. Thus it is simplistic to say,
as Johnpoll does, that "the basic differences between the old-line
Socialists . . . and the new breed . . . were over tactics rather than
principles." If Norman Thomas, for example, at one stage of his
career believed in an "inclusive" party, it was both a matter of
ideology derived from certain principles about what a Socialist
Party should be and a tactical statement of what he felt would be
more successful politically. Only a recognition of the seriousness of
the ideological differences, leading to differences in tactics and
strategy, permits one to understand the character of Socialism in
the 1930's, which is ultimately to understand the hard choices that
radicals faced in that period. To refuse to acknowledge these real
issues, as distinct from pseudo-issues simply masking generational
differences and power drives, is, in the end, the luxury of an era
which cannot grasp the fact that some of the best men of the thirties
believed that capitalism was going to collapse in the foreseeable

future and that it really did make a difference what kind of party—in organization and in ideas—existed in this situation.[12]

The hotly contested 1934 Declaration of Principles (see Appendix) should be seen in this light. That men should have fought so bitterly over a document whose most controversial clauses pertained to conjectural situations not yet in existence may seem difficult to comprehend thirty-five years later. Even by 1940, six brief years after the controversy, the emotions the Declaration generated seemed puzzling to some of the participants in the struggle. Writing in 1941 to Norman Thomas, his former ally, from whom he was now separated over the war issue, a tired and older Louis Sadoff said that if he had it to do over he would not have gotten so upset over the Declaration of Principles. But in 1934, for a Socialist, the statement was important. For the capitalist world appeared to be collapsing; in desperation capitalism was turning toward fascism and war. And what had been the response of the German Social Democrats when faced with the rise of fascism? If not inaction, at least not militant resistance. It seemed to many thoughtful Socialists that it would simply be suicidal to repeat the strictly parliamentary approach of the German Social Democrats if the United States were faced with a similar crisis. It became necessary for them to delineate their differences from the course the German Social Democrats had followed. And the 1934 Declaration of Principles, whatever Thomas's reservations about its precise wording, was a statement of this necessity. Stating that *if* Socialists were faced with a collapsed and disintegrated capitalism, they would not abjectly wait for the next election to seize power, the document at once raised the issue of violent revolution and armed insurrection. This was hardly what was meant by either Thomas or the vast majority of Militants. Even those in the Socialist Party closest to subscribing to armed insurrection, the Revolutionary Policy Committee, did not subscribe to immediate insurrection and qualified the conditions under which such action might take place (the Revolutionary Policy Committee supported the Declaration, while criticizing it as a completely inadequate statement). To Thomas, it simply was a warning that Socialists would not roll over and play dead under all possible circumstances and that the history of German Social Democracy would not be repeated.[13]

It is easy to ridicule the Militant position. Since capitalism did not collapse, the internal threat of fascism seems exaggerated today. The whole idea of a small band of Socialists, led by an essentially nonviolent man, resisting fascism by seizing power and establishing socialism, seems a silly kind of revolutionary posturing. But these judgments are again much easier to make in 1960 or 1970 than they were in the 1933–34 world of disarray. If the Militant phrases of the Declaration of Principles draw smug grins, the nature of the Old Guard's hysterical response to it is apt to draw analogous comments on the order of "much ado about nothing." That the document might be preposterous is granted; that it was anarchistic, Bolshevist, and insurrectionist seems equally preposterous. But, not to defend the hysterical Old Guard response, consider their position. The leaders of the Old Guard had grown up in democratic socialism; they had lived through the I.W.W. issue, and, even more important, the Bolshevik split. They had battled fiercely with the Communists in the needle trades in New York during the 1920's, and they were now living through a period in which the Communists were arguing that violent revolution was the only answer. They had seen their fellow Russian Social Democrats jailed in and exiled from a country whose ideology disdained the peaceful and parliamentary approach to Socialism. The world in which they operated—with its ties to the international Socialist movement—seemed to reinforce their belief that the parliamentary approach to socialism was the only answer. This was compatible with their experience and their Marxism, which held that only a conscious working class could create socialism. The German Social Democrats might have made some mistakes, they believed, but nowhere near as fatal mistakes as their Communist rivals, and, despite any mistakes, the general outlines of their approach remained valid. Given this experience and beliefs about the process of socialism, it is understandable—if not acceptable—that the Old

Guard should have interpreted the Detroit Declaration of Principles in such a drastic manner.[14]

The section of the Declaration relating to war raised the same kind of emotions and responses that the section on the road to power did, though not to quite the same lengths. Again, the issue was conjectural: what Socialists should do when faced with the next imperialist war. The argument that the Socialist Party should meet war with resistance again seemed a necessary statement to the Militants and to Thomas. It seemed necessary to accent the Party's refusal to accept the imperialist solution to the capitalist crisis. Moreover, it was a warning that the Party would not follow the path of European Social Democracy during the World War, and that it would follow the tradition of the American St. Louis Proclamation of 1917. Further, it was a warning the Militants and Thomas felt was necessary, with threats and statements of war being reported daily in the press. But to the Old Guard the phrasing raised again the image of armed insurrection as the road to power, and for those who had lived through the Wilsonian "democracy" of the war years, its refusal to be bound by capitalist definitions of legal action opened the possibility of suppression of the Socialist Party. The Old Guard was opposed to imperialist war, but it refused to risk the suppression of the Party by placing the Party on record as favoring illegal actions should war occur.[15]

When World War II came most of the Militants and all of the Old Guard supported it; the Socialist Party itself wrote a compromise statement that did not openly oppose the war; and the antiwar members of the Socialist Party did not engage in antiwar activities, such as the general strike, that seemed to have been foreshadowed by the Detroit Declaration of Principles. Again, it is easy to take the attitude that it was not ideology at issue, but mere power, and that it was all a silly business anyway, since it had nothing to do with "objective reality." But it was ideology that was the issue in 1934 (ideology that obviously led to tactical differences). And what was "objective reality" in 1933–34? Is it too extreme to suggest that the radical perception of the fascist danger came closer to the truth than the complacency of the American people or the American government? The Socialists were clearly wrong about the imminent collapse of capitalism (a point that will be developed later). They were too certain that their comprehension of the First World War would remain, despite their fears of fascism, the same for any future war. But neither mistake was unwarranted in 1934, and they hardly compare to the mistakes in the American government's comprehension of capitalism's problems or of the dangers of fascism.

No single word in the Declaration of Principles upset the Old Guard more than the phrase "bogus democracy," used to describe the workings of democracy under capitalism. To the Old Guard it seemed an unwarranted attack upon democratic rights that workers had fought for. To the Militants, it was an apt description of how democracy worked in a capitalist nation, especially a capitalist nation facing crisis and seeking to maintain power. Norman Thomas insisted that the phrase did not mean that he and the Socialist Party wished to give up democracy, political action, or the struggle for the extension of democracy in favor of dictatorship, proletarian or otherwise. But to the Old Guard the phrase suggested the Militants' admiration for Russia, their desire for the Party to proclaim itself in favor of the dictatorship of the proletariat, the Revolutionary Policy Committee's antiparliamentarianism, and the whole tendency in the Socialist Party to move beyond parliamentary democratic forms on the road to power. The phrase, which culminated in inner party debate over the issue of democracy, engendered bitter emotion. A veteran Marxist like Haim Kantorovitch could cut through some of the rhetoric to chastise the Militants for joining in the reactionary attack on democratic rights that workers through the ages had struggled for, while, at the same time, as one aligned with the Militants himself, he could reveal the bogus nature of how democracy did in fact operate under capitalism. But the emotions surrounding the issue seem once again difficult to understand.

However, in this case, recent analogous debates over Herbert Marcuse's theory of "repressive tolerance" might suggest that the earlier debates involved serious and substantive issues.[16]

The substantive nature of the internal party debate is perhaps better revealed by examining at length a less volatile issue than the Declaration of Principles, but one that played an equally significant part in the party split: the attitude of the Socialist Party toward labor unions. For one of the main reasons why the Old Guard was so upset about the Detroit Declaration was the negative effect it believed it would have on the Party's relations with the trade unions. And it was the Old Guard's attitude toward the trade unions that played a prominent role in persuading Norman Thomas that continued Old Guard leadership of the Party would be disastrous, thus persuading him to align himself more closely with the Militants at Detroit.[17]

II

The Socialist Party
and the Labor Unions

WHAT should be the relation of a radical socialist party to the trade-union movement? This has not been an easy question for radicals to answer. The question derives its difficulty, in part, from the fact that the interests of a socialist party have not necessarily coincided with the predominant sentiment in the trade-union movement. Is the duty of the socialist trade unionist primarily to his trade union or to his party? Should party policy be coordinated and centralized in the trade unions, or should basic policy be left to each socialist operating within his union? Should socialists work within the organized trade-union movement, or should they form rival dual unions where the trade-union movement seems lethargic, antisocialist, or reactionary in character? These and similar questions have constantly confronted the radical.

Before the depression, the Socialist Party had operated on the policy of working within the American Federation of Labor, despite the fact that a number of Socialists had been prominent in the formation of the I.W.W. The Socialist campaigns within the A.F. of L. had varied in success. In the early 1900's the Socialist Party had had considerable influence. But by 1929 the conservative hierarchy of the A.F. of L. was in solid control and, despite Socialist centers of strength, particularly in the needle trades, the Party had a minimal influence in any policy decisions. The Socialist Party had, in 1924, joined with a number of important unions to back Robert LaFollette's insurgent candidacy. But the campaign only served to demonstrate the differences between the Socialist desire for a permanent Labor Party and the Unions' desire to use the La-Follette movement as a lever on the two old parties. If anything, it pointed anew to the fundamental question of what the relationship should be between a socialist party, ostensibly radical and social-ist in its ideology, and a trade-union movement, which subscribed to the capitalist ethos.[1]

All of the elements within the Socialist Party were convinced that the advance of socialism depended primarily upon the working class becoming socialist in its consciousness and in its politics. In its practical political application, this belief meant that the organized working class should pursue a policy of independent political ac-tion on the part of labor. But this policy of rejecting the two old parties in favor of labor's own politics ran directly counter to the political policy of the A.F. of L.: nonpartisanship in politics on the part of labor, while rewarding one's friends and punishing one's enemies. Given this difference in political ideology, there was bound to be tension between the A.F. of L. leadership and the Socialist Party. Compounded by the A.F. of L.'s social philosophy, which feared radicalism more than it did the power of business, this ten-sion was intensified by the general inactivity of the A.F. of L. on the issue of industrial unionism. Despite their ideological differences with A.F. of L. policy, however, the Old Guard elements within the Socialist Party had not pressed these substantive differences. The Old Guard had contented itself with a kind of détente with the A.F. of L. that gave it hegemony over the needle trades, at the price of not pressing socialism within the official labor movement. This uneasy marriage of convenience was helped by the Socialist belief that, whatever the faults of the A.F. of L., Socialists should work through it rather than pursue a dual-union policy as the Com-munists were pursuing with disastrous consequences. But if a com-mon opposition to dual unionism could bring the Socialists and the

A.F. of L. into what, in its practical consequences, amounted to a truce, there were other forces that could upset this delicate relationship. In particular, there was the Socialist commitment to industrial unionism, a commitment that could, at any moment, push the Party toward a more critical stance. And there was also the embarrassment to the Socialist-A.F. of L. alliance caused by the probusiness activities and ideology and the intense antiradicalism of Matthew Woll, one of the vice-presidents of the A.F. of L. and, at the same time, acting president of the probusiness National Civic Federation.[2]

For a short time in 1928 and early 1929, Woll's activities threatened to upset the détente between the Socialist Party and the A.F. of L. Woll's critique of the Brookwood Labor College as anti-A.F. of L. and pro-Communist, combined with the founding in 1929 of the Conference for Progressive Labor Action by A.J. Muste, one of Brookwood's original founders, temporarily drove the Socialist Party to a more critical posture in relation to the A.F. of L. The Conference for Progressive Labor Action's program was what the Socialist Party was officially committed to and what Norman Thomas had long been urging: industrial unionism, the democratization of union structures, nondiscrimination in the unions, unemployment and old-age insurance, and a general orientation toward militant class struggle, rather than class cooperation through such organizations as the Woll-led National Civic Federation. In late 1928 and early 1929, both the Old Guard *New Leader* and Norman Thomas began to step up their critiques of Woll and the National Civic Federation. For a brief period it seemed possible that the Socialist Party as a whole was going to take a strongly critical position toward the A.F. of L. leadership. In an article in March of 1929 Morris Hillquit described the A.F. of L. leadership as "incredibly reactionary" and accused it of ceasing to organize new groups of workers. Criticizing restrictions on union membership and labor political begging ("doormats in the legislative halls"), Hillquit joined Muste in urging a campaign to "awaken American Labor." In July of 1929, however, the United

Hebrew Trades condemned the Conference for Progressive Labor Action for its critical position on the A.F. of L. and for its supposedly dual-union tendencies. Following this, the *New Leader* began to increase its criticism of the C.P.L.A. and to tone down some of its harsher criticism of Wollism in the A.F. of L. By June of 1930 the *New Leader* was accusing the C.P.L.A. of seeking a "revolutionary leadership" of the trade unions instead of a "cooperative and fraternal" relationship.[3]

The United Hebrew Trades' condemnation of the C.P.L.A., however, was not the decisive force in reestablishing the working relationship between the Old Guard Socialists and the A.F. of L. leadership. Even after the condemnation, articles and editorials appeared in the *New Leader* criticizing the A.F. of L. In August of 1929, James Oneal criticized William Green's nonpartisan political stand and his view that labor was generally well off, and in July of 1931 Morris Hillquit's analysis of the backwardness of American labor contained critical references to the A.F. of L. But the tone was becoming milder. Still, the turning point was the 1932 convention of the A.F. of L., where the body officially dropped its "individualism" and came out for government unemployment insurance. It was this turning point that confirmed the Old Guard in its belief that its position had been right all along, that its criticism of the Militants, the C.P.L.A. and others impatient with the A.F. of L. leaders had been justified. Whatever Old Guard criticism of the American Federation of Labor occurred between the 1932 convention and the A.F. of L.-C.I.O. split, it was consumed in the philosophy and belief that the organized working class was moving in its—the Old Guard's—direction.[4]

This confirmation of their position in the minds of the Old Guard Socialists brings us to the basic ideological differences between the Old Guard and the Militants, and to Norman Thomas's position in this dispute. The Old Guard's attitude was based on the position that the trade-union movement must be independent of the Socialist Party. Socialists in the trade unions were to work to increase the socialist consciousness of the rank and file, but the Socialist Party was not to form trade-union policy for the Socialists in the unions. The Party should function as the political wing of the socialist movement; the trade-union movement would be the economic wing as workers began to understand better the principles of socialism and the failures of capitalism. The two structures were to operate in a parallel, though cooperative, manner. Any steps that might lead to Socialist Party control of the labor movement were seen by the Old Guard as modern examples of DeLeonism or a variation on the Communist philosophy of tight party control.[5]

This Old Guard position, on the surface, had "democratic" overtones. In practice, however, it could mean acquiescence in conservative and undemocratic union policies. The democratic element revolves around its assumption that outside domination of the trade unions by political parties implied that the problems of workers and unions were going to be solved from on high. "The organized workers," James Oneal wrote, describing the Militant point of view, "are regarded as irresponsible human beings that must be led. The union democracy which he [the Militant] claims as his aim is rejected at the very outset of his crusade. His view does not differ from the one ascribed to the conservative leaders. Both think in terms of leaders to lead a mass that is considered incapable of directing itself. The 'saviour' and the conservative leader have no confidence in the members." How could change come, then, according to Oneal? How could a conservative union become progressive? Change would have to come, he argued, from the members—the rank and file—and only through education; insurgency without a basic education of the members would not make lasting changes.[6]

The Old Guard wrote off the body of Militant criticism and policy recommendations. Should there be a special Socialist trade-union organizer in New York to stimulate activity? No, answered Oneal, such a move held the "dangerous possibility of leading to party interference in trade unions." A special organizer might become an agency to "dominate" unions. Were American workers backward? Yes, answered Hillquit, but you couldn't "force" Socialist ideas on them as the Militants would do; to think so was a form of middle-class radicalism, not working-class radicalism. The Militants, wrote Oneal, were "high-hatters," always thinking of the leaders and not of educating the rank and file; they were sectarians, willing to flirt with dual unionism in their disgust with the A.F. of L.; and "strategists" with grand strategies and programs to impose on the unions. The Militants' attitude assumed, he wrote in October, 1932, that "trade unions will come to the Socialist position if we as a white-collar brigade stand on the frontiers of the unions and continually cry their shortcomings."[7]

In contradistinction to outside party domination and interference in the work of the unions, Oneal offered the generality of "frank cooperation with the organized workers in their struggle for organization and better conditions." All the agencies of the Socialist Party—its press, its relief agencies, its speakers—should support "every important strike." Here, Oneal sought to give his theoretical analysis of the correct relationship between the Socialist Party and unions a historical basis by pointing to past periods of Socialist cooperation. The Socialists, he maintained, had through following his suggested policy of support gained "the sincere respect of thousands of organizations" before World War I and they had had considerable influence in a number of unions. Now, through a renewed policy of such cooperation, Socialist influence could reemerge. He pointed to the "turning point" in the "estranged relations between the party and the trade unions": the 1932 Convention at Cincinnati, where the A.F. of L. had "scrapped its 'individualist' philosophy" by coming out in support of unemployment insurance. Pressured from below by the rank and file, the delegates had taken this decisive action, an action which offered Socialists "a splendid opportunity for cooperation with the unions." If Socialists would enter into this "class struggle," old barriers to understanding and cooperation would fall; but if Socialists tried to play the role of "strategists" and "high-hatters," they would remain isolated sectarians.[8]

Once the A.F. of L. had modified its long-standing oposition to unemployment insurance, the Old Guard was carried on the tide of optimism. "The progressive tide has set in," the *New Leader* wrote in announcing the story. "All forces of American capitalism," it continued, "will compel further advances in the same direction. Old fears, prejudices, and complexes are being dissipated. It is the duty of Socialists and progressive workers to work with and encourage the new trends." Though there was an occasional natural "hangover of old ideas," a historic step forward had been taken at the Cincinnati convention. Nonpartisan politics would likely be the next old idea left behind, and any Militant gibing at the reactionary politics of the A.F. of L. was so much "sectarian high-hatting." The Old Guard looked with confidence on the continued growth of progressive ideas in the A.F. of L.; its defense of William Green became clearer. He was not a reactionary, Oneal claimed; he was not holding back industrial unionism. That was being done by the structural type of affiliation with the A.F. of L. To change this would require a change in attitude by members and officials. But with the breakthrough on government insurance, the possibility of subsequent progressive changes was easily envisioned by the Old Guard. Even as the A.F. of L. continued to drag its feet on the issue of industrial unionism and the split by the C.I.O. became firmer, the *New Leader* still read the signs in the A.F. of L. as moving toward progressive social policy.[9]

I have suggested that the Old Guard policy was ostensibly democratic in that it argued that change came through the growing social consciousness of the rank-and-file worker, and could not be imposed by an outside "enlightened" party. The Socialist Party's chief work should be educational and supportive—educating the rank and file in socialist ideas and supporting the union's trade-union actions. But a policy that seemed on the surface to be democratic could also have deeper conservative implications, implications that easily supported the status quo and prevailing power relations within the union movement. For the supportive aspects of the policy meant supporting trade-union decisions that had been arrived at by the trade-union leadership, rather than attempting to formulate policy within the unions. It meant, in fact, avoiding any coordinated policy within the A.F. of L. to pressure it in a more democratic direction. It was just this kind of pressure that the Militants wished to place on the A.F. of L. Their own philosophy was not as developed as that of the Old Guard. Their decisions on what the Socialist Party should do in relation to trade unions were not primarily based on a theoretical position of the correct relationship between a Socialist Party and the trade-union movement, but rather were arrived at by a shared disgust with the existing A.F. of L. policy and the Socialist Party's complicity in that policy. The Militants were upset by the continued political backwardness of the A.F. of L. They were upset by its undemocratic structure, and they were upset by its economic backwardness on such issues as industrial unionism. They believed that Socialists as Socialists should play a role in changing these policies, and they came to believe that this required more coordination by the Socialist Party of its trade-union work. The Militants perceived that many nominal Socialists in the trade unions acted no differently from non-Socialists and they wanted to pressure them too. This again required a more coordinated policy.[10]

In reply to the Old Guard's fear that this kind of coordination would mean outside control along the lines of the Communist Party's trade-union work, the Militants professed that they did not want to "run" the trade unions, or to control them "mechanically" as did the Communists. One can argue, of course, that the end result of the Militant policy would have been such control. But nowhere does a reading of the Militant writing suggest that they were instituting reforms in order to make the trade-union movement an appendage of the Socialist Party. What it does suggest is the need for reforms that would better enable Socialists in the trade unions to fight for what was the official labor policy of the Party, subscribed to by both Old Guard and Militants: industrial unionism, independent political action on the part of labor, an end to labor racketeering, the democratization of union structures. Such reforms required coordination, and so the kind of reform the Militants worked for organizationally was the establishment of a special Labor Committee with a National Secretary; the hiring of a special organizer for New York; the establishment of Socialist labor leagues in New York; and, in general, for a more activist posture in implementing the Party's official labor policy. In large part, this is what the Militant position amounted to: faced with the inaction of the Old Guard with respect to pressing the Party's official labor policy on the A.F. of L., they were proposing activity geared in this direction.[11]

The Militants, then, knew what they were against: foot-dragging on the professed policy of the Socialist Party in the trade unions. They had concrete proposals in terms of suggestions for coordinating that policy. But their theory tended to be an "anti-theory"—that is, anti-the Old Guard theory of "labor right or wrong." When Julius Gerber, Old Guard Secretary of the New York City local, said, quoting his friend, Ben Hanford, "Organized labor may it ever be right, but right or wrong, my place is with organized labor," the Militants correctly perceived that this policy, in practice, led to an acquiescence in the policy of the American Federation of Labor. Beyond that, there was little attempt by the Militants to define the theoretical relation of the Socialist Party to the trade unions. Haim Kantorovitch, the Marxist editor of the *American Socialist Quarterly,* attempted to furnish the Militants with a more detailed theoretical underpinning, as Oneal and others did for the Old Guard. But Kantorovitch's views on the relationship cannot be used to express a Militant consensus. Kantorovitch was able to see through many of the pretensions in the Old Guard theory. He recognized that the theory of "labor right or wrong" meant, in practice, that the Socialist Party would be "with the leaders, right or wrong, whoever they may happen to be—very often with the labor leaders against the rank and file." This last point—which should not be confused with a DeLeon-like condemnation of all labor leaders as labor fakers—may have been overly optimistic in positing a rank and file purer than the leaders. Nevertheless, it pierced the inner contradiction of the Old Guard "democratic" position: the "democratic" appeal in theory to the rank and file and the everyday tacit acceptance, in practice, of the leadership. Refusing to accept the labor litany of the Old Guard, Kantorovitch insisted that Socialists are "with labor only when it is right." They are against it when it endorses the Democratic Party, or engages in witch hunts, or clings to the "old and obsolete form of organization."[12]

Kantorovitch believed that the Old Guard's policy of refusing to criticize the A.F. of L. leadership, except in the mildest of manners, had resulted not in greater Socialist influence in the trade-union movement, but in less. "To the broad masses in the unions," he wrote, "we are the eternal supporters of the leadership; to the leadership, we are nothing at all." This situation he traced back to a basic attitude toward socialism which, in turn, led to the existing relations between the Party and the trade-union movement. Kantorovitch argued that the Old Guard position derived from a purely parliamentary approach to socialism. Having accepted this as the only path to socialism, the Old Guard's whole strategy was designed to win votes by whatever means. Following this strategy, the line of least resistance pointed to winning the friendship and endorsement of the labor leaders (though he felt the Old Guard was mistaken in believing they had much political influence over the rank and file). On the other hand, Kantorovitch argued, the Militant Socialists fought for progressive policies for the sake of the unions themselves. But he also believed that their policy was determined by their analysis of the path to socialism. Believing that the road to socialism would be harder than the purely parliamentary path, the Militant perceived the necessity of preventing a reactionary-controlled labor movement when the "decisive struggle" arrived. In such a struggle, the trade-union movement might be the decisive key, and therefore it was necessary to have its support for the socialist movement. This task required planning; it required organization; above all it required winning "the masses of trade-union workers in the direction of socialism." This could not be done by "playing up to the leadership of the union," but only by acting upon the slogan "to the workers instead of the leaders."[13]

Kantorovitch's appeal over the heads of the union leaders went further than some Militants and Norman Thomas were prepared to go in their criticisms of the A.F. of L. leadership. His connection of trade-union strategy with a specific nonparliamentary road to power was never made by Thomas. But in both cases, Kantorovitch caught the spirit of the Militant thrust in labor-union policy, a spirit and thrust which were supported by Norman Thomas.

Two brief letters from Norman Thomas suggest the two key elements in Thomas's thoughts on the Socialist Party and the labor movement. In a letter to Julius Gerber in September of 1929, Thomas wrote: "In general I feel strongly that we have a right to expect Socialists in labor unions to act as Socialists and not as Republicans and Democrats. Certainly we may expect them not to use the tactics of political compromise with dubious elements that so often are used. At the same time I agree with the proposition that we ought not to interfere in the day to day internal affairs of the unions." And in a January 10, 1935, letter to B.C. Vladeck dealing with the possibility of a farmer-labor party, Thomas declared: "I want a farmer-labor party. I think we have to be on decent terms with the leaders of the A.F. of L. to get it. But I think the kind of a party we want will come nevertheless by converting masses of farmers and workers, and we shall not get the right kind of a party unless we are demanding something a great deal more than the A.F. of L. leaders themselves will demand or even at first desire."[14]

The first letter reveals Thomas's constant concern that Socialists within the trade-union movement act upon Socialist principle and policies; that they openly support Socialist political candidates; that they not make deals with old-line politicians; that they fight racketeering within their unions; that they support union democracy; that they support industrial unionism. Most of the cases that led him into conflict with the Old Guard revolved around these issues. One important case involved rival union factions in the fur industry. The Socialist faction obtained a court injunction against a Communist-led faction. Thomas did not deny that the Socialists had grievances against the Communists, but he insisted that as Socialists they could not use this capitalist antistrike weapon against their union's rivals.[15]

The second letter, aside from the particular issue of a farmer-labor party, reveals Thomas's attitude toward the A.F. of L. It was important, he felt, to try to be on friendly terms with its leadership, but this desire could not be permitted to determine *Socialist* policy. It was necessary for Socialists to go beyond the policy of the A.F. of L. if the Party was to be successful; it was necessary to be critical of the A.F. of L. if the Socialists were to help bring about the kind of union movement that could help socialism triumph. Thus, in discussing strikes—the role of the A.F. of L. in the textile strike of 1934, its opposition to the 1934 San Francisco general strike—or in discussing A.F. of L. policy on issues like industrial unionism, Thomas was quick to adopt a critical attitude. He was not as vociferous as some of his party allies, but certainly he was more critical than the A.F. of L.-oriented Old Guard. He had praise for the A.F. of L.'s support of unemployment insurance, but he did not see it in as euphoric terms as the Old Guard did. In his published writings on labor, he consistently combined the two themes of how a Socialist should act and what it was necessary for Socialism to demand of the A.F. of L. in terms of reform: Socialists should push for industrial unionism, the end of racial discrimination, union democracy, the end of racketeering, an organized strike-relief and labor-defense policy.[16]

Thomas and the Militants may never have worked out as carefully defined an ideological statement of the correct relationship between the Socialist Party and the trade unions as did the Old Guard. But it would be a mistake not to see important ideological differences here. For if much of the difference involved the difference between a placating and a critical posture toward the official labor movement, this difference in policy suggests a difference in ideology. The Old Guard, despite urging Socialist education in the unions, wanted to keep a clear line between the two prongs of a socialist movement: the unions and the Party. The Militants, without urging a party-controlled union movement, believed that a union movement adequate for the building of socialism required much more party coordination. That this was not an inconsequential difference, that it remains a serious question for radicals, is seen by the fact that Socialist Party relations with the official trade-union movement are still at issue today.[17]

Moreover, it is inadequate, if not altogether wrong, to look at the differences between Norman Thomas and the Old Guard in terms of "morality" vs. "practicality." Bernard Johnpoll writes that Thomas's views on labor "were based on moral premises; the Old Guard, many of whom were union officials or union attorneys, based their attitudes on practical, personal considerations. When the moral and the practical collided, Thomas sided with what he assumed to be the correct moral position, while Old Guard Socialists generally favored the position that best suited their practical position in the union involved." This view focuses on Thomas's moral opposition to labor racketeering and the Old Guard's toleration of such racketeering if it was useful in a "practical" fight with rival left-wingers in the unions. Because of this focus, it misses the larger ideological dimension in Old Guard thinking. The Old Guard's theories on correct Socialist Party relations with unions may have been self-serving, "practical" rationalizations to defend its members' own acquired positions in the union movement. Even if this were true, the theory was much more rigid, less flexible, more schematic and abstract than any moral premises that Thomas brought to the problem.[18]

Even more important, by rigidly bifurcating the "moral" and the "practical," Johnpoll misses the larger practical dimensions of Thomas's view. Thomas's opposition to labor racketeering was certainly moralistic. But Thomas was also absorbed in building a socialist movement, and he realized that, practically, it could not be built on the back of a tolerant attitude toward racketeering. Another kind of movement might be built—but not a *socialist* movement. If one looks at the labor movement as a whole, one realizes that, if anything, Thomas and the Militants were more practical, and the Old Guard more rigid in holding to a set ideology. For Thomas perceived that the Old Guard position led, in practice, not simply to a failure of Socialism to grow, but to a failure of the union movement to grow. It led to the détente in which Socialists, in exchange for hegemony over a few unions, might have the privilege of gently chastising the A.F. of L. for its inadequacies, but would continue support of its essential policy. This was hardly practical in terms of the growth of socialism; it was hardly practical for bringing pressure on the A.F. of L. to organize the mass industries. It clearly derived from a sense of what was practical and possible in the given situation, but like so many derivations of the "art of the possible" it was thoroughly impractical. Even more, it derived from a rigid ideological position that said that Socialists must not interfere in inner-union affairs. Thomas and the Militants were certainly moved by ideological considerations. Moreover, Thomas and many Militants were also moved by "moral" considerations. But in addition, they knew that a Socialist Party without a mass base in the mass industries would be a permanently weak Party, and that any socialist movement that developed without this mass base would also be weak. Pressure in this direction was a practical necessity. But it was also a necessity if there was even to be industrial unionism without a socialist base. That this resulted should not obscure the fact that between 1929 and 1935, Thomas's and the Militants' critical posture toward the A.F. of L. was the only practical course of action for Socialists.[19]

III

The Moral and the Practical:
Of Being "In" and "Of" the World

THE ISSUE of the Socialist Party and the labor unions shows that Thomas's ideological and moral beliefs and practical considerations were not separate, but rather were constantly interwoven. It is artificial to label a particular decision as resulting either from absolutist ideals or from practical considerations of what was possible in a given situation. But this interweaving of the practical and the moral should not be used to suggest that there is never a tension between the two. Certainly there was with Thomas. He was often faced, as all men are, with a choice between what he believed was necessary morally and what he believed was required practically. Far from constantly opting for the former, however, he often leaned in the direction of the latter. And far from being most in error as a political leader when he chose the moral course, he was more often wrong when he let practical concerns of party building override his moral concerns. This latter aspect—the practical concern of party building—requires emphasis. For if one is going to discuss Thomas (or any Socialist—Old Guard or Militant—in the 1930's for that matter) in terms of practicality and morality, one has to be clear about what the practical task for them was. And here one must stress Thomas's constant absorption in and dedication to the building of the Socialist Party. Although he was inclined

35

to believe that ultimately a farmer-labor party, with the Socialist Party as a constituent element, would be required to bring socialism to the United States, Thomas believed that this, in turn, required a strong Socialist Party. The development of the Socialist Party was, for Thomas, part of the development of a larger farmer-labor movement. When, in the late 1930's, Thomas concluded that direct party building should no longer be a prime focus, it was only with the greatest reluctance that he adopted this position.[1]

There were elements in the Socialist Party (especially the Trotskyists during their brief stay and the post-1936 Clarity faction) who thought more in terms of a vanguard party—a party which would have required the extension of activity and influence in many directions, but which would not necessarily have required concentrating on extending membership. Thomas, however, until his series of political defeats pushed him toward the conception of the Party as an educational, rather than a direct political force, concentrated on enlarging the Party. This was one of the reasons why he favored the all-inclusive party (which ironically brought the Trotskyists in). In short, for Thomas, the practical task was to win people to socialism in general, and to the Socialist Party in particular. Most of his decisions were made in terms of this practical task, and if he failed it was not because he let abstract ideology or morality govern him. Thomas's correspondence shows this constant attempt to present Socialism in a practical light. His interest in Paul Porter's Commonwealth Plan was one attempt to present Socialism in concrete terms, but to distinguish it from the unsuccessful reformism of the New Deal. The establishment of a Washington Bureau by the Socialist Party was largely designed to keep the Party both on top of the news and in the news. Thomas's interest in the Workers Rights Amendment was certainly a matter of principle, but he viewed the publicity as a practical way to get the Socialist Party before the eyes of the American people. I have already suggested that his critique of the A.F. of L. on the issue of industrial unionism was not simply a theoretical critique, but was conceived of in terms of establishing a form of unionism that might be more receptive to the Socialist message. Thomas's cooperation with anti-Stalinist radicals in establishing the Non-Partisan Labor Defense Committee and eventually the Workers' Defense League came from a moral concern that strikers and other workers needed such support. But it was also due to the fact that he realized the Socialist Party could get credit from the workers for its strong defense of them, and that all of the credit would not go to the Communist International Labor Defense. Even in his debates with Upton Sinclair over the latter's running for governor of California as a Democrat, Thomas was not scoring solely ideological points. He acknowledged that if he were convinced that Sinclair's strategy was furthering socialism, he might support it. But, very practically, he felt it was damaging the cause of socialism. At the same time, it was wreaking havoc with the California Socialist Party; it was therefore damaging to the practical task of party building.[2]

In this task of party building, Thomas reached out in many directions. The Old Guard liked to chide the college boys and ministers from a "working class" point of view. They kept insisting that their perspective was of a working-class party, while Thomas and the Militants thought in terms of a middle-class party. It is quite true that Thomas consciously sought to win young middle-class college-educated men and women to Party membership—for both ideological and practical reasons. It is doubtful that this discouraged many workers from joining the Party, as the Old Guard claimed. There were too many other reasons for the lack of a working-class base. Besides, Thomas did more proselytizing among workers and strikers across the nation than did the Old Guard.[3]

Party-building permeated all of Thomas's actions and attitudes. This can be seen even when one examines an issue such as the attitude of the Socialist Party toward Russia—an issue that might seem to be largely ideological, but was inextricably tied to the issue of how to build the Socialist Party.

It is not entirely true (more will be said about this later) that the Militants' and Thomas's attitude toward Russia was, as Johnpoll claims, more liberal than radical. Nor is it true that the Old Guard saw the terror and brutality in Russia before Thomas did; they saw it more *fully,* though not necessarily first. Thomas never apologized nor tried to cover up the terror in the same way that a number of liberal apologists did. He simply continued to feel that economic progress was being made and that this should not be ignored in criticizing the political repression. There is no reason to doubt his sincerity on this issue—that he genuinely believed that economic production for use was advancing, while at the same time believing that the dictatorship was a threat to the whole enterprise, and that democratic socialists should find a better way. There is no reason to doubt his sincerity, but along with this must be recognized that he was trying to reach out and win to the Socialist Party many young people who were tremendously impressed by Russia's achievements. In this, Johnpoll is right and the Old Guard was right in saying that Thomas did not want to alienate liberals by taking, and having the party take, a completely hostile attitude toward the Russian "experiment." He wished to bring some of these liberal-minded progressives toward socialism. Moreover, he was afraid that if the Party adopted a completely hostile attitude, many younger members would leave it.[4]

One can see this dilemma at the time of the formation of the American Committee to Defend Leon Trotsky. Thomas agreed to join the committee, but he emphasized that he did so not out of agreement with Trotsky (though by this time he was coming to feel many of Trotsky's criticisms of Stalin were valid), but to ensure his right of asylum and to assure a fair hearing. Despite his endorsement of the committee's activities, Thomas became upset when some of his fellow members—Max Eastman, in particular—used a public meeting of the committee for the opportunity to criticize all aspects of the Russian regime. Thomas was still determined, in 1936, not to pursue a completely hostile stand. One suspects that it was not so much misplaced idealism or ideology that led him in this direction as his continued desire to reach liberal opinion and keep some of the younger radicals in the Socialist Party. By this time, however, many of the younger radicals were criticizing him for not stating more firmly that the trials were a frame-up. Other associates, like Alfred Baker Lewis, cautioned him not to become associated with the Trotskyists in their anti-Stalinist activities, and urged him to play down the issue of the trials. Clarence Senior, the former national secretary of the Socialist Party, gave him the same advice. The tension between morality and practicality was clearly there. Thomas walked a thin line. He was too "moral" a man to take the practical course offered by Lewis and Senior. Besides it was no longer so clearly a practical course. To ignore the trials in order to maintain party harmony and prevent the alienation of un-affiliated liberals, as Lewis and Senior suggested, would damage the party from the other direction—the growing anti-Stalinism of the Party's left wing. Thomas's role in 1936 regarding the trials was not a dishonorable one, as it would have been if he had followed Lewis's and Senior's advice. But he did not speak with the kind of unambiguous condemnation that he could use against a General Hugh Johnson or that was being used in regard to the Moscow Trials by younger party members like Gus Tyler. Two years later, even a year later, all ambiguity was gone; the course of Stalin and the American Communist Party had resolved the tension between the "moral" and the "practical." They now appeared as one. But if Thomas temporized on Russia in the early thirties, it was more out of thinking as a "practical" leader trying to build and to hold his party together than as an impractical ideologue and evangelical moralist.[5]

Indeed it seemed to many Militants in the early thirties that it was the supposedly practical Old Guard that was determined to ignore the practical problem caused by widespread sympathy for Russia within the Socialist Party in order to score abstract ideological points. For much of the Old Guard's position on Russia was based on *a priori* assumptions about the nature of industrial development. It is true that a major part of the Old Guard's position also resulted from simple moral indignation at the brutality and political terrorism practiced by Stalin. Such practices were incompatible with Socialist ideals or with maintaining a friendly attitude toward the Soviet Union. Nevertheless, much of the Old Guard's hostility to Russia also derived from its interpretation of economic development according to Karl Marx. Hillquit, Oneal, and their European mentor, Karl Kautsky, all contended that the capitalist stage of economic development could not be skipped. The capitalist stage was necessary for industrialization, as well as for the future of socialism. Capitalism, in the Old Guard view, created the economic structure and the class—the working class—which would create socialism as it came to full consciousness by perceiving its condition and its power. To attempt to impose industrialization, even socialized industrialization, led to brutality and, ultimately, to failure. In many articles written by Russian Social Democrats and the Old Guard, this theme was constantly emphasized: Russia was recklessly trying to skip a stage of history.[6]

It is easy to understand why the Militants were so impatient with this theory. Whatever its theoretical merits, it could only strike them, in the midst of a capitalist depression, as the worst kind of theoretical rigidity to argue that Russia was required to go through the same agonies that accompanied the development of capitalism. A number of Militants accused the Old Guard of subscribing to "iron laws" of economics and of being theoretical metaphysicians. Algernon Lee sought to defend the Old Guard position by maintaining that it was not a matter of "iron laws" or preordained charts of development. All that Marxism predicted, he said, was general developments. And it was these general trends that Russia was violating; those who denied it were dualists who sought to separate human will from the materialist modes of development. Such characterizations hardly went far in persuading the Militants of their historical errors; the Old Guard attitude still seemed to derive from a historical rigidity—as indeed it did. The "practical" Old Guard, however right they were about Stalin's practices, came to their conclusions about the nature of the Russian state from ideological theories about the process of socialist development as much as they did from the evidence of those practices. And though they were convinced that the American workers would never listen to a Socialist Party sympathetic to Russian Bolshevism, they were much less motivated by practical concerns of party building and much more concerned with theoretical purity than was Norman Thomas.[7]

The tension that existed in Thomas's mind between the moral course and the practical course can also be seen in two incidents related to the Socialist Party and the Spanish Civil War. The Socialist Party was, of course, pro-Loyalist. At the same time, it was becoming increasingly critical of Russia and Communist activities in the United States. The Trotskyists in the Socialist Party and the Clarity group urged the Party to adopt a policy of criticism of the Spanish Popular Front government from a revolutionary perspective. However, Thomas and many of his former Militant associates hesitated. Thomas was convinced that too vociferous a criticism of the Spanish Loyalists would aid the cause of fascism, and he was anxious that the Communist Party not have the reputation among American radicals and liberals as the only true friend of Loyalist Spain. The issue of Spain seemed to many to demand an unambiguous commitment, and Thomas, as a party builder, was afraid that too much ambiguity on the part of the Socialist Party could cost it support among Loyalist sympathizers. Yet he could not be completely silent at the increasing evidence of Communist influence in the Spanish government.[8]

The May, 1937, uprising in Barcelona placed Thomas in a peculiar dilemma. He was genuinely convinced that it hurt the Loyalist cause, but I suspect that he was also convinced that too great a sympathy for the insurgents might damage the Party. At the same time, he knew the insurgents had genuine grievances. And so he chose a middle course, arguing for the genuineness of the grievances and urging that the insurgents be given fair trials, but also criticizing them for hurting the cause. He was not able to perceive, at this stage, as Orwell did, that the insurgents were not the betrayers, but the betrayed.[9]

In 1937, the Socialist Party sent Sam Baron to Spain, where he was arrested by the Loyalist government and jailed. Through the protests of Thomas and others, Baron was finally released. But he returned to the United States a bitter man, filled with a kind of Orwellian insight into Spanish events. In November, 1939, Baron was called to testify before the Dies Committee about Communist activity in Spain. He knew that his testimony would embarrass the Socialist Party because of the Party's anti-Dies Committee stand. But he chose to testify, at the same time resigning from the Party. In a moving letter, he described the vision into the "chamber of horrors" he had seen in Spain, and he defended his decision to testify on the ground that he could use the testimony as a vehicle for allowing the American people a glimpse into these depths. Thomas was visibly shaken by Baron's decision. James Loeb, who headed the Spanish Committee of the Socialist Party, disagreed with Baron and continued to defend the Loyalist government, while protesting some of its actions against anti-Stalinist radicals. The left wing of the Socialist Party—the Clarity group—disagreed with Baron's decision to testify before the Dies Committee, but it was convinced that his analysis of Spanish events was more nearly correct than Loeb's. Thomas, however, sided with Loeb. He demanded a strong repudiation of Baron; he was even prepared to resign as national chairman if the National Executive Committee did not strongly repudiate Baron. Thomas was willing to acknowledge that there was some "truth" in Baron's charges, but he argued that Baron had overstated the case, that he did not see the whole picture.[10]

And what was this whole picture? The indications again are that it was not so much the whole picture in Spain, as in the American Socialist Party and in the United States generally. Thomas was distraught because he felt that Baron's decision to testify had hurt the Party in the eyes of the progressive community. And he was right to have opposed Baron's decision, as an eloquent letter to Sam Baron from Liston Oak, who had seen the same "chamber of horrors," makes clear. But Thomas was also concerned that Baron's testimony—not simply the fact that he testified, but what he said —would damage the Party's cause. It would create too great an ambiguity to win commitment to the Socialist position, and it would damage the Party's reputation as a friend of Spain. Finally, it would reduce the Party's and Thomas' influence with the Spanish ambassador—an influence which he hoped could in part moderate the Stalinist excesses in Spain.[11]

In all this, I do not suggest that Thomas ignored the anti-Stalinist purges in Spain, like the liberals around the *New Republic* and the *Nation*. He wrote persuasively against these purges, and he protested privately to the ambassador as well as publicly. But I do suggest that when Thomas was faced with the moral dilemma caused by what Sam Baron had to tell, he chose what seemed the most practical for the Party in its political circumstances. He would have done better to have repudiated only Baron's decision to testify, and not what he had to tell.[12]

The erroneous view that Norman Thomas consistently opted for a "moral" choice over the "practical" derives from the conception of the Socialist Party as standing on a moral plane, outside the realm of practical politics. Thus it is necessary to briefly analyze this conception, a conception which draws much of its force from Daniel Bell's distinction between being "in" or "of" the world.

Daniel Bell, contrasting the pre-World War I Socialist movement with Socialism in the thirties, correctly perceived that the latter, shaken by the World War's disruption of its faith in the inevitable process of history, was forced "to take stands on the particular issues of the day." But he feels that while taking these particular stands, the Party also "rejected completely the premises of the society which shaped these issues." Hence, he says that the Socialist Party "lived 'in' the world, but refused the responsibility of becoming part 'of' it." And this was impossible politically: the Socialists were forced to "duel with no choice as to weapons, place, amount of preparations. . . . Each issue could only be met by an ambiguous political formula which would satisfy neither the purist, nor the activist, who lived with the daily problem of choice." It would be hard to deny Socialism's inability to choose the ideal battleground or to deny that its answers were often ambiguous. But more is at stake here than simply a critique of Socialist tactics and Socialist planks. For if Bell can be deciphered (and such a strict dichotomy between "purist" and "activist" in American Socialism makes little sense), what he seems to have done is to have placed the Socialists in a position where they simply cannot win.[13]

Bell knows that the Socialists proposed solutions to the problems of the day; thus they were "in" the world. In fact, at one point, he writes that unlike the Communists, they shared "responsibility for the day-to-day problems of society." But, he says, by ultimately rejecting society because of their chiliastic expectations, the Socialists were still not really "of" the world—by which one must assume that he includes their rejection of capitalism's political premises: pragmatic compromise among competing interest groups through the political structure.[14]

But all this is too vague, since Bell is writing not only of American Socialists, but of the Socialist movement in general. Were the premises of the Spanish Socialists too different from those of the American Socialists? And can one say that the Spanish Socialists did not share in the "responsibility" *of* the world? In Bell's definition it would seem that he has the American Socialists primarily in mind. And why? Because they failed even more miserably than foreign Socialists. This is important because it points to *failure* as the primary criterion for ultimately not being *of* the world. For what Bell is saying is that Socialists, unable to reconcile the tension between their millennialism and their immediate demands, were ultimately irrelevant to American politics. Theoretically, they could have been irrelevant in two ways. Either they were irrelevant in that they offered poor answers to the problems of the depression or they were irrelevant because they failed. It is doubtful that Bell really wishes to say the former, since there is nothing in his writing that would indicate that he would not have preferred, say, the Unemployment and Labor Section of the 1932 Socialist platform to the National Recovery Administration of the New Deal (or even its entire platform). Where Roosevelt comes off better is in his ability to implement his program. Thus the irrelevancy of Socialism in the 1930's is not so much that its programs were not designed to cure the unemployment problem, but that the Socialists were not able to implement them, to pressure others into implementing them, or even to be members of a compromising team where they could neatly gain support for their program by ignoring segregation, as Roosevelt did in order to get Southern support. In short, the Socialists, like Godkin, Villard, and other intransigents, just didn't "get things done."[15]

Aside from being what must remain a narrow conception (which I hope to show more fully later) of getting things done and of being "of" the world, Bell's analysis leads directly to what is central to his approach: no matter how the Socialists reacted, they cannot win in Bell's "in-of" world. If they did not compromise, they did not confront "the problem of social compromise"; they failed to appreciate the responsible tradition of reform: the tradition of Theodore Roosevelt's "give-and-take" politics. Hence the rigid adherence to class struggle as the *only* way toward Socialist advancement, the forecasts of approaching victory, the refusal to desert Socialist politics for larger labor-reform politics are all indications that the Socialists refused to be "of" the world. But when they tried to be "responsible" and reached a policy of "critical support" of World War II, a policy that was based on compromise, that tried to confront the feelings of the factions within the Socialist Party, the need for domestic reform, and the sensibilities of the American people; when they reached, as Bell recognizes, " an elastic and ambiguous" compromise, but a compromise which in its qualitative essentials was no different from hundreds that the major parties had made to avoid unpleasant issues ("I am for big business, and I am against the trusts," said Woodrow Wilson), they still cannot win Bell's approval. They are damned if they tried to come to terms with the premises of their society and damned if they did not.[16]

PART TWO

The Problem of Alternatives

IV

Theoretical Strategies

DANIEL BELL'S schematic "in-of" conceptional framework placed the Socialist Party of the thirties in a position where it could not win—that is, win Bell's approval. But this was hardly the Socialist Party's problem in the thirties. In this decade, the Party was faced with the problem of real alternatives in terms of basic strategy. And, in terms of this problem, Bell's analysis, ironically, given his views, tends toward an antihistorical approach. As Bell knows, politics deals with possible alternatives. Third parties, no less than the major parties, must continually face this problem. In American history, the Populists of 1896 faced the classic dilemma: to fuse with the Democrats and risk being swallowed up by them, or to refuse and risk isolating themselves from the mainstream of politics. Compared to the Socialist choice, this one was relatively easy, for the Populists, despite recent attempts to make them proto-Socialists, were, at heart, reformers, albeit radical ones. But the Socialists of the thirties, whose main attempt was to create a socialist society—what could they do? Bell's analysis constantly drives toward this conclusion: give up their Socialism and function as another liberal-reform pressure group within the two-party system. This is exactly what many socialists did, especially when faced with the choice between the direction in which the labor movement was going and the direction in which the Socialist Party was going. But what needs emphasizing is that, for all practical purposes, this was not a choice for Socialists who wished to remain socialists; it was a choice that meant giving up socialism. Thus, ex-Socialists became members of the Union for Democratic Action, later the Americans for Democratic Action, and now function as liberal reformers, but they are no longer Socialists and no longer either expect, or want, a socialist society. And this is exactly what makes Bell's analysis antihistorical for Socialists: as long as they had Socialist expectations in the thirties, it is historically irrelevant to say they should have become liberal reformers. For the Socialists were *socialists;* for whatever reasons—chiliastic, rational, psychological—they had come to believe that socialism made for a more humane society than did capitalism. Given this premise, then, what were their alternatives?[1]

Let me set forth the alternatives simply and crudely, and then explore the matter in greater detail. Starkly put, the Socialists could rest their case on the classic Marxist analysis and attempt to build the Party and propagate their ideas from a working-class base. If the Marxist analysis proved wrong (either temporarily or permanently), if for instance, the middle class did not disappear, then this choice would obviously prove unsuccessful. Since this was, to a great extent, the choice that was made, and since it ran head on into the stubborn existence of the middle class and the bourgeoisification of the proletariat, many historians are inclined to suggest other choices. Any choice that would have meant direct support of the Democratic Party would have been out, given the desire for Socialism and the facts of the depression; for historians to expect otherwise would be antihistorical. The only other alternative was another kind of third party. Here, the only kind of national third party that would be significantly different would have been either a Labor Party (modeled, perhaps, on the British Labor Party), a Farmer-Labor Party, or a Socialist Party that not only strove for middle-class support (Norman Thomas, practically speaking, did that for the Socialists), but one that rested its theoretical analysis on the permanent existence of the middle class—i.e., a party based on a theory counter to Marxism.

These are the simple alternatives, but one cannot see the full dimension of the problem unless one examines first the theoretical problem of analyzing historical developments and developing large strategies and then the practical problem the Socialists faced in terms of responding to the various third party movements of the 1930's.

The theoretical problem requires going outside the immediate realm of the Socialist Party, a fact that might indicate one of the Party's chief weaknesses: a lack of theoretical-historical analyses of American society and American history. There is very little radical ideological work in the thirties of lasting significance if one is talking about a development of the larger economic and social trends of the twentieth century and the relationship of these trends to the whole realm of American history and culture. Norman Thomas's work, like much of the radical literature, notes some important developments, but there is no attempt at systematic analysis. There were some important books on Marx; there were a few systematic attempts at Marxist analysis (Lewis Corey's works being the most impressive), but these are characterized more by the ponderousness of their prose than by their creative profundity. Indeed, the kind of Marxism that characterized much of the writing of the 1930's, which could be very useful in evaluating particular events or positions, became, when transformed into a historical-analytical tool, a series of apparently self-evident propositions that approached history in search of evidence. Thus capitalism was believed to be, by definition, contradictory, its ultimate disappearance foredoomed; the middle class was assumed to be disappearing—either dropping down into the working class or appending itself to the capitalist class; the working class was assumed to be growing. The New Deal was assumed to be an impossible attempt to preserve the system, an attempt that would fail and give way to imperialist war and fascism. Radicals might differ on what to do about this scenario of the future, but these rough trends were assumed to be valid. The central element in all this was the working class; to prevent fascism the working class would have to come to power—a reliance on another class was a reliance on the forces that would lead to fascism. An eclectic radical like Thomas did sense that the matter was of greater complexity. But his attempts at theoretical and historical analysis went little beyond the recognition that the middle class was an important element that could not be ignored, went, in the last analysis, little beyond appeals to the workers of "hand *and* brain."[2]

One of the few men on the left to seriously question this simplistic Marxism was Alfred Bingham, an editor of the magazine *Common Sense,* and a kind of intellectual activist in attempting to organize indigenous state farmer-labor parties into a national farmer-labor party. In his key book, *Insurgent America* (1935), Bingham analyzed the emergence of certain economic and social patterns which, according to him, rendered Marxism in need of serious revision and which pointed in the direction of the possibilities of social change based largely on the middle class.[3]

Bingham's assault on a philosophy of social change based on the working class centered, on the one hand, on what he believed to be the historical facts of the case, and, on the other hand, on the psychological consciousness and the culture bred by these facts. In the first place, Bingham argued that the labor movement—the organized working class movement—did not have the potential for radical action that Marxists attributed to it; indeed he saw it as a conservative force. Drawing from various studies, Bingham focused on the job-securing mentality of a mature trade-union movement; the more labor gained in strength in a developed capitalist country, the more it became conservative. The most powerful unions, Bingham believed, had developed "vested interests" that took precedence in policy decisions. The A.F. of L. was used as a prime example of the kind of union structure that was most concerned with protecting previous gains. Radicalism in the labor field, he argued, existed chiefly in the "newly and insecurely organized."[4]

Moreover, Bingham continued, even if labor was more disposed toward radicalism than his analysis might indicate, it was losing its dominant position in society. One of the few radicals of the 1930's to take seriously the rise of the "new" middle class, Bingham focused on the development of this "distributive" class. The distribution of goods, he argued, was becoming as important, if not more important, as their production. And in the wake of the rise of the distributive sector came "a host of new 'business' occupations." These were the "salesmen, advertising men, brokers, jobbers, agents, collectors, credit men, and the like." And as this distributive class increased in terms of numbers and in its power in the economy, the manual working class declined. Along with the development of the distributive class also went the proliferation of managerial functions in the corporate structure and the growth of the engineer and the expert, and, generally, the salaried worker as opposed to the wage-earner. These groups grew numerically (they were at least equal in number to the working class, Bingham argued), and, more important, they grew functionally. Their dominance in urban centers, and even more, in suburban centers, placed them in the key centers of the economy, creating a development that radicals could not ignore ("The type made famous by Briggs' 'Mr. and Mrs.' cartoons has come to set the pace for America. Trim front yards, petty snobbery, gossip, and the *Saturday Evening Post,* may be discouraging soil for revolutionary doctrines, but the radicals would have done better not to ignore them"). The growth of this new class in key areas of the economy had given them, in the end, functional dominance. "The middle class expert," Bingham wrote, "has become the most important functional element." From there it was only one step to predict a future dominated by this new class. Relying for the moment on the Marxian concept that "political supremacy" follows "functional supremacy," Bingham predicted that "the technical and managerial middle-classes" would be the next "ruling class"—unless, of course, radical social changes were to occur.[5]

To compound the difficulty in bringing about radical social

change, there had developed out of this middle-class dominance a whole middle-class psychology that permeated all classes in the United States—in buying habits; reading habits (*Woman's Home Companion, Saturday Evening Post, McCalls*); talking habits; attitudes toward sex, the woman, the home, toward "law and order"; joining habits. Encouraged by "every social institution, from the daily newspaper to the sale of washing machines on the installment plan," these middle-class habits were impossible to break by proletarian class-struggle theories and propaganda: "Imagine the task involved in turning any sizable portion of the readers of *Liberty* or the *Saturday Evening Post* into readers of the *Class Struggle!*—to realize that those who try it are merely butting their heads against the wall."[6]

At this stage in Bingham's analysis, the opportunity of radical social change looked bleak. The strength of the working class was declining; its trade-union organization was making it increasingly conservative; its class consciousness was being increasingly merged into a middle-class consciousness. In short, the working class could not be expected to take the lead in any serious social transformation.

Bingham made one of the few serious attempts to probe and grapple with economic and social trends in the United States. A second attempt, more cultural in its orientation and more concerned with the broad scope of American history, was made by an almost totally ignored American Marxist and sociologist, Leon Samson. Samson, who wrote a series of books in the early thirties —*The New Humanism* (1930), *The American Mind* (1932), and *Toward a United Front* (1934)—, might be considered loosely in the category of those radicals who tried to Americanize Marx. But his work far transcends, at its best (at its worst, it is perverse and crankish), the usual attempts to do this. There was an awareness on the part of the American Left during the thirties that their message was not making contact with the masses; the conclusion was often drawn that this was due to the foreignness of their message to American ears. There was, then, a realization that the radical message must appeal to American traditions, speak the American language—in short, a realization that Marxism must be Americanized. But the end result of this realization was usually worse than the original product. It generally led either to the mechanical appeals to Jefferson and Lincoln of the Communist Party Popular Front period or to analyses that focused almost entirely on terminology or vague warnings that the farmer should not be ignored, even though the worker must lead. There was in all of the talk about Americanizing Marxism very little serious exploration by Marxists of what America was all about or what America's relation to radicalism was or might be. This was what Samson attempted to do.[7]

Samson's first book, *The New Humanism,* can, for my purposes here, be practically ignored. In many ways his most scholarly work, it is a general critique of relativism as it manifested itself in sociology, economics, and philosophy. His second book, *The American Mind,* is a strange combination of analysis and general put-down, insight and crankishness. The basic argument is that the American social mind is immature, undeveloped, infantile. Samson follows this with a description of how infantilism permeates the entire American scene—the working class, the businessman, American socialism, liberalism, art, religion, letters.[8]

According to Samson, this infantilism manifests itself on an *individual*—or personal—level in the absence of a "social sense" and in the presence of a belief in "individual omnipotence." On the *social* level, it can be seen in the absence of "class" feelings. The two—the individual and the social level—come together, of course, to produce American infantilism. The American, Samson writes, "loves to be 'big.' " This is the "well-known wish of the infant . . . to be a man, to be big." But the American is unable to satisfy this in the social sense (he is in the psychosexual sense) because he does not develop "an understanding of the objective laws and limits that are at work in one's social universe." An understanding of these laws and limitations would prevent the American "from attempting to achieve by individual effort" what in actuality can only be achieved through social effort. Lacking this knowledge of social laws and limits, the American believes he can achieve everything privately. As he makes the impossible attempt to achieve social or collective goals by individual effort, American behavior and gestures become "big," grandiose—in short, infantile. The Horatio Alger myth is thus viewed by Samson as a prime example of infantile wish fulfillment:

> No limits here, and no laws. All he needs is nerve and grit and pep and persistency, and above all, a wish to succeed and the social moon is in his hands. The average American discovers soon enough that between his achievement and his wish there are stern barriers that no belief in magic can brush away. This discovery, however, does not seem to un-deceive him, so that on the aftermath of every failure, instead of blaming the barriers, he blames himself, and true to his socio-neurotic nature, after a flush of buoyant expect-ancy, he drops back into his brooding over his own deficiency, drops from his omnipotence back into his incompetence. Drops, but does not stay there long. The Presidential perora-tions on equal opportunity see to it that he does not. He reads and is convinced. His hopes run high. Once more the world is waiting on his wish. And so the American—the average American—tosses and turns from dream to defeat and from defeat to dream.[9]

And so Samson turns from illustration to illustration of Ameri-can immaturity and incompetence. He analyzes the presuppositions behind American patriotism and finds that it is based on the idea that we ought "to sacrifice our 'all' for America, because America is the land of opportunity for all." But he dismisses this kind of patriotism as "greenhorn gratitude" and the most self-centered in the world. "Frenchmen die," Samson writes, ". . . for 'la belle France.' Englishmen die for 'King and Country,' Germans for the 'Fatherland,' Americans for the land of—equal opportunity." Thus, he concludes, "they identify their country's culture as their own comfort and project their own comfort as their country's culture." Similarly, he dismisses the American concept of freedom as "the absolution of an abstraction." It tells us, he says, nothing about the nature of the social world and the structure of its relations. Consequently, the word "freedom" has "done more to obscure our social vision than has perhaps any other word."[10]

Samson considered himself a Marxist. He believed that the working class had the power to transform the United States from what he called "the gaseous stage of its evolution" into an integrated and organic whole. Yet (perhaps *because* of this faith in the working class), some of his bleakest comments on American infantile social thinking are reserved for what it has done to the working class. In the first place, it has eliminated the concept of class. By positing an extreme individualism and an equality of opportunity, and by denying the existence and meaningfulness of social class, the American creed has made the working class unreceptive to radical ideas and doctrines. Suffering from its "fatal social infantilism," the working class has not had the collective energy for the kind of thought and action that would break the bonds of the capitalist society. Instead, the proletariat and its struggle is transformed into the "poor man" and his complaints; instead of proletarian class formation and ferment one has "private sorties" against society by "Hairy Apes"; instead of a revolution against private property one has individual "criminal adventures"; instead of the working class being anticapitalist, it is "anti-social."[11]

Samson's conclusions in *The American Mind* were hardly reassuring to anyone who believed in a future for socialism in the United States. Most radicals shared his belief in the infantile nature of the working class, in its undeveloped class consciousness. But most attributed this relative ideological backwardness of the working class to the lack of the full economic development of capitalism and its institutions. American capitalism, beginning later than European capitalism, had yet to mature completely; with the maturation of capitalism would come the ideological awakening of the working class, the development of a revolutionary class consciousness. When one considers that Samson was not attributing the working-class or the general American infantilism to an undeveloped capitalist system (it was infantilism in the *face of* a thoroughly developed and matured capitalist economic system), one glimpses the stark pessimism of his picture. A 350-page illustration of the United States' social, intellectual, and artistic incompetence was surely a "weapon of criticism" as he wrote in his introduction, but it certainly offered no way out. Indeed, there are parts of the book that, in their descriptions of the incompetence of American culture and the pathos of the American intellect, read as if they came from the pen of a conservative elitist; stripped of their covert Marxism, there are passages in the book that could have been penned by the anarchist elitist, Albert Jay Nock. From a reading of its bleak and pessimistic commentary, one could hardly imagine that the United States was potentially fertile for socialism; in fact, one could hardly imagine anything more alien to the United States.[12]

Toward a United Front, written two years later in 1934, was subtitled "A Philosophy for American Workers." Its purpose, among other things, was to show that socialism in the United States had a future, and to provide the working class—still the one vehicle for socialism—with a philosophy and tactic for achieving it. It might be imagined that Samson's ideas would have undergone significant shifts in two short years in order to move from a compilation of American infantilism to a book which ended on a rather optimistic note about the possibilities for radical transformation. However, it was not so much a shift in ideas as the placing of his previous ideas in a new context. In Toward a United Front American infantilism is placed within the context of what Samson called America's "substitute socialism." Substitute socialism is analyzed as both an impediment to the real thing (in the same way that American infantilism was an impediment to real social thought), and an illustration of the potentiality for real socialism. In the hidden recesses of substitute socialism there lingered a potential anticapitalist thrust. In short, socialism—the real thing—was not alien to America; it had simply been distorted into a fake form.[13]

In this work, Samson again begins with a statement of the

backwardness of the American working class: the objective conditions (production, etc.) were ripe for revolution; the working class was far from revolution. He rejects as causes for this backwardness such standard ideas as the greater prosperity of the American working class, the frontier (though he sees certain important conditions arising out of geographic expansion), and the betrayal by working-class leaders ("even if they are being sold out constantly, why do they allow themselves to be?"). He concludes that it is impossible to find the cause for working-class backwardness in any purely objective conditions; the reasons, he says, "must be sought elsewhere—in the mind of the American." His subsequent investigation of the "American social mind" leads him to an examination of the meaning of Americanism—and into the whole concept of substitute socialism.[14]

What is the meaning of Americanism? Samson asks. It is not, he says, a tradition or a territory as France would be to a Frenchman or England to an Englishman. Rather it is a *doctrine*—what socialism is to a socialist. Americanism, he argues, in an apparent contradiction to his previous analysis of patriotism, is not looked on patriotically—"as a personal attachment." Instead, it is viewed as "system of ideas" or as "a handful of final notions." These ideas or notions—democracy, liberty, opportunity—are adhered to "rationalistically" by the American. Samson stresses this because he is trying to draw a comparison between the thought processes of a socialist subscribing to socialism and an American subscribing to Americanism. The two thought processes, he insists, are similar. Like the believer in socialism, the adherent to Americanism subscribes to his belief "because it does him good, because it gives him work, because, so he thinks, it guarantees him happiness." In this manner, by offering an alternative to socialism, Americanism has functioned as a substitute for it. And that is why it has been so difficult for the socialist message to be accepted by Americans. "Every concept in socialism," he writes, "has its substitute counter-concept in Americanism, and that is why the socialist argument falls so fruitlessly on the American ear."[15]

The mutual existence of a capitalist societal structure with the ethos of substitute socialism helps explain, for Samson, many of the paradoxes he found in American society. The United States was a capitalist society with all the characteristics of a capitalist state— "a strong political state—a profit-wages system of imperial dimensions—a religion—a navy." Yet Samson found a decidedly uncapitalist element in American culture. "In the minds of its inhabitants," he declared, "in their manners, their rhythms, their style of life, this American civilization appears to be in no sense capitalistic, appears, on the contrary, socialistic, proletarian, 'human,' . . . far from imperialistic." Again, this paradox helped explain the weakness of true socialism; the "socialistic fantasy in the mind of the American" closed his mind to true socialism, since the American thought—in his mind—that he already had the genuine article.[16]

How could this be? Socialism is offered to the American as a new world—"a new social universe"—displacing the old; but America is for the American already the "new world"—the land of the future, isolated, aloof, "a new social planet that has torn itself off and away from the old-world system." "Workers of the world unite—you have nothing to lose but your chains" is the disinherited's cry of socialism; but "to go to America" has been the road open to the disinherited (America again appears as a substitute for socialism—"the one new world which proletarians do not have to rise to, but run to. But a new world nevertheless").[17]

In this new world, old ideals take on new forms. Using the image of a prism, Samson attempts to demonstrate what happens to capitalist ideals when they confront Americanism. The ideals themselves—"Liberty, Equality, Democracy" are, according to Samson, capitalistic, imperialistic, bourgeois "in origin and essence." In this, they are like the system itself. But "refracted in the prism of Americanism," liberty becomes more than laissez faire. It becomes, instead, "human self-emancipation." It becomes "individualism," but not simply "bourgeois" individualism. Rather, it becomes "collective" individualism. And here lies its pseudo-socialist element, for the ideal of a collective or a "universal" individualism is a "socialistic conception" of individualism.[18]

Similarly, the whole American ideal of opportunity, originally a capitalist concept, no longer remains a capitalist concept. Opportunity was, in capitalist theory, to be restricted to the bourgeoisie. But in the American prism, it is "brought down . . . to the broadest layers of the population" and thereby takes on its socialistic connotations. "The idea that everybody can become a capitalist," Samson writes, "is an American conception of capitalism. Socialism is of all systems the only one in which everybody is in it. Capitalism is, in theory, and in Europe, for the capitalists—just as feudalism is for the feudal lords."[19]

In the United States, however, it is capitalism for all—that is, in the American mind. In reality, of course, capitalism is not for all; it is as oligarchic and brutal and exclusive in the United States as it is everywhere else. Similarly, one does not have democracy for all in the United States; that would only be possible under socialism. Democracy in the United States remains, in reality, democracy for the ruling class. But as the concept of democracy works its way through the prism and refracts into the American mind it overrides the reality of class, conceals it, substitutes for it "an amorphous and intangible all-around democratism—a general, good-natured camaraderie of the spirit that here goes hand in hand with a most dis-spirited, oligarchic, unprincipled violation of the democratic ideal in the actual relations of life."[20]

What does one have then? According to Samson, every single bourgeois concept is transformed into a substitute pseudosocialistic form as it "passes through the prism of Americanism." Laissez faire comes out "individualism"; "simple democracy" becomes "equalitarianism"; instead of "plain competition" there is "competitive opportunity." Indeed, Samson writes, "nothing in America is capitalistic except the capitalism. The people, their temper, their tastes, are socialistic. A socialistic spirit in a capitalist system. This is America. And this is what the comrades will have to take into account in their calculations."[21]

Despite the fact that substitute socialism masks a hidden desire for true socialism (the American assertion of classlessness reveals an unconscious wish that there were no class struggles and no classes), what exists, for Samson, remains *substitute* socialism. From "democracy" and "opportunity" to the flappers (the pseudo-socialistic parallel of free love), the existing article is fake. And as such, it is oppressive. Harking back to *The American Mind,* Samson reminds the American that in settling for the substitute, he reveals himself as "socio-neurotic, infantile." In *Toward a United Front,* Samson tries to analyze some of the reasons for this infantile satisfaction with substitutes. His reasoning involves the role of the frontier in diffusing European ideology and the counterpull of Europe in ideologizing this now negated and diffused ideology. The end result is that the social energy necessary for true revolution has, under the belief in Americanism, run off into individual adventurism—into land, money-making, politics, work itself. What becomes necessary in order to redirect this energy is a large dose of political realism injected into the American scene in order to reveal the pseudo quality of the socialism and to lay the basis for genuine socialism.[22]

The need for a redirection of energy leads into the area of solutions. Here Bingham and Samson offered clearly distinct paths to the attainment of socialism, or, as Bingham chose to call it, "production for use." This differentiation in strategies is important because the two men were quite close in their diagnosis of American culture. What Bingham called middle-class attitudes and habits, especially the absence of class feelings, Samson diagnosed as substitute socialism. In order to illustrate the middle class's potential stake in socialism and its lack of a permanent stake in capitalism, Bingham emphasized its concern for security rather than, strictly speaking, capitalist property. Samson similarly emphasized security, arguing it was a socialist idea, but one which, in typical American fashion, had been "pseudo-ized" and "infantilized" into "family insurance." Indeed, the conjunction of their two analyses is shown by Bingham's specifically citing Samson in support of his own analysis:

> Leon Samson coined the phrase 'substitute socialism' to cover the whole range of American phenomena with which we are here concerned. Not only has the American hidden the realities of exploitation and class rule by adopting manners of a classless society, but in his attitude toward the community in every respect, from the insignificant social group to the nation as a whole, he behaves more as one would expect a member of a cooperative socialist community than of an individual in a competitive acquisitive society. The phrase is a happy one. It suggests at once that middle-class America is more ready for Socialism, as regards national characteristics and habits, than other countries.[23]

But if Bingham's and Samson's analyses of American society frequently touched, their solutions were very different. Bingham's solution was based on a theoretical analysis, as we have seen, that ran counter to the Marxism that characterized Samson and most radicals and radical parties in the thirties. So did his solution. Because he believed the growth of the middle class and the diminution of the proletariat contradicted Marxist theory, Bingham was desperately afraid that the middle classes would go fascist if a straight working-class appeal was used by radicals. The middle class in his analysis had little stake in the capitalist system *per se,* but it was definitely afraid of a proletarian revolution that would rob it of its personal security—its job and its home. If it were fearful of a proletarian revolution, the middle class would rush to fascism, which Bingham diagnosed as the pseudo-revolution of the middle classes against capitalism *and* the proletarian revolution. A straight Marxist theory of class struggle, then, might easily drive the middle class, in reaction, toward fascism. To avoid this, it was necessary to avoid a split between the middle classes and the working class. This meant playing down the class struggle, eschewing straight proletarian appeals, reaching out into farmer-labor parties, emphasizing working-class *and* middle-class common interests.

Specifically, in terms of making appeals and planning a strategy for radical change, Bingham suggested: (1) "Devotion to security and to property (in the sense of possessions) must not be outraged." Negatively, this meant minimizing the "emphasis on revolution, civil war, domestic turmoil, class struggle, confiscation, expropriation, destruction." Positively, it meant "an emphasis on greater security, a higher standard of living, wealth for everybody (except those who are already wealthy), protection of home and farms, and . . . a promise of a peaceful transition with a minimum of disturbance of the even course of the average man's way of life." (2) "The American characteristics of optimism, sentimentality, patriotism, and Puritanism must be respected." This meant "cheerfulness, good humor, hopefulness—the 'booster' qualities—are more important than hate and savage or brutal attacks, in winning popular support." To emphasize this "positive" approach, Bingham wrote:

> Americans are sentimental, and no movement will get far that does not pledge unswerving allegiance to the protection of America's soft heart and its fetishes, the home and the family. A 'proletarian' appeal is almost necessarily hard-boiled, and immediately rouses anxiety among other elements of the population. Finally, the association of radical thought with pacifism, internationalism, sex freedom, and other ultimate desiderata, not immediately involved in the transformation of the national economy, has offended certain American prejudices, for the most part unnecessarily. A sound radical movement will be one-hundred-per cent American, defending the home, the family, the church, and the nation.

(3) "A constructive, practical plan for thorough-going change is essential." What this meant was more emphasis on ultimate aims than on immediate objectives. Finally, demonstrations and mass action would be necessary, but any specific direct action—especially if rife with "the suggestion of violent class struggle"—which has a greater "divisive than unifying effect should be ruled out." Political campaigning, educational activity, and the joining of fraternal groups should be emphasized.[24]

Farmer-labor politics, the ballot, economic plans and blueprints for shared wealth, a little "flag-waving"—these were the essence of Bingham's strategy for socialism. Samson's strategy involved the leaders of the American working class injecting the aforementioned dose of political realism into the majority (at present under "the spell of the thousand-headed American ballyhoo"). American capitalism was bound to run its course and only the party that had talked "sober reason" and had a "reputation for realism" would be listened to. At this point, when capitalism ran its course, the working class would reject the ballyhoo with cries of " boloney."[25]

What political realism involved ideologically was the "establishing of the class line in the American social mind, the crystallizing of the ideological divisions to correspond to the realities of the economic division." This, for Samson, was the real battle—not the organization of productive forces, not the bourgeois-feudal resistance. The former was already accomplished and the latter was largely absent in the United States. The belief that the real battle was the ideological battle was directly related to his concept of pseudo-socialism. The American mind was a classless mind, so it would not stand a class society if it perceived that there was, in fact, a class society. Hence, "the establishing of classes in the American mind is the abolishing of classes in American society." The initial step was the all-important step; once the class line was established, once the workers saw that the failures of the American dream were directly attributable to capitalism, then because of their deeply ingrained Americanism (previously an impediment to socialism), they would move toward socialism. And so would the majority of Americans, since they too were pseudo-socialists all the time. "So long as Americanism is intact under capitalism," Samson wrote, "they will not listen seriously to socialism. Let, however, their Americanism be violated by capitalism, and they will go the full length and logic of socialism."[26]

To develop this class line, Samson suggested a United Labor Front, and, in particular, an American Labor Party—a party founded "on the broad base of the working class" and mirroring "the needs and nature of the American working class." This party would both unite all "honestly proletarian groups, parties, sections" with one another and also connect them all to "an American vanguard." Samson stressed the need to fuse the American revolutionary heritage with Marxian revolutionary theory in this party. But the essential point here is that Samson's diagnosis, which had touched Bingham's on a number of points, departed from his when it came to prescriptive suggestions for the radical way out, when it came to remedies for answering the perennial question for radicals: "What is to be done?" For though his Labor Party would try to draw out American revolutionary energy and not be content with parroting Marxist slogans, Samson nevertheless had proposed a *labor* party. And any such suggestion, to Bingham, would run the terrifying risk of splitting the working class and the middle class and setting the stage for fascism.[27]

It was these alternatives (with obviously a number of individual variations) that presented themselves to radicals in the thirties as theoretical possibilities for social change: a program oriented toward the middle class and middle-class sensibilities which would play down proletarian and revolutionary slogans, and a program that emphasized working-class activity, that made a working-class appeal that would confront this middle-class sensibility. Each had its attractions. But there were fundamental problems in each view that neither author faced, and which meant that each course, rather than being filled with possibilities and opportunities for radicals, was precarious and filled with problems and dilemmas for them.

Bingham was cogent when it came to noting the development of the new middle class and interpreting the habits of the American people. But he exaggerated the potential for basic change in the middle-class mind, overread its dissatisfaction with capitalism, failed to see that many of the economic trends he discussed were barriers to—not possibilities for—radicalism. In stressing "ultimate aims" and minimizing immediate demands when appealing to the middle class, Bingham failed to realize just how these grandiose aims, schemes, and plans—technocracy, utopian societies, even

Townsend plans—led off into vagueness and generality. In short, he failed to recognize how they led off into a vague kind of talk about the future, while leaving the participants still wedded to the system and the system free to continue its operations smoothly.

Moreover, Bingham never faced the fact that his sentimental approach, which was designed not to alienate the middle class, would only serve to reinforce many of the very attitudes that made it shy away from basic social change, and thus inevitably negate the movement's radicalism. In addition, there was a fundamental psychological fact he passed over: the type of person who would respond most to his kind of appeal was generally not the type of person who responded to socialism in the thirties. For most Socialists had turned toward socialist politics in order to escape this inflated rhetoric of hearth, home, and country. The type of person who would more readily respond to Bingham's mixture of radical economics and homegrown corn was the type of person who would more easily see this blend and feel more comfortable in the fuzzy generalities of Franklin D. Roosevelt and the New Deal. In brief, Bingham's solution led almost inevitably toward liberal reform. It is not surprising that Bingham, by 1937, was arguing that the New Deal was as revolutionary as could be expected.

And Samson's analysis and solutions? For all the perceptiveness and suggestiveness in much of his analysis, he was overly optimistic about the possibilities of transforming substitute socialism into true socialism. He failed (probably because of his faith in the ultimate collapse of capitalism) to reckon fully with what he "theoretically" realized—that pseudo-socialism, simply because it was pseudo-socialism and not a feudal, or even a capitalist, exclusionary ideology, was the strongest barrier to true socialism. While he perceived how the proletariat had been bourgeoisified in mind, he failed to perceive how a "democratic" "pseudo-socialistic" form of capitalism could also "bourgeoisify" the worker in practice by taking him into the corporate structure. The union movement and the New Deal together would do this in the 1930's and 1940's. And as this process developed, those who clung to Samson's working class orientation in politics—working-class parties, independent political action on the part of labor, a Marxian critique of capitalism—found themselves more and more isolated from political power.

This last point returns us from the realm of theoretical strategies to the historical events of the 1930's. The analysis of Bingham and Samson has attempted to delineate two broad theoretical directions in which radicals, including the Socialists, might go. Theoretically, they could have gone with Bingham's approach, in which case they, like Bingham, would have wound up no longer Socialists, but New Deal reformers. Or they could have clung to their Marxist analysis and isolated themselves from the American public. Neither alternative pointed toward success—and by success I mean socialist success, for that was what they were interested in historically.

V

Parties

TO SUGGEST that Bingham's and Samson's solutions were the two large alternatives between which Socialists were caught in the 1930's does not demonstrate the problem in its full historical dimension: the practical problem that the Socialists faced in terms of third party movements and/or quasi-Socialist attempts to redirect the politics of the Democratic Party. In the early thirties, the Socialist Party contained a number of diverse attitudes toward the issue of third parties. Following the unsuccessful attempt to transform the Progressive Party of 1924 into a Labor Party, the Socialist Party as a whole was determined not to participate in third parties that were simply capitalist reform parties. At the same time, there was a great deal of sentiment within the Socialist Party for a broader labor party or farmer-labor party, which might not be fully socialist as yet in its politics, but which had widespread labor support and at least a semi-socialist orientation. It was felt, however, that if such a party developed, the Socialist Party should enter it on a federated basis, keeping itself intact; any possible third party cooperation should not be a vehicle for liquidating the Socialist Party.[1]

In the late twenties and early thirties, Norman Thomas was especially sympathetic to the idea of a larger farmer-labor party into which the Socialists might enter as a constituent part. But he was insistent that the Party should be allowed to enter as a unit, and that any third party the Socialists joined should not be merely an insurgency movement by groups within the two old parties or an attempt to bring pressure on the Democrats and Republicans. It had to be a genuine third party, willing to break clearly with the capitalist parties, even if it was not yet willing to adopt a full Socialist ideology. Thomas had no wish to repeat the 1924 experience.[2]

To a number of Socialists, the League for Independent Political Action looked like a genuine attempt to transform American politics. Formed by a number of liberals and radicals (including Socialists) in 1928, the League appeared to be a vehicle for launching a larger farmer-labor party that would decisively break with the capitalist parties. Thomas was eager for the Socialists to cooperate in this John Dewey-led organization. And a number of Socialists did play a role in its organization. However, a letter from John Dewey to Senator George Norris in 1930, inviting him to withdraw from the Republican Party and to lead the L.I.P.A. in the 1932 presidential election, quickly ended the Socialist enthusiasm—and with it, the L.I.P.A.'s promising beginning. Right-wing Socialists, suspicious of Thomas's "progressivism," urged Socialists to withdraw; left-wing Socialists felt Dewey's letter indicated the liberal nature of the League for Independent Political Action and withdrew.[3]

Though this initial Socialist cooperation with an incipient third party movement came to naught, the experience indicates the outlines of the Socialist Party's attitude toward third parties in the early 1930's. The major support came from Norman Thomas and the non-Marxian radicals within the Party. The major opposition came from the Old Guard on the right and the Marxist Militants on the left. Theoretically, the Old Guard subscribed to the need for a labor party. But in 1931 Morris Hillquit, the Old Guard leader, was speculating that perhaps a labor party might not be a necessary stage on the road to socialism in America. Some of his disinterest in a labor party was the result in his experience in 1924, but part of it resulted from his belief that a labor party, controlled by the Socialist Party, might become a vehicle for Socialist control of the labor unions. The left-wing Socialists, for their part, felt that too much attention to third party movements pointed the Party away from its revolutionary function. They were convinced that any possible labor party on the horizon would be a reformist party and that this would make the Socialist Party dependent on reformist ideas.[4]

At the same time that the left wing and the right wing of the Socialist Party showed little interest in a farmer-labor party, the Milwaukee Socialists, the least ideological group within the Party, were, for their own reasons, hesitant to cooperate with the Wisconsin Progressive Party. Daniel Hoan, the Socialist mayor of Milwaukee, had a solid Socialist base and was optimistic about the possibilities throughout the state. Therefore, he, as well as Wisconsin Militants like Andrew Biemiller, viewed with suspicion Easterners who urged cooperation. The Eastern Socialist who was most active in urging the Milwaukee Socialists to cooperate with the LaFollette Progressives was B. C. Vladeck, who was on close terms with Norman Thomas, although he eventually sided with the Old Guard when the Party split. Vladeck was enthusiastic about the possibilities for a national farmer-labor party and he saw great opportunities for beginning it in Wisconsin and the rest of the Midwest. He was in correspondence with Thomas Duncan, a former Socialist and secretary to Mayor Hoan, who had left the Socialist Party to become Governor LaFollette's executive secretary. Duncan encouraged Vladeck's optimism about joint cooperation.[5]

In late 1933 and early 1934, Vladeck communicated to Hoan his belief that the Wisconsin Socialists should seek cooperation with the LaFollette forces. Vladeck argued that by itself the Socialist Party in Wisconsin could not gain power, that the Progressives were moving in the direction of Socialism and had centers of strength in areas where the Socialists were weak, and that, functioning in cooperation, the two groups could control the state.

Vladeck, arguing always that what one should be concerned with was a socialist *movement,* rather than a Socialist Party, saw possibilities where the Wisconsin Socialists saw drawbacks. Daniel Hoan, Andrew Biemiller, and other leading Wisconsin Socialists accused Vladeck of taking his information from Wisconsin Progressives who could not be trusted. The Wisconsin Progressives were not moving toward Socialism, Hoan and Biemiller argued. They were attempting to hop on the Roosevelt "bandwagon," minus the Democratic Party. The Socialists, on the other hand, were growing every day and picking up new centers of strength.[6]

Norman Thomas believed that a genuine farmer-labor party or labor party had to have a solid labor base and be more than a capitalist reform party. He was anxious for the development of such a party and had high hopes for the new developments in Wisconsin. He encouraged the Wisconsin Socialists not to remain aloof from the Wisconsin Progressives. But faced with resistance from the Wisconsin Socialists, he refrained from bringing pressure after his gesture. One suspects that, involved in the intraparty dispute over the Declaration of Principles, he was thinking of keeping allies and not simply of his own beliefs on when Socialists should cooperate with third parties. Daniel Hoan was an influential "centrist" figure that Thomas needed on his side, and Andrew Biemiller was a close ally of both Hoan and Thomas. Still, one should not exaggerate Thomas's enthusiasm for farmer-labor parties. He was, as I have argued, always very conscious of what was good for building the Socialist Party and socialism, and he was not about to sacrifice Party interests by rushing into ecumenical cooperation with spurious third parties. In any case, there was no further pressure on the Wisconsin Socialists from Thomas in 1934.[7]

The issue of Wisconsin Socialist cooperation with a third party came up again in 1935. The newly formed Wisconsin Farmer-Labor Progressive Federation endorsed a "production for use" platform and all candidates endorsed by the Federation were required to subscribe to its platform. The Wisconsin Socialists participated in the formation of the Federation and actively cooperated with it. The National Executive Committee of the Socialist Party granted approval in 1936. A promising beginning, where joint tickets were run, and, in 1936, any endorsement of Roosevelt was set aside, soon gave way to deep problems. The Wisconsin labor movement was moving closer to the New Deal. So was Senator Robert LaFollette. Governor Philip LaFollette made an abortive attempt to form a national third party in 1938, but even its progressivism—much less any socialism—was suspect. The Socialists within the Federation, rather than leading it toward socialism and leading labor toward independent political action, found themselves swallowed up in the liberal reformist tide. Their strength deteriorated. Hoan was defeated for mayor of Milwaukee in 1940, though his defeat cannot be blamed solely on the disappearance of Socialist strength. By the early 1940's, the few remaining Wisconsin Socialists were blaming Hoan and many of the old Socialists for having destroyed the Party. Hoan and others, they argued, had, once they were in the Wisconsin Farmer-Labor Federation, shown little interest in party building, much interest in job-seeking, and the cause of socialism had been forgotten. Hoan himself, over the protests of many Socialists, accepted a job on Roosevelt's National Council of Defense, and later in the 1940's ran unsuccessfully for various offices as a Democrat. One episode of the Socialist Party attempting to follow an alternative along the lines suggested by Bingham's theories had led to little in terms of building Socialism, except a liberal organization of ex-Socialists. And even it could not exist separate from the Democratic Party for long.[8]

The problem of cooperation with other political parties could take a variety of forms. In 1933 Fiorello LaGuardia ran on a fusion ticket for mayor of New York against the Democratic Tammany candidate. The Socialists had been consistent and vociferous critics of Tammany. In 1932, Thomas and Paul Blanshard had co-authored *What's the Matter with New York*. They had severely criticized Tammany's corruption and Governor Franklin D. Roosevelt for temporizing with it. Thomas's focus on corruption as a political issue had been so strong that many Socialists, especially among the Old Guard, spoke disparagingly of this "liberal" approach. LaGuardia's reform approach, his promise of clean government, held an appeal then to Socialists who had viewed corruption as a key issue in local Socialist politics. When Thomas's close friend, Blanshard, resigned from the Socialist Party in order to support LaGuardia for mayor, he embarrassed Thomas, since he had been associated with the Militant wing of the Party. But Thomas did not waver in his belief that fusion was not the answer to New York's problems. Whatever the weaknesses of the Wisconsin Progressives might have been, they at least were a third party, running candidates against the two old parties. But the fusion candidacy of LaGuardia was backed by Republicans. For the Socialist Party or Thomas to have supported the LaGuardia candidacy would have meant supporting a candidate supported by one of the old parties. And, in the early thirties, this was a step that the Party was determined to resist. Blanshard, of course, justified his action by arguing that more steps could be taken in the direction of implementing his ideals through LaGuardia than through the Socialist Party, which remained small and isolated. Thomas, whose interest was socialism, was more perceptive than Blanshard in seeing that whatever good Blanshard might achieve on specific issues, his ideal of socialism would not be furthered by his course of action.[9]

An even more dramatic example of attempting to further socialism in conjunction with one of the two old parties occurred in 1934 when Upton Sinclair attempted to win the governorship of California on his EPIC platform. Sinclair's candidacy had a disastrous effect on the Socialist Party in California. Members from both the right wing and the left wing deserted the Party to support Sinclair. Many Socialists throughout the country, particularly from the West, wrote to Thomas urging him to support Sinclair. Sinclair's supporters argued that his End Poverty in California Plan was at least quasi-socialist, if not completely socialist. Moreover, they argued that the masses of people were with Sinclair. The task of the Socialist Party was to convert the masses of people to socialism.

For the Socialist Party to repudiate Sinclair, then, would mean not leading the people to socialism, but turning them away from it. Only by actively participating in his campaign could Socialists perform their educational task for socialism. For Thomas, who shared many of the premises about the need to reach masses of people, the argument was difficult to counter.[10]

Thomas exchanged many letters with Sinclair's supporters and with Sinclair, in addition to his famous Open Letter to Upton Sinclair. He also sent the EPIC plan to Party economists in order for them to evaluate it. Constantly he reminded Sinclair and his supporters that, while some of the individual planks had merit, the EPIC program was not socialism. And for Thomas, to lead people into thinking it was socialism by supporting Sinclair would not perform the necessary education for true socialism. Moreover, he argued, Sinclair's program would not work; thinking it was socialism, the people would be harder to convince the next time around. Thomas insisted that he would support Sinclair if he could be convinced that he was somehow advancing socialism, even if his program was not itself socialistic. But all he could see was that Sinclair was advancing the interests of the Democratic Party—and himself. In order to get elected, even after winning the primary, Sinclair would have to at least reassure the conservative Democrats. Rather than bringing the Democratic Party to socialism by his course, Sinclair and the Socialists would be absorbed in the Democratic Party. Thomas's prediction, of course, came true. Some Socialists returned to the Party. But most were absorbed into the Democratic Party and whatever liberal reformism it could muster, and little was heard from them for the cause of socialism.[11]

The Sinclair issue was a bitter one in the Socialist Party. The bitterness derived not from the fact that any of the major groups within the Party supported Sinclair—they were all opposed—but because the Old Guard sought to use it to embarrass Thomas and because it ripped through the California State Party so dramatically. The Old Guard attempted to show that the forces aligned with Thomas, in particular the *American Guardian,* published in Okla-

homa and edited by Oscar Ameringer and his son, Siegfried, had
taken a tolerant and sympathetic attitude toward Sinclair. The Old
Guard struck gold when Dr. Michael Shadid, elected to the National
Executive Committee from Oklahoma in 1934, and aligned with
Thomas and the Militants in the fight over the Declaration of
Principles, wired his congratulations to Sinclair for his primary
victory. The succeeding uproar in the Party forced the N.E.C. to
insist on Shadid's resignation. The Ameringers protested, but
Thomas felt he could not let the Old Guard have the Sinclair issue
as their property at a time when he was attempting to enforce
Socialist discipline on the Old Guard in New York City.[12]

The Sinclair issue was clearly not an Old Guard-Militant issue,
since one of Sinclair's chief lieutenants was the former Old Guard
member of the National Executive Committee, John Packard. Still,
the issue, like most issues, became associated with the internal feuds
of the Party. Part of its major import was, in this way, lost in the
thirties. But not all. For Thomas understood that more was at
stake than preventing the Old Guard from having a political issue
to use against his supporters. He understood the real problem that
the Socialists were faced with in California. He saw that if Sinclair
was defeated, it would assure a reactionary governor. He saw that
individual parts of Sinclair's program might be progressive. He
saw that if the Socialist Party ran a candidate for governor against
Sinclair, it would take votes away from him, as well as gain for
the Socialist Party a reputation for being a spoiler. Among liberal
people who might be inclined toward sympathy with the Socialist
Party and its program, this could prove damaging. Indeed, Thomas
even wrote privately to Milan Dempster, the Socialist Party candidate for governor in California, saying that though he favored
running a Socialist ticket, if Dempster and the other Socialist
leaders in California felt it was in the best interest of the Party
there, they could withdraw Dempster's gubernatorial candidacy
(though they should not under any circumstances positively support Sinclair). Thomas understood all this. But he also understood
the fact that the Democratic Party, not socialism and the Socialist

Party, stood to gain from Sinclair's candidacy. He understood that the Socialists who were deserting the Socialist Party for Sinclair were benefiting the Democrats and not socialism. He understood, then, the risks of absorption within the folds of the Democratic Party. That later he was to support a move by Socialists in New York which, in its practical effects, was not so different only shows the desperate weakness of the Socialist Party as the thirties progressed.[13]

American Labor Party

The story of the Socialist Party's relations with the American Labor Party in New York cannot be told in full. Yet it must be examined in detail. For it epitomizes the problems faced by the Socialists in relation to third parties. It is connected with many issues—with internal party feuds, with theoretical proclamations and viable options, with the Party's connection with the labor movement, with high hopes and diminished expectations.

The American Labor Party was formed in 1936 by a number of New York unions which wished to support Roosevelt, but not on the Democratic line. The recently formed Social Democratic Federation, composed of the Old Guard Socialists, gave it immediate support. The Old Guard-Militant feud had decimated what new support Thomas had succeeded in winning for the Party since he had become its presidential candidate in 1928. At the beginning of the 1930's the Old Guard had accused Thomas of trying to turn the Socialist Party away from a workers' party and into a liberal-reform party. As the bitter feud developed in the early thirties, however, the Old Guard came to view the reformist New Deal with less hostility than did either Thomas or his Militant allies. Before 1936, the Old Guard, for the most part, still maintained a high level of criticism of the New Deal. However, in 1936 it became apparent to the Old Guard that many of the unions from which it gained support were aligning themselves with the New Deal. As yet, still nominally in the Socialist Party, the members of the Old

Guard were unwilling to give outright support to a capitalist party. But if a vehicle could be created which at the same time had labor support, would back Roosevelt, yet was outside the two-party structure, then the Old Guard was willing to jump on it.[14]

When the Old Guard left the Socialist Party following the Cleveland Convention in May, 1936, it formed the Social Democratic Federation. With the formation of the American Labor Party in New York, the Social Democratic Federation saw the opportunity for helping build a labor party, supporting Roosevelt, and still remaining outside the Democratic Party. Theoretically, the American Labor Party was to work for a national party, though this was soon forgotten.[15]

The Socialist Party, however, did not greet the American Labor Party on such a positive note; in fact, their attitude was negative. The reasons for the Party's criticism are connected with its more critical attitude toward the politics of the labor movement and with its theoretical position on what a labor party should be in order to gain Socialist support. In February, 1936, Thomas proclaimed the necessity for a farmer-labor party, but he recognized that there was no opportunity for a national party in 1936. He also recognized that the recent mine workers' endorsement of Roosevelt was an indication of the direction in which the labor movement was moving in 1936. He understood the reason for the policy the mine workers were following: the union received concrete benefits from the administration, which in turn faced hostile opposition from the mine owners. However, he insisted the policy was dangerous; it was a defensive strategy that had not worked in the past. The American people had voted for Wilson because he kept us out of war, and they had gotten war. "To vote for Roosevelt in 1936 because he kept us out of reaction or fascism will prove equally futile," he declared. Labor would never free itself from "its house of bondage" if it remained satisfied with the crumbs from the Roosevelt administration. The *Socialist Call* spoke in even more critical terms of labor's support for Roosevelt. In either case, the Socialist Party's position was clear: the labor movement and its political vehicles for supporting Roosevelt, like Labor's Non-Partisan League, were making a mistake.[16]

The theoretical position was more difficult to arrive at. There were numerous problems complicating the formulation of a position that would satisfy the vast majority of Socialists. On the one hand, there were various indications from around the country that local and state farmer-labor and labor parties were emerging. Thus it seemed that Socialist cooperation with them might be a logical step in the attempt to develop a socialist consciousness among the masses. On the other hand, it was quite clear that these parties would not merge into a national party in time for the 1936 election. Hence an over-concentration on working out relationships with them could divert attention away from the prospective Socialist campaign. Norman Thomas, who looked with sympathy on the development of a national farmer-labor party and believed the Socialist Party had to work out relations with the emerging local farmer-labor parties, especially felt the need to concentrate, during the campaign, on the Socialist Party. In addition, the Party itself was badly divided on the issue. The Trotskyists, who were entering the Party in 1936, were adamantly opposed to any of the local farmer-labor parties. Believing that the United States was entering a revolutionary period, they argued that all of these parties were reformist, and maintained that the Socialist Party should build itself as the revolutionary party. The Trotskyists were opposed to the relationship that the Wisconsin Socialists had worked out with the Wisconsin Farmer-Labor Progressive Federation. But even non-Trotskyists had very mixed feelings toward the whole issue of farmer-labor parties, and were hesitant to rush in to embrace them uncritically.[17]

In May of 1936 Norman Thomas took note of the increase in local and state labor parties in 1935–36 and the problems that they posed for Socialists. There were, he said, certain principles on which all Socialists could agree: no coalition was possible which included "candidates or groups on the old party ticket" or which supported such tickets or candidates. In addition, Socialists should not consider coalitions that were not anticapitalist and that were not supported by large groups within the labor movement or organized farmers. Socialists also should make certain that they kept their "own ranks firm" in any coalition. Even guided by these principles, Socialists would still have difficulties. Here, Thomas noted the "awkwardness" in Wisconsin of the coalition supporting a candidate for governor who in turn was supporting Roosevelt for president, even if the coalition itself did not support the President. He expressed fears that, especially with local labor parties, the Socialist organization and propaganda would be weakened "with no corresponding gains." He urged the Socialists not to form local labor parties, but to concentrate on building their own party. Despite all these cautions, Thomas was not, like the Trotskyists, prepared to close the door entirely on cooperation and coalitions. "Nevertheless," he wrote, "where there is a real labor demand for such coalitions from labor unions, and real hope of educating them and organizing them for Socialism, I do not believe Socialists should draw into their own shells and say: 'We'll keep ourselves pure.' That drives eager folks away from us and it loses us an educational opportunity. Nothing venture, nothing have." As long as Socialists were prepared not to sacrifice their own organization, to work hard for the party and platform, Thomas was willing to permit cooperation with the emerging parties.[18]

Thomas's acceptance of the possibility and necessity for coalitions, however, should not be interpreted as a blanket endorsement of coalition with any and all "labor" or "farmer-labor" parties. It was still necessary to judge each case for itself. And it was still necessary to be guided by the basic principles of no support for capitalist candidates and wide support for the labor party by the state or local labor movement. The resolution on farmer-labor parties at the 1936 Socialist Party Convention reflected the ambiguities in the Party's position. The Convention defeated a resolution, supported mainly by Trotskyists, that would have closed the door on Socialist cooperation with all farmer-labor parties. The resolution which passed acknowledged that it would have been

preferable for workers to have been won directly to a revolutionary
Socialist Party, but that it was apparently inevitable that the next
stage in developing socialist consciousness in the working class
would necessitate the development of farmer-labor parties. For
Socialists to cooperate would require that the parties be formed on
a federated basis in which the Socialist Party could join as a
constituent part; it required that the parties be grounded in
genuine labor and labor-farmer support and that they completely
"cut loose from capitalist parties and politics"; and it required that
the parties have control over their candidates. The resolution
warned against premature attempts at forming farmer-labor parties,
and ended by asserting that the best way to build a genuine farmer-
labor party in 1936 was to increase the Socialist Party vote in the
election.[19]

The resolution reflected the crosscurrents of feeling within the
Party and within its leader, Norman Thomas. It showed the re-
ceptivity of the Party to the *idea* of a farmer-labor party, but it
showed the care with which, at this time, it couched its support for
the ideas in terms of establishing clear guidelines. It revealed both
Thomas's belief in the historical necessity of a farmer-labor party,
and also his dedication to the Socialist Party and his desire that
energy and activity not be channeled off from it into short-lived
third parties.

It was with this "mixed" attitude that the Socialists entered the
1936 campaign. It was a loose enough resolution to permit the
Wisconsin Socialists to cooperate in the Wisconsin Farmer-Labor
Federation. At the same time, it was stringent enough to lead the
Socialist Party to ridicule the new American Labor Party and its
Social Democratic Federation allies. In July, Norman Thomas
reported that the Waldmanites were negotiating with Labor's
Non-Partisan League to form a labor party. The terms, he pre-
dicted, would be the endorsement by Waldman and the Social
Democratic Federation of Roosevelt and Lehman, and the oppor-
tunity to run candidates in a few Assembly districts against
Tammany candidates. He ridiculed the move as similar to the

Communist desire to form a labor party in 1936, and dismissed it with a prediction that the Waldmanites might pick up a little leftover Jim Farley patronage for their support of Roosevelt. "The farmer-labor party that we want," he wrote, "the only farmer-labor party worth getting is a farmer-labor party entirely free from capitalist old party alliances." But, he went on, there was "no chance of building such a party this year, certainly not in a state where labor is going to endorse a Democratic candidate for Governor as well as for President."[20]

The Party's official newspaper, *The Socialist Call,* joined in the criticism of the proposed labor party in New York. The labor party that was being planned was a "Trojan horse." Labor leaders knew that millions of workers would not vote in the Democratic column, so they were planning a "labor party" designation for the Democratic candidates. The labor leaders were creating a "disguise" for Democratic candidates by placing them on "a so-called labor ticket." Roosevelt on a labor ticket was still the same as Roosevelt on the Democratic ticket. The labor leaders thought that move was the start of a labor party. But, the editors argued, experience demonstrated that a labor party could only be created on "the basis of a complete rejection of capitalist parties and capitalist candidates." The editors skillfully cited Morris Hillquit on the need for labor to break with capitalist parties and to directly challenge them; the Social Democratic Federation, the heir of Hillquit's Old Guard faction, was doing the exact opposite. The only way that was left to lay the foundation for a true labor party in 1936 was to vote for Thomas and the Socialist Party.[21]

The Socialist critique mounted with the actual formation of the American Labor Party. Norman Thomas accused it of being tied "to Roosevelt's coat-tails" and of endorsing his bad labor record. John Ball criticized it for not breaking clearly with the capitalist parties; as such it was part of the "lesser evil" that the labor movement had come to accept in 1936. It and Labor's Non-Partisan League had become "apologists" for Roosevelt. In September, the State Executive of New York issued a statement on the question of whether the American Labor Party was "genuine." The American Labor Party, the statement said, was started by Labor's Non-Partisan League leaders because they believed that thousands of workers would not vote for Roosevelt on the Democratic ticket. The reelection of Roosevelt and Governor Lehman was set forth in the A.L.P.'s Declaration of Principles as the prime objective. There were, it said, even some who desired the party to be temporary—to end after the election. There were others in the A.L.P., however, who did want it to develop into a "bona-fide labor party."[22]

At this time, the S.E.C. statement went on, this development was clearly not taking place. The A.L.P. met none of the Socialist Party's tests for a genuine labor party. It was not created to elect "labor-controlled candidates," but it was created by the "councils of the Democratic Party" to elect Democratic candidates. It was not "committed to the principle of independent political action," but continued "the futile and discarded principle of non-partisanship." No group such as the Socialist Party could affiliate with the A.L.P. as a group and only those pledged to vote and work for Roosevelt could join. After detailing the ways in which the American Labor Party failed to meet the Socialist litmus test for labor parties, the S.E.C. ended with a critique of nonpartisanship as a form of company unionism, a pledge that the Socialist Party stood ready to work with all those in the labor movement who were committed to independent political action, and a reaffirmation that the best way to bring about a genuine labor party—"the next step for American workers"—was to support Norman Thomas and the Socialist Party in the coming election.[23]

Despite its apparently optimistic campaign statements that the future of the labor movement lay with the "revolutionary" Socialist Party and despite its quick dismissal of the American Labor Party, the Socialist Party was in more serious straits than would appear on the rhetorical surface. Seriously hurt by the Old Guard defection, all groups in the Party had united on running Thomas for president in 1936, though even here there was a dispirited and fatalistic attitude toward the results of this enterprise. The rhetorical flourishes were, in part, to boost the Socialists' own spirit. Below the unanimity for the Thomas candidacy, the Party was badly split. A number of leaders, formerly associated with the Militant faction, like Jack Altman in New York and Paul Porter in Kenosha, Wisconsin, read the signs pessimistically for the future in terms of Socialist Party political campaigns. In particular, those in New York, led by Altman, looked with more favor on the American Labor Party and were increasingly eager to come to terms with it after the election campaign. Others, formerly associated with the Militants in the struggle with the Old Guard, were emerging as a new left-wing group. Calling itself the "Clarity" after their paper, the *Socialist Clarity,* the group was led by Frank Trager, the National Labor Secretary of the Party, Gus Tyler, editor of the *Socialist Call,* Robert and Max Delson, and Herbert Zam. The Clarity group viewed the American Labor Party with deep suspicion. Adherents of revolutionary socialism and of an antireformist, anti-Popular Front line, they saw correctly that those who composed the A.L.P. were either Old Guard Socialists, pro-New Deal union leaders, or Communists who, entering the Popular Front period, were now joining Old Guard Socialists in supporting the New Deal. In theory, the Clarity group, like the Socialist Party as a whole, was not opposed to labor parties and farmer-labor parties, but they were more insistent than the Altman Militants that any labor party wanting Socialist support have a wide labor base and have broken completely with capitalist-reformist politics. Complicating the picture and strengthening the Clarity group on the labor party question were the Trotskyists, who, at this time, insisted that any third party would automatically be a capitalist reform party (in 1938, after they had left the Socialist Party, the Trotskyists would do a complete about-face on the issue). Although the Clarity was not prepared to go to this length and could join with the Militants in writing the 1936 Party statement on labor parties, they lent support to the Trotskyist position in the everyday resistance to cooperation with the American Labor Party.[24]

The conjunction of the Clarity and the Trotskyists on the labor party question could not, however, be sustained on other issues. The Trotskyists' support of the Fourth International, their ultra-revolutionary line on Spain, their failure to adhere to Party decisions, their publication of their own journals, brought them into conflict with the National Office, Thomas, and the Altman-Porter Militants. Somewhat reluctantly, the Clarity agreed with the Militants that the Trotskyists had to go, and, in 1937, they were purged from the Party. The Trotskyist dispute marked another severe blow to the Socialist Party. In addition to expending energy in another bitter intra-party struggle, the Party also lost many of the younger Socialists in the Young Peoples Socialist League when the Trotskyists left the Party. In terms of the issue of the labor party, the internal struggle with the Trotskyists took place while the Party was reevaluating its relation to the American Labor Party. The victory of Altman in pushing his hard-line position against the Trotskyists strengthened the position of his followers within the Party and placed the Clarity opponents of the American Labor Party on the defensive. The Altman Militants were further strengthened because they had the support of Norman Thomas in their desire to reevaluate the Socialist Party-A.L.P. relationship.[25]

The first major decision toward establishing a new relationship would not come until 1937 when Norman Thomas withdrew as Socialist candidate for mayor of New York, leaving the way clear for LaGuardia's fusion ticket to be unopposed from the left and for the Socialists to support A.L.P. candidates in local elections where they were not also candidates of either of the two major parties. This decision, however, did not come easily. Following the election of 1936, Thomas reiterated his disappointment in the American Labor Party and his belief that while a genuine national farmer-labor party need not be completely Socialist, it still needed to cut its ties with the two old capitalist parties. But an increasing difference in tone can be distinguished between Thomas and the Clarity-dominated editorial board of the *Socialist Call*. On November 21, 1936, while the editorial board of the *Call* was reasserting the need to build the Socialist Party, criticizing the A.L.P., demanding independent political action on the part of labor, and proclaiming that a revolutionary program was the only way out, Norman Thomas was posing the question: if Socialists can't enter a labor party on a federated basis, how can they enter it? He was not prepared to give up the hope of entrance on a federated basis, but the posing of such a question suggested that there was a possibility of reappraising the Socialist answer to it.[26]

In December the National Executive Committee issued a resolution which stressed that farmer-labor parties were part of the Socialist work in mass organizations. The Party should attempt to enter state farmer-labor parties on a federated basis; the state parties should insist on a federated party conducting its affairs democratically; they should not hide their revolutionary Socialism and should try to advance Socialist propaganda; but they should also abide by majority decisions and support the farmer-labor platform on immediate demands. The resolution stressed the need for a Socialist Party whether or not a farmer-labor party existed and urged Socialists to conduct independent campaigns where a farmer-labor party had not been formed. Approval by the N.E.C. was required for Socialist joint action with state and local farmer-labor parties. There was again nothing in the resolution that in any way specifically repudiated the established principles by which the Socialists were to judge the genuineness of a farmer-labor party. Still, by comparing work in farmer-labor parties to that in other mass organizations like unions, unemployment leagues, and anti-war organizations, the resolution tacitly loosened the conditions for Socialist cooperation with the American Labor Party, since participation in none of these other organizations was guided by the rigid principles previously established by the New York State Executive Committee for judging the genuineness of a farmer-labor party.[27]

Also, in December, 1936, in his *Socialist Call* column, Thomas analyzed the American Labor Party not simply to criticize its inadequacies, but to argue how it might become a true labor party.

He said that the main reason the A.L.P. was formed was to help Roosevelt, but he acknowledged that there were some members who were interested in its becoming a genuine labor party. He continued to feel that the A.L.P. decision not to admit existing parties as a bloc and to require individual members to renounce all parties was a handicap in depriving the A.L.P. of leaders who could move the party in the direction of a genuine labor party. He urged the unions affiliated with the A.L.P. to "speak out for a democratically federated party cut entirely loose from old capitalist parties." He ended by noting the readiness of Socialists to cooperate in building such a party, and stated that the necessity of not abandoning the Socialist Party did not preclude "proper arrangements governing tickets for the election campaign."[28]

What the "proper" arrangements would be was still open to question at the end of 1936. Though Thomas was closer to the Altman Militants than to the Clarityites in general philosophy, there is some evidence that he was resisting pressure to be even more conciliatory on the labor party issue. In a letter to Maynard Krueger, in November, he acknowledged the difficulty of the Party's reaching a general agreement on proper relations with a farmer-labor party. He saw no great demand for a national party, but he pessimistically concluded that the Socialist Party's own weakness and "the vague sentiment" for a labor party meant the Socialist Party would have to make "terms" with it. He was not prepared to spell out these terms—though they had to include preserving the Socialist Party's "identity." And then he went on to say that he was not prepared to "play the kind of game" that some New Yorkers were ready to play with "a very unsatisfactory labor party." The reference was obviously to the pressure from the Militant group in New York that was demanding coming to terms with the labor party. Thomas did not want to play with "Hillman, Lewis, and company" in the manner they suggested. He hoped an agreement could be reached, but he threatened at that time to retreat from Party leadership if the Party followed the New Yorkers' advice.[29]

By early 1937, however, Thomas was taking most of his advice from Altman and his supporters. Paul Porter wrote him in February, 1937, complaining about the Zam-Tyler Clarity position in the *Call,* defending the Wisconsin Socialists, and supporting the Altman-Murray Gross faction in New York. In March, 1937, Dan Hoan wrote him with the same complaints against the Clarity faction. Whatever the reason, Thomas's temporary dissatisfaction with the Altman group had ended by early in 1937. Perhaps he had only been worried that they would surrender too much of the Party's activities and independence and, having received assurances that they were not proposing this, acquiesced in their position. Certainly he was closer to their general ideology than to the revolutionary Socialism of the Clarityites. Probably, however, his basic reason for siding with the Altmanites was that he accepted their diagnosis of the problem and believed that unless the Socialist Party came to terms with the American Labor Party, it would isolate itself in sectarian purity.[30]

In late February, 1937, Murray Gross, a follower of Altman, sent Thomas a long letter outlining the basic arguments for the Altman position. Gross said that the sentiment for a labor party was rapidly increasing, and the Socialists had to get in on the ground floor. Thus far, the Party had remained content with slogans, but had "no plans for actual work." This led to a position where the Socialist Party was becoming irrelevant in the struggles of labor and consequently would disintegrate. The emphasis for the Party should be shifted from "useless parliamentary campaigns" to a role of influence within a labor party. The Party needed contact with the masses and it could only conduct an educational campaign if it had contact with them in mass organizations. Instead of concentrating on all the necessary principles that a labor party should have, principles that were rapidly dividing Socialists, there should only be one criterion: the labor party should consist of *labor.* It must have a trade-union base. By worrying about other theoretical aspects, the Socialist Party was alienating the labor movement, and satisfying only its revolutionary theory. Even a federated party—

one of the original Socialist principles—was "no guarantee of anything." The Socialist Party had to adopt a "whole-hearted, active, non-sectarian approach" in order to win the masses and gain influence in the labor movement. Otherwise, the Party would remain "a pure revolutionary sect."[31] Although Gross did not mention the American Labor Party directly, the thrust of his argument pointed toward Socialist cooperation with the A.L.P. in the coming political campaign of 1937.

Thomas, while perhaps not prepared to go to Gross's lengths in giving up the Party's political identity, was increasingly moving closer to his position on the American Labor Party. The Party itself continued to restate its official position on Socialist relations with labor parties. In the month preceding the special Socialist Party Convention in March of 1937, the *Socialist Call* reiterated its earlier criticisms of the American Labor Party, Labor's Non-Partisan League, the Popular Front, and all other varieties of reformism. The Convention's resolution on labor parties may have had a stronger sense of urgency for cooperation than the 1936 resolution, but essentially it restated the Socialist position on independent political action, a labor base, joining on a federated basis, and a general commitment to production for use as essential requirements for Socialist cooperation with a labor party.[32]

Perhaps it was significant that the 1937 resolution, unlike the 1936 platform, did not demand that a labor party "completely cut loose" from capitalist parties and politicians. In any case, the grounds of discussion were moving from the area of Party resolutions and theoretical statements to the practical problem of what to do in the coming New York City mayoralty campaign. The Socialist Party had opposed fusion in the 1933 campaign, as we have seen, and Thomas had strongly criticized Blanshard for breaking with the Party to support LaGuardia. It had argued that fusion was a form of capitalist "good government" reformism and that LaGuardia was closely connected with business interests. The Party had insisted on the need to run a *socialist* campaign in a city with a large labor force.[33]

The necessity of running a socialist campaign was not a position to be surrendered easily. Even before the Party's special convention in March, 1937, the *Socialist Call* printed a story denying that the Party was about to support LaGuardia and Fusion. Jack Altman, the secretary of the New York local, and the Public Affairs Committee of the Party issued a statement saying that Fusion, like the two old parties, existed to serve the capitalist class, and that the Socialist Party's purpose was to abolish capitalism. The statement warned that workers could not rely on well-intentioned "good men"—an obvious poke at LaGuardia. "The Socialist Party," it read, "has never supported and never will support any capitalist political party or any capitalist nominated by a capitalist political party." It modulated this strong wording by indicating that the Party would not adopt a "sectarian" position and was willing to take part in organizations looking toward independent political action on the part of labor. But any such "tendencies" in that direction still needed to be "completely divorced from all capitalist parties and from candidates of such parties." The statement ended on an ambiguous note: "Although we can't foresee all contingencies of the confusing municipal campaign, we can now say with certainty that the Socialist Party will not support LaGuardia or any other candidate who is nominated on a ticket of a capitalist political party."[34]

This last statement seemed to make clear that there would be no direct Socialist support for LaGuardia and Fusion. But what about indirect support that might result from the Socialists not running a campaign of their own? Although the Party still went ahead in the spring and summer of 1937 with plans to run a Socialist ticket headed by Norman Thomas for mayor, private discussions with the American Labor Party were already under way. In November of 1936, Thomas had written a memorandum to Clarence Senior, Jack Altman, and Harry Laidler suggesting that discussion with the A.L.P. about the coming election begin. In March, 1937, Thomas designated Harry Laidler as his deputy in discussions with the American Labor Party. In his instructions to

Laidler, he indicated his own mixed feelings. On the one hand, he admitted LaGuardia's was the best administration since he had lived in New York. On the other hand, because of his desire to seek support from Democrats and Republicans and because of his stand on the sales tax, LaGuardia did not qualify as "proper for a Labor party man." If he had run on a straight American Labor Party ticket and reversed his stand on the sales tax, Thomas might have endorsed him. But now it was impossible. At the same time, however, he suggested that if the American Labor Party endorsed LaGuardia, the Socialist Party should not run a mayoralty candidate against him because it would bring the Party into a collision with the labor movement. Such a move, he argued, would not jeopardize the Socialist place on the state ballot and it would still allow for the possibility of making the Socialist views clear through the city council races. Where A.L.P.-endorsed candidates did not also have old-party nominations, the Socialist Party stood ready to join in endorsing them. Finally, if the party decided to follow this course, it should issue a statement making clear that it did not endorse LaGuardia's campaign "in full," especially his acceptance of old-party endorsements.[35]

Thomas did not formally withdraw from the race until October, 1937. Negotiations had been going on with the American Labor Party during this time. In addition, intraparty differences forced a referendum by local New York on the course that Thomas proposed to follow before the negotiations toward his withdrawal could be completed. From March until October the issue of whether Thomas should withdraw was fought inside the Party. The opponents of withdrawal—the Trotskyists and the Clarity—saw the issue in terms of a growing "reformist" trend within the Party. The Clarity controlled the Party paper, the *Socialist Call*. The *Call* printed several articles so critical of LaGuardia that Norman Thomas had to threaten specific repudiation of its policies in his column if it did not desist. In its editorials, the *Call* connected the American Labor Party with Labor's Non-Partisan League and the Communist Party as an advocate of Popular Front reformism.

Capitalism, the paper argued, was entering a period of decline with the possibilities of a fascist reaction. The Socialist answer should be an "aggressive struggle for Socialism." These other parties and groups, however, were adopting "a defensive alliance" with a "lesser capitalist evil." The time was ripe for independent working-class political action in New York; the two old parties were discredited and the labor movement was strong. The American Labor Party, instead, was backing LaGuardia. Only a labor party committed to labor candidates and struggling against Popular Frontism and endorsement of "good men" deserved Socialist support. "Where labor tags along behind capitalist candidate," the paper said, "the Socialist Party must call upon workers to vote for their class candidate, the candidate of the Socialist Party."[36]

In a series of articles in the *Socialist Call* at the end of August and the first week in September, Gus Tyler, of Clarity, attempted to put the problem in its long-run perspective. The immediate problem, he said, was coalition with capitalist candidates. But, compounding this, was the whole drift to a "PERMANENT coalition of lib-Labism." As the old New Deal coalition split, a new coalition was developing. The anti-New Deal Democrats were departing, new groups were being "grafted on" from the left: old Guard Socialists, Popular Front Communists, the American Labor Party. A. A. Berle was quoted as saying that the A.L.P. was the "true Roosevelt Democratic Party." The problem with this new coalition from the point of view of Socialism, however, was that it could not go beyond the liberal capitalists with whom it was allied. It would be a "party of capitalism with a liberal outlook." To free workers only a working-class party and a party of class struggle would do. What was required at this time was not a "good capitalist party" or a "liberal party" or a "party of labor's friends," but a "party of labor."[37]

While the *Call* kept up its criticism of the American Labor Party (without actually specifying the tactic of withdrawing Thomas), the Clarity struggled internally within the Party. Prominent Clarity spokesmen like Lillian Symes from California and the National Labor Secretary (until he resigned in the middle of the struggle), Frank Trager, wrote Thomas protesting against the "liquidationist" trends in the Party. They had been unhappy with Wisconsin's entrance into the Farmer-Labor Federation and the Party's strategy there of not running a Socialist candidate against Governor Philip LaFollette. Now, they saw a similar tactic emerging in New York in relation to the American Labor Party. They felt that the signs clearly indicated that the Party was ceasing to be a revolutionary party committed to class struggle and was preparing to merge itself with vague labor reformist parties throughout the country. The Clarity issued a stinging attack on Altman and Thomas for surrendering the revolutionary struggle by their New York strategy.[38]

The Clarity's position within the Party was both strong and weak. On one hand, the Party's 1936 platform and resolutions on the farmer-labor party question reflected Clarity positions. On the other hand, the centers of key Socialist strength like Wisconsin, New York, and Massachusetts were predominantly anti-Clarity in their outlook. The Clarity did have a strong voice on the National Executive Committee and it was only because a non-Clarity alternate to the N.E.C. was chosen that the N.E.C. approved the New York referendum by a vote of 8 to 7. Despite its apparent strength, however, the Clarity was handicapped by being associated with the Trotskyists. The Clarity's struggle against the Altman-Thomas strategy in New York was going on at the same time that the most outspoken foes of the strategy, the Trotskyists, were coming under increasing criticism in the Party for their sectarianism and factional politics. In August, the New York Socialists expelled a number of leading Trotskyists. The Trotskyists opposed any labor party at this time, while Clarity accepted the necessity of a labor party, but a labor party cut loose from the old capitalist parties. The theoretical distinction did not do the Clarity much good, for what they stood to gain from the Trotskyists in numerical support on the issue they stood to lose by being associated within the Party with extreme factionalism. Besides, the Trotskyists were not particularly interested in helping the Clarity; they were mainly concerned with advancing their own theoretical position. Finally, of course, the Clarity faced the opposition of Thomas.[39]

And Thomas's opposition on this issue was strong. Not only did Thomas attempt to answer Clarity's objection to the course the Party was pursuing in New York, but he also brought strong internal pressure on the Party to accept the New York decision. He pressured the N.E.C. by implying that he would withdraw from a strong role in the Party if it overruled the results of the New York referendum. He insisted that strong state parties be given a certain flexibility in meeting their local problems, and he warned that the excessive discipline that Clarity sought to impose on the Party would drive people away from the Party. In defending the course that the Party proposed to follow in New York, he argued that the A.L.P. did not meet the standard of a labor party in terms of Socialist membership. But, he claimed, it had made tremendous strides toward becoming a genuine labor party. If the Socialist Party, in this situation, antagonized the A.L.P. by running a candidate against LaGuardia, it would stand to lose the support of the working masses. Moreover, if it were on friendly relations with the American Labor Party, the Socialist Party could bring more pressure to bear on the weak spots in LaGuardia's candidacy, especially on the sales tax. LaGuardia's weaknesses came from a lack of "proper labor support" and this support could come more easily from friendly relations with the A.L.P. than from "unnecessary hostility." To those critics who said that withdrawing a candidate against LaGuardia meant supporting him, Thomas replied that it did not, that Socialist criticism of him would continue. Unlike in the 1936 presidential election. Thomas argued, it was not necessary to run a mayoralty candidate to conduct a Socialist campaign. To those, like Tyler, who said the Party was adopting support of capitalist candidates, Thomas replied that the Party was not endorsing any A.L.P. candidate who was also endorsed by a capitalist party. Moreover, they were running their own candidates against capitalist-party-backed A.L.P. candidates except in the case of

LaGuardia. Why except LaGuardia? Again it was primarily a matter of moving the A.L.P. in the right direction by not antagonizing the labor movement; in addition, LaGuardia, as mayor, had, through the police force, a much greater effect on labor than the other city candidates.[40]

The whole strategy that Thomas argued for during the summer of 1937 was theoretically based on successful negotiations with the American Labor Party. It is not going too far to say, however, that while Thomas apparently took the negotiations seriously, it would have taken a serious and direct repudiation of Socialist support by the A.L.P. in order for the plan to withdraw Thomas to be rescinded. In September, Thomas wrote Laidler, Altman, and James Lipsig, who were negotiating with the A.L.P., that under no circumstances would he personally be a candidate, although if negotiations failed it might become necessary to run a candidate. He did suggest using the "threat of a Thomas candidacy to wrest concessions." The area of concessions, however, could not be large. The Socialists were not about to endorse LaGuardia directly; the A.L.P. was not about to give up the support of its candidates by capitalist parties. All the Socialists could do was to agree to support A.L.P. candidates in races where they were not backed by a capitalist party, in exchange for vague assurances that the A.L.P. would move toward running its own slate in future elections. Thomas professed happiness when the American Labor Party criticized LaGuardia's endorsement of Colonel Harvey's candidacy for Queens Borough President. But it is fair to say that this was not a large concession, and that for the Socialists to have changed their course after midsummer of 1937 would have taken more than silence on the Harvey candidacy.[41]

In October of 1937 Norman Thomas withdrew as mayoralty candidate; a satisfactory understanding had been reached. The supporters of the Altman-Thomas position had carried the day. The Socialist Party would not be running its own candidate, carping and criticizing, splitting the progressive vote, alienating labor, making the Socialist educational task more difficult. It would be cooperating with the A.L.P., running its own candidates only where unsatisfactory A.L.P. candidates were running. The decision catapulted the Socialists off of the sidelines of the American Labor Party's political field, but it did not solve the problem of where they were going to land. The Party was still badly divided on the issue. The Clarity continued to have deep misgivings about the decision and the Party's direction. The Altman Militants looked ahead optimistically. Thomas wrote optimistically of the election results. Altman declared that the election of three Socialist-supported A.L.P. candidates to the State Assembly demonstrated that labor was ready for independent political action. Thomas felt "progress" had been made. Murray Gross wrote Thomas urging an almost complete merger of the Socialist Party with the American Labor Party. The Party's branches would become "some sort of League centered around the American Labor Party neighborhood clubs." He did not propose literally liquidating the Socialist Party. But the thrust of his argument was that the emphasis of Socialist Party work should be in the trade unions and the A.L.P. If the Socialist Party identified with the A.L.P. and a national labor party, the class-conscious worker would be drawn toward the Socialist Party affiliation. "Eventually," Gross wrote, "we will be on the road to building socialism in the United States and the Labor Party shall be the medium." If the American Labor Party nominated an acceptable candidate for governor in 1938, the Socialists should support him. The 1940 presidential election was too far away to predict, but the Socialists should cease worrying about losing their electoral line on the ballot and wholeheartedly work at building a Labor Party.[42]

Thomas was not prepared to have the Socialist Party become some kind of league; he stressed the need to maintain a strong, unified, all-inclusive party. But he argued that in light of the results of the mayoralty campaign, the Socialists should agree to support all American Labor Party nominees in 1938 that were not also endorsed by the two old parties. He urged cooperative action in the city council with the American Labor Party. Most important, he suggested that a very tentative and careful exploration be made of the possibility of admitting certain individual Socialists into the A.L.P. Thomas, like the Party, had long insisted on the need for affiliated membership of the Party within a labor party. This had been one of the principles in determining what was a genuine labor party. But he realized that the A.L.P. was not about to accept the Socialist Party as an affiliated unit.[43]

On November 30, 1937 the New York State Committee of the Socialist Party of New York appointed a subcommittee (including Thomas, Laidler, Altman, and Gross) to examine the political situation in New York and make definite recommendations on future Socialist Party cooperation with the American Labor Party. Its recommendations would then be sent to the New York membership for a referendum. The State Committee was not neutral in appointing the subcommittee; it expressed its belief that "definite steps should be taken toward active participation of the Socialist Party and its individual members in building the American Labor Party and toward possible affiliation of the Socialist Party with the American Labor Party.[44]

The State Committee's step precipitated another lengthy negotiation and debate that was not settled until December, 1938. The negotiations followed a precarious course. The Socialist Party wished the American Labor Party to adopt a position of independent political action on the part of labor; barring this, it was not prepared to surrender its right to run candidates against A.L.P. candidates with Republican or Tammany backing. The A.L.P., for its part, wished the Socialist Party to do exactly that: surrender its own candidates and support all A.L.P. candidates. The Socialists, in addition, realized the difficulty of joining, on a federated basis, a party structure like the A.L.P.'s based on individual membership; yet they also wanted to be able to have an arrangement where they could function as a unit or at least be admitted as a whole. The A.L.P. leadership, strong factionalists themselves, and already faced with a tightly knit Communist group, were not prepared to allow the Socialists to enter as a unit. The A.L.P. leadership

wanted the Socialist Party members for their strength in its internal struggle with the Communists; it did not want them as a
party within a party.[45]

The debate over Socialist affiliation with the A.L.P. followed
some of the usual pattern. John Newton Thurber of Clarity wrote
Gus Tyler about the opposition to the Thomas-Altman-Gross line
throughout the country, and Tyler renewed his attack on "lib-
Labism" in the *Socialist Review* in January. However, other
voices, with somewhat different or surprising emphases, were
beginning to be heard. Samuel Verne, who was not in the Clarity
group, but did oppose Altman's leadership, argued against joining
the A.L.P. unless dual membership were permitted. If it were
permitted, then entrance by individuals with special Party permission should be granted. The emphasis of his analysis was on the
need to protect the Party as an entity and not rush headlong into
the A.L.P. But the stress on dual membership left the issue a
pragmatic one: could this be arranged? More important and surprising, Lazar Becker, who had been associated with the Clarity,
made a report on Party membership in February, 1938 in which
he supported Socialist affiliation with the American Labor Party.
Arguing against the sectarians who opposed the A.L.P. on principle
and the liquidationists who would dissolve the Socialist Party,
Becker said that the issue revolved around three key questions:
federation, independent political action, and intraparty democracy.
The issue of federation, he argued, was not applicable to the
A.L.P.; even opponents of affiliation accepted the fact that the
structure of the A.L.P.—with its individual membership basis—
made the issue of a federated affiliation a moot question. The
A.L.P. was committed to independent political action in its Constitution; but it did not put this provision into practice. The
question then became: who could pressure it in the direction of
independent political action—Socialists staying outside the A.L.P.
or Socialists working within A.L.P.? Given the conditions of the
Socialist Party—its financial weaknesses, its lack of coordinated
press and activity—Becker argued that the latter could bring the
most pressure. Similarly, the A.L.P. did not function democratically

in its decision-making. But could this be changed most easily from the inside or the outside? Again, Becker argued for the inside. Socialist members, functioning in a disciplined manner, could bring the right kind of pressures from the inside more easily than from the outside.[46]

Despite the continued internal in-fighting among the Clarity and Altman's supporters in New York, the fact that Thomas could endorse Becker's arguments as sound indicated that the issue was becoming a question of the terms on which to enter—not whether to enter or not. This meant that the issue would be settled less by debate than by circumstances. Thomas had hopes in February of 1938 that the American Labor Party would accept the entrance of Socialists as a party. The negotiations subsequently became more difficult. The Party Convention at Kenosha wrote a statement which reiterated the historical inevitability of labor parties as the next step forward in the struggle for socialism, the need for these parties to be independent of capitalist politics, and the failures of People's Frontism and "lesser evilism." The resolution laid down ground rules for Socialist cooperation. Though the document reflected the Clarity position and was too stringent for Thomas, it did not rule out Socialist affiliation. Wherever labor organized parties of its own, Socialists should seek out ways to affiliate with them, at the same time insisting on their right to maintain their own organization and run their own candidates against capitalist candidates. And wherever there were labor slates, controlled by labor and independent of capitalist parties, but short of a labor party, the Socialists should give them full support.[47]

Thomas would have preferred more flexibility. But the resolution did not have a significant adverse effect on Socialist negotiations with the A.L.P. Indeed, though the N.E.C. passed a somewhat looser set of provisions to attempt to cover the variety of individual cases, Thomas himself insisted on the right of the Socialists to continue to run candidates—a point which led to a temporary standstill in negotiations in the summer of 1938. By summer, it was also becoming clear that other developments were impeding Socialist affiliation. The American Labor Party, instead of moving toward independent political action, had taken further steps at "horse-trading" with the old parties—even accepting the support of Tammany in one case. Thomas criticized these "power politics" in the *Call,* and despite Socialist endorsement of some A.L.P. candidates, the two parties did not genuinely cooperate during the 1938 elections. Thomas ran for governor against Lehman, who was backed by the A.L.P. The results for both the A.L.P. and the Socialists were disappointing. The A.L.P., after its encouraging vote in 1937, suffered serious setbacks in the city elections. Thomas did so badly that the Socialists lost their line on the ballot.[48]

Ironically, the loss of the electoral line solved some problems; one could no longer insist that it was necessary to run a Socialist campaign in order to protect the line—it had been lost, and prospects for recovering it in the near future were not encouraging. The referendum to the Party membership to approve affiliation won the support of the key members of the Altman and Clarity groups. Robert Delson, Ben Horowitz, Frank Trager, and Herbert Zam for the Clarity issued a statement giving their reasons for voting "yes." They argued that the referendum did not call for affiliation of the Socialist Party as a party, since the A.L.P. was not a true independent labor party and such affiliation was impossible under its structure. The Socialist Party would continue to exist and carry on its work. All the referendum did, they said, was to "enable the party to decide which members are to join the A.L.P." In a national labor party, affiliation would have to be on a federated basis. But, here, Socialists could work in the A.L.P. and also carry on their own party work. The Delson group urged that there be no unplanned rush into A.L.P. Careful planning was necessary to assure that Socialists would lead the A.L.P. toward independent political action. Finally, the Socialist Party was still a political party; it was not a legal electoral party in New York State, but the referendum did not decide on future electoral action. The Socialist Party should stand ready to support the A.L.P. completely if its 1939–40 campaigns were independent of the

old capitalist parties. If not, the Socialist Party had not surrendered
—and should not—its right to run independent candidates.[49]

Jack Altman, Harry Laidler, Aaron Levenstein, and Brendan
Sexton urged support from the perspective of the Altman Militants.
They stressed the need for the Party to be close to the working
class and emphasized that the A.L.P. marked a step toward independent working-class action. It was imperfect, but a militant
Socialist membership could push it in the right direction. The problem of the Socialist Party's place on the ballot, they said, was no
longer an issue: a new electoral agency was needed and the A.L.P.
was "the best in sight." All other, nonelectoral, activities of the
Socialist Party would continue. A few voices were raised in dissent.
The pacifist Jessie Wallace Hughan urged a "no" vote on the
ground that the American Labor Party was not an independent
organization of the working class; it accepted support from both
capitalist parties. The A.L.P.'s program was a liberal reform program, already endorsed by liberal capitalists, and hence Socialist
educational activity was being sacrificed along with Socialist political activity. Marion Severn, a Socialist lawyer, argued that Socialist
affiliation with the American Labor Party would inject A.L.P.
politics into the Socialist Party and into the work that the Socialist
Party was trying to do in other organizations.[50]

With the two key groups lined up behind the referendum, there
was no question of its passage. On December 25 the Party released
a statement that the referendum had passed and that Socialists
would join the A.L.P. as individual members. The quickness with
which the Party approved the referendum, following a long year of
negotiation, was, in part, due to the disastrous results in the 1938
election. Thomas emerged from the Socialist setbacks in New York
and Wisconsin with a belief that the main area of Socialist activity
should no longer be electoral, but educational. Education for
socialism in mass organizations was the immediate prospect for
the future. With that prospect in view, a prospect that all Socialists
of whatever faction could not help but share emotionally—if not
intellectually—the way was clear for approval.[51]

It was hardly an ecumenical coming together behind the American Labor Party. But what had once seemed, at least to the Clarity group, a matter of principle had become, under the pressure of events, a matter of tactics. Presented with the Altman-Gross argument that running a Socialist candidate for mayor in 1937 would split the progressive vote, alienate key unions, and lead to a Tammany comeback, the Clarity had argued that withdrawal would mean covert cooperation in the American Labor Party's pro-New Deal position and would mean the Socialist seal of approval of LaGuardia. The Clarity group had viewed the withdrawal as a step in the liquidation of the Party. Rather than furthering independent political action on the part of labor, it would be a step away from it, tying labor—and in this case the Socialist Party—to the New Deal. They viewed Altman, Gross, Paul Porter, Alfred Baker Lewis, even Norman Thomas with suspicion and increasing hostility, feeling they were taking the Socialist Party, through the vehicle of the American Labor Party, down the road toward a variety of liberal reformism. That was what the Old Guard Social Democratic Federation had become; but a revolutionary party, they insisted, should be a vanguard party, leading the masses toward socialism and away from the pits of reformism. Now, at the end of 1938, here they were, rationalizing the entrance of Socialists into the American Labor Party—a party which, in the intervening year, had managed to pick up a Tammany endorsement for one of their candidates to go along with Republican endorsements for others.[52]

What caused the Clarity adherents to accept the decision was the fact that they were dealing from weakness. This was not simply in terms of their internal situation in the Party (where they were probably the majority, but a majority minus the decisive influence of Norman Thomas). It was the weakness they shared with their opponents and with Thomas—the weakness of the Socialist Party. From the very beginning, the Socialist Party was handicapped by this weakness both in its negotiations with the A.L.P. and, from the Clarity viewpoint, in its power to resist cooperation and affiliation. The Socialist Party had far too little to offer in negotiations to make the final terms really satisfying to them; it had far too little power to be a threat on the outside of the American Labor Party. The American Labor Party wanted the support of the Socialists, but they were not about to end the "power game" they were playing with the Republicans on a local level and with the Democrats on a national level and seriously move toward independent political action in order to get it. After the Socialist defeat in 1938, the situation was compounded; weakness was added to weakness. Entrance into the American Labor Party became a kind of salvaging operation—to save what little share of influence in the labor movement that the Party might have. The Altman supporters could talk about the possibilities of getting in on the ground floor of a half-genuine working-class party as it moved toward becoming a genuine party. The Clarity could talk of the possibilities of disciplined Socialist activity in the A.L.P. winning the masses to socialism. But all the brave talk by both the Clarity and the Altman supporters about the possibilities deriving from affiliation could not hide the fundamental weaknesses of the Party. They were a weak group of individuals in a party which from their own point of view was highly unsatisfactory.[53]

By 1940, the situation had gotten worse. New factors had entered the American Labor Party situation in New York; none of them was helpful to the Socialist Party. Norman Thomas was again caught between a series of conflicting forces and loyalties. On the one hand, he was eager to cooperate with the A.L.P. leaders in their internal fight with the Communists. It was impossible to do this if Socialists were outside the A.L.P. or if they withdrew because of other unsatisfactory tendencies. On the other hand, there were the unsatisfactory tendencies: the American Labor Party was more than ever tied to Roosevelt, had made deals with Tammany, and was showing no progress in building a national farmer-labor party. Not only was it supporting Roosevelt's domestic policy, but also—and even worse to Thomas—his foreign policy. Roosevelt's foreign policy, his desire to aid the Allies, had begun to separate Thomas from his old Altman allies. This was a very difficult predicament

for Thomas. For, in addition to all the tactical and strategical reasons he had used to win Socialist support to his position on the
A.L.P., there was also the fact that, in this struggle, the men he
trusted most—men like Altman and Paul Porter—were supporting
increased American aid to the Allies. These were the men with
whom he had been closest in the Party, and, generally, they were
the first to split with him on the war issue. Altman was now allying
himself more closely with the Old Guard Social Democratic Federation people in the A.L.P. who supported all-out aid to England.
The war issue had been the chief stumbling block in negotiations
that the Socialist Party, urged on by Thomas, had been conducting
with the Social Democratic Federation. Any possible reunion had
gone down before the issue of Roosevelt's foreign policy. And now,
by mid-1940, segments of his party were moving in the direction
of all-out aid to the Allies.[54]

The Altman Socialists had grave reservations about running any
Socialist campaign against Roosevelt, much less a Socialist campaign in which the war was the prime issue. The unions were clearly
behind Roosevelt; Thomas was pursuing what they believed was
a suicidal foreign policy. His insistence on running could only once
again, as in the 1937 mayoralty campaign, drive a wedge through
the progressive forces. The Altman Socialists began to drop away
from the Party and from party activity. Some lingered through the
1940 campaign, but played a silent role in the campaign. A number
of former Clarity supporters began to join the exodus over the war
issue. Many of these former Socialists wound up in the liberal
Union for Democratic Action. The Socialists in the American
Labor Party who remained loyal to Thomas still found themselves
in a dilemma. To push for A.L.P. endorsement of Thomas in the
face of the union attitude and Thomas's foreign policy position
seemed suicidal and foolish; it could only mean their loss of influence within the A.L.P. While Thomas recognized this fact of life,
he was also determined that Socialists—even those within the
A.L.P.—should not simply acquiesce in an A.L.P. endorsement of
Roosevelt. Such a strategy would be bad Socialist theory; even
more important, at this stage it seemed bad to Thomas because of

his adamant opposition to Roosevelt's foreign policy. Therefore, once he had decided to run for the presidency in 1940 (largely because of the foreign policy question), he urged his followers in the A.L.P. to attempt to get a nonendorsement resolution through for all presidential candidates, leaving the Socialists free to support worth-while local candidates. This attempt failed. And Thomas's A.L.P. supporters were forced into deeper dilemmas and predicaments. Thomas expected Socialists to act as Socialists and support his candidacy. Yet it was very hard for Socialists, whose unions supported Roosevelt on the A.L.P. line, to buck the union sentiment. Even Thomas realized that certain exceptions had to be made. Harry Laidler, running for city councilman from Brooklyn with A.L.P. support, was more or less excused by Thomas from speaking publicly for him, though Thomas continued to insist that all Socialists in the A.L.P., including Laidler, should not endorse Roosevelt. Again, this simply accented the drift away from the Socialist Party. Many of the former Socialists remained in the A.L.P. until the Liberal split and then wound up in the Liberal Party or out of politics altogether. By then, the high hopes of making the A.L.P. a vehicle on the road to socialism had long since come to naught.[55]

The New York Socialists were not, of course, the only ones faced with the problem of how to relate to their state labor movement in the late 1930's. In Detroit, the Michigan Socialists supported a labor slate of candidates in the local elections of 1937. The labor slate was headed by a liberal Democrat named Patrick H. O'Brien, but the election was a nonpartisan election. O'Brien agreed to run on the platform of the labor movement. The Michigan Socialists endorsed O'Brien and argued that this was a labor candidacy free from all capitalist ties. The Michigan Socialists were Clarity-oriented and contrasted their course with that of the New York Socialists in the New York elections. Thomas supported the course Michigan Socialists had adopted, but he could not see where their strategy was "purer" than that of the New York Socialists. O'Brien had been a Democrat and the labor slate was not even a labor party. Ben Fischer, the young chairman of the Michigan

Socialists, wrote to Thomas explaining the difference. Essentially, Fischer's argument was based on the "class alignments" in the two cases. The program of the labor candidates in Detroit might be no more socialistic than the American Labor Party, but, freed from all ties with the capitalist parties, the class alignment behind the labor slate was strictly a working-class alignment. Tied still to the capitalist parties, the class alignment behind the A.L.P., Fischer said, was a mixed alignment. The 1937 local Detroit contest entered indirectly into the A.L.P. issue in New York. But, in terms of a strategy for Michigan Socialists, it did not create the kind of drastic problems that the gubernatorial election of 1938 did.[56]

In 1938, Frank Murphy ran for governor of Michigan, and the national figures in the C.I.O. were anxious that the U.A.W. support him. This put pressure on the Socialists within the union (in particular, Walter Reuther), who needed the support of Lewis and Murray in their internal struggles with Homer Martin. Although the issue did not involve a labor party, the situation was roughly analogous to the 1937 A.L.P. mayoralty problem in New York. All the unions in Michigan were lined up in support of Murphy. Not to support him, to run a Socialist candidate for governor, meant to split the pro-union vote and risk defeating Murphy. It also would create hostility to the Socialist Party within the U.A.W. To support Murphy would mean to support a capitalist party candidate, and this was against the principles of all Socialists. Even to withdraw the Socialist candidate for governor would mean, especially for Clarity supporters, another apparent step in the liquidation of the Socialist Party as a political party and a step toward turning it into simply an educational agency. In addition, there was the problem of Socialist discipline. If the Socialists were to run a candidate for governor, what should the party's attitude be toward those Socialists in the unions who, because of their union position, felt they had to either keep quiet or support Murphy?[57]

In the end, the Michigan Party fudged through. The Socialist Party ran a candidate, but no enthusiasm was put into his campaign, and no action was taken against Socialists who, for union reasons, endorsed Murphy. Some were allowed to quietly resign from the Party; others simply escaped censure. Thomas, who had approved of the course followed in New York, was deeply disturbed about the developments in Michigan. There were three possible options, he said: running a straight Socialist ticket with discipline enforced down the "line"; running a straight ticket with "special dispensation" to some trade-union leaders who could not support all candidates; nominate candidates for all offices but governor and run a vigorous Socialist campaign, criticizing Murphy but explaining that no candidate was being run against him because of his labor support. The second alternative, for Thomas, was the worst. Either of the other two was acceptable (depending on local conditions), although he leaned toward withdrawal as preferable. It was especially preferable to the campaign that was finally conducted—a campaign that followed the second, and worst, option. In correspondence with Michigan Socialists after the election, Thomas insisted that if one was going to run a political campaign, one ran it genuinely and with effort. To run a half-hearted, lackadaisical campaign was worse than running no campaign at all. And to permit prominent Socialists to endorse the Democratic candidate when there was a Socialist candidate running without taking disciplinary action was absurd.[58]

In taking a critical line on the Michigan Socialists, Thomas was being harsher in his judgment of them than he was of his Altman friends in New York. For the dilemma of the Clarity-oriented Detroit Socialists was similar to the problem confronting the Altman Militants with the A.L.P. To keep their revolutionary political line of independent political action on the part of labor and no compromise with capitalist parties, the Detroit Socialists had run their own candidate for governor. But as with the Altman group, the pressures from the direction in which the unions had moved and were continuing to move proved too great to withstand. The unions were moving into the New Deal. The Socialists believed in independent political action on the part of labor. Between the facts of the union movement and the beliefs of the Socialists, the prospects for the Socialist Party were dim. Cooperation with an unsatisfactory pro-New Deal labor party and running a half-hearted campaign against a labor-supported Democrat were two answers. Neither solved the problem.[59]

It is this series of tragic dilemmas that confronted the Socialist Party in the 1930's. All revolved around the alternative courses charted by Bingham and Samson: the course of fusion in a larger liberal-reform movement, party, or organization, or the course of independent political action along working-class lines. Many Socialists helped form the C.I.O. with the hope that this would be the mass base for independent political action on the part of labor. But as the C.I.O. grew and eschewed independent labor politics, the Socialists who clung to this perspective found themselves lonely voices in the C.I.O. wilderness. Those who traveled the road of the C.I.O. ceased to be Socialists and radicals and became liberal reformers. The whole history of the Socialist Party's agonizing attempts to reach out for a larger base without surrendering socialism —the fluctuating relationships with the Wisconsin Farmer-Labor Progressive Federation; the results of Sinclair's EPIC movement; the dilemmas and consequences of the Party's relation to the American Labor Party; the predicaments faced by the Michigan Socialists—all these point to the stark alternatives of isolation or surrender of socialism and absorption into some kind of liberal reform parties, politics, and perspectives. Independent political action, the persistent clinging to a Marxist perspective, the reliance on working-class action, Samson's vision and alternative—this meant isolation. The optimistic may insist it was temporary isolation, but it was isolation nevertheless. Blanshard's and Henry Rosner's fusion into the LaGuardia movement, the exodus into the Sinclair movement, the union leaders' move from the Socialist Party to the Democratic Party, the absorption of Socialists into the American Labor Party, the transference of Socialists into the Union for Democratic Action—this meant liberal reform. The optimistic may insist it was "realistic" and "practical," but they should have the decency not to confuse the results with the advance of socialism.

VI

The Problem of Failure

ISOLATION and absorption. These two roads lead us to the perennial question of why the Socialists failed in the 1930's. Obviously, this is a larger part of the question of why radicalism failed, and it is probably better to attempt to answer the question without restricting the discussion entirely to the Socialist Party— though this will be the main focus. Too often historians have singled out the mistakes of one or another radical party as explanations of their failures. The basic faults and various blunders of the Communist Party should not be confused with root reasons for its failure, no matter how serious they were. Nor should the "disintegration" of the Socialist Party be taken to be synonymous with the causes for its failure. Yet, when treating the causes of Socialism's failures this is what most historians have done: they concentrate on the internal weaknesses of the Socialist Party, which caused it either to splinter or to fail to win adherents. All historians, however, have not focused on socialism's own internal failure. David Shannon, for one, while acknowledging socialism's mistakes, attributes its main failures to outside forces: the lack of class consciousness among American workers, the relative absence of a feudal tradition, the wealth of the United States, the relatively high degree of mobility, the ethnic heterogeneity of American workers, the strong two-party system, the correlation of Socialism and Communism in the public mind, and the ingrained American philosophy of pragmatism. As overriding reasons for socialism's historic failure, these reasons have varying degrees of validity. What they do tell us is that factors outside of the Socialist movement itself can account for its failures; what they do not tell us is which reasons apply—and how—to the concrete historic situation of the 1930's. When the failures of socialism in the 1930's are analyzed specifically in terms of outside forces, it is usually in terms of the New Deal robbing radicals of their potential power by siphoning off protests with a series of liberal reforms; this is not untrue, but does not go far enough.[1]

However, the main burden of post-mortems on socialism in the 1930's has not been on the outside forces, but on the internal failures. And it is interesting—and worth while—to explore these lines of reasoning. David Shannon, while not stressing them, does suggest three internal failures of the Socialists which might be applicable to the 1930's: (1) the blundering of the Socialists in their approaches to labor; (2) their failure to build strong local and state organizations, to organize machines on a local level; (3) their drive to become homogeneous.[2]

That the Socialist Party lacked a labor base can hardly be denied, despite its often heroic—and important—efforts in helping to organize the C.I.O. The blame should not fall entirely on the Socialists (as Shannon realizes), since labor's hostility toward socialism was of a deep-seated and often irrational nature. But Shannon does suggest that the Socialists were particularly ineffective in their attacks upon the A.F. of L.: they "neither reformed that body nor attracted it to the Socialist Party." Without examining each incident of Socialist criticism of the A.F. of L. between 1900 and 1940, or each example of cooperation, one thing would seem clear: at best, given the nature of the A.F. of L. leadership, its conservatism, its ties in the twenties with organizations like the National Civic Federation, its ties with Roosevelt in the 1930's, its verbal and actual hostility to radicalism, the exclusionary policy of many of its crafts, and the lack of democracy

in many of its locals, the relationship between the Socialist Party
and the A.F. of L. could only have been ambiguous at best. For not
to attack that leadership would have meant not to have been a
socialist in any meaningful sense of the word. The Socialist strategy
of participating in the struggles of the workers and at the same
time criticizing the conservative A.F. of L. policies may not have
been carried out as successfully as possible in all instances. Nor
was it a strategy that was designed to win the Socialist Party
popularity with the A.F. of L. leadership. But a much different
strategy, a capitulation to the conservative leadership, would have
meant surrendering the struggle for socialism. This indeed was the
policy which the Old Guard, as we have seen, ended up adhering
to in practice. Its attempt to mollify the A.F. of L. leadership by
tempering its criticism of its conservative policies accomplished
two things of a negative quality: the Old Guard eventually gave
up the struggle for socialism, and little change developed in A.F.
of L. policy as a result of the more temperate relationship. Even
on the issue of, say, union democracy there was bound to be a
tension between the C.I.O. and the Socialist Party. Again capitulation to the absence of union democracy would have meant the end
of a struggle for meaningful socialism.[3]

Shannon argues that the striving for homogeneity, most prominent in the thirties, also weakened the Party. Here he finds that "it
violated one of the most basic principles of American political
parties." The two major parties, he writes, were not homogeneous,
but were, rather, "coalitions," with platforms that were arrived at
by compromise and bargaining. First, despite the loss of the right
wing after 1936, the Socialist Party never became homogeneous in
outlook. After the split, Norman Thomas argued for an all-inclusive
party and during 1936–37 the Altman Militants, the Clarity, and
the Trotskyists vied for leadership. With the departure of the
Trotskyists, the Clarity's brand of revolutionary socialism and the
Militant brand of reformist socialism constituted the two main
groups. But there existed pacifists, the Hoan followers in Milwaukee, personal followers of Norman Thomas, and a various

assortment of radicals that reached into both camps. To a large extent diversity was maintained throughout the thirties, and with it, factions. The problem was not so much the lack of diversity, but the lack of sheer numbers. Even with the outbreak of the European war, when the Party suffered large losses of members, there still remained a degree of diversity. Shannon says that they were almost all "social democratic pacifists." I am not certain whether this phrase refers to Thomas or to his critics within the Party. In any case, there remained absolute pacifists like Jessie Wallace Hughan and Winston Dancis, revolutionary socialists like Travers Clements and his wife, Lillian Symes, as well as "critical supporters" of the war, like Norman Thomas. The revolutionary socialists wished to oppose the war politically; the absolute pacifists could not support any war. Socialists like Thomas, who had a strong, but not absolute, pacifist strain and who felt that wholesale political opposition was futile, argued for an acceptance of the need to defeat fascism, while maintaining a strong criticism of the capitalist system and the domestic and foreign policies of the Roosevelt administration. Again, numbers, not diversity, were the main problem.[4]

The continued existence of factions and diversity within the Socialist Party does not mean that the issue of homogeneity is a bogus issue. Its importance lies, however, not in the *fact* of a homogeneous party, but in the thrust toward strict party control that could easily have led to such homogeneity. The whole issue of party control, then, is directly connected to Shannon's charge of an excess of homogeneity. For the assumption is that a uniform demand for adherence to party programs and policy drove members from the Party. The insistence, for example, that members not openly oppose the Party's antiwar stand during the 1940 election campaign obviously caused many members to drop out. But the issue of party discipline, party democracy, and party control is not a simple matter by any means.[5]

The problem faced by the Socialists, that of maintaining democracy within the Party and yet presenting a unified and disciplined program, while at the same time avoiding the centralization and "line" of the Communist Party, was hardly an easy one to solve. In the early thirties, young Militants like Paul Porter, Amicus Most, and Andrew Biemiller urged Thomas to enforce a stricter party discipline, even where it might apply to actions with which they had some sympathy. When the Party decided against participation in the Communist-dominated American League against War and Fascism, it was Militants (who were more sympathetic, at this time, to United Front activities) who encouraged Thomas to enforce discipline against errant Socialists like J. B. Matthews, who continued their participation. These Militants believed that it was possible to have Party discussion, but that once decisions were made by the National Executive Committee, the policy should be followed by all groups. They argued that a party that went in all directions, with no discipline, would diffuse its energy and would be unprepared to meet the coming crisis. Thomas, for his part, feared that their kind of discipline would lead to the kind of rigid, centralized discipline associated with the Communist Party. And it would drive young people from the Party. Yet Thomas also acknowledged the problem and the existing lack of discipline within the Party. He was disturbed by what seemed to him undisciplined actions by Party members, particularly Old Guard members. He felt that these actions embarrassed the Party both with the public and with radicals who were potential members. Louis Waldman's criticism in the *New York Times* of an unemployment demonstration led by David Lasser, a Socialist, in Mayor LaGuardia's office seemed like a typical instance of a lack of party consideration. During the whole battle with the Old Guard over the Declaration of Principles, Thomas and the Militants constantly believed that the Old Guard broke the limits of socialist discipline by taking its case outside the Party and into the capitalist press. The Old Guard, on its side, found many instances of what it believed was un-Socialist conduct by Thomas and the Militants.[6]

After the Old Guard left the Party, the problem continued. The

Party expelled David Lasser in 1938 for not following the Socialist
Party policy in the Workers' Alliance. The Young People's Social-
ist League did the same to Joseph Lash in the American Student
Union. Sam Baron was censured for his testimony before the Dies
Committee, with Thomas playing a leading role in pressing charges.
Later, charges were brought against Jack Altman over the issue
of the Socialist Party war policy. Throughout the late 1930's, the
Clarity group was the most insistent on party discipline. Clarity
spokesmen like Frank Trager argued for the need for a more
centralized Party. Trager argued that the composition of the
N.E.C. should reflect the majority sentiment in the Party and that
geographic representation should be ignored in order to obtain it.
All the national organs of the Party should similarly reflect the
majority sentiment. Indeed, when Trager decided he could no
longer support the Party's war position, he resigned from the
N.E.C. because he felt that his minority position would interfere
with the Party's coordinated work. The Clarity group's stress on
discipline placed it in a position where it had to support the purge
of the Trotskyists, who had broken party discipline, despite the
fact that the Trotskyists were closer to them ideologically than the
Altman Militants. At the same time that the Clarity emphasized the
need for discipline, it also stressed the need to maintain intraparty
democracy. Trager warned against turning the Socialist Party into
a structure in which the Communist brand of monolithic discipline
prevailed.[7]

Norman Thomas, in theory, held a more flexible position than
the Clarity. But he was not averse to acting, as in the Baron case,
when he felt that too many transgressions had occurred. The Socialist Party, in short, was struggling with a fundamental problem that
faces any radical party: what are the limits of public dissent from
the party's position. On the war issue, the Party tried to compromise. It was hoped that by not making support of the repeal of the
neutrality legislation and later support of the Lend-Lease bill
matters for Party discipline, the Party might hold together its antiwar and pro-aid-to-the-Allies forces. As the war crisis developed,

this temporary relaxation of discipline did not end the problem. Again, the Party tried to compromise by relaxing discipline far enough so that members were not required to support publicly the Party policy, though they still were expected not to oppose it publicly. But the compromise did not work; the war issue was too fundamental and controversial to be confined to intraparty debate.[8]

I am inclined by disposition and principles to lean always in the direction of utmost flexibility, autonomy, relaxed discipline. But to defend this position, one must acknowledge that there do seem to be cases where flexibility in discipline may lead to a diffusion in purpose, and autonomy may lead to undirected activity. I personally am prepared to accept these as risks, or simply as "facts of life." The thrust to eliminate them by centralization and discipline creates larger problems. It never succeeded in creating a homogeneous party for the Socialists in the thirties, but the drive in this direction, whether it was the Old Guard demanding the expulsion of Militants or Militants demanding expulsion of members of the Old Guard, created constant discord. Finally, it would seem necessary to recognize that this is a problem which, while not peculiar to radical parties, is a special problem for them. A Socialist Party is not a capitalist party, and it would seem that there are limits beyond which an ideological difference is incompatible with membership in the party.

Whatever the answer to the problem of radical discipline may be, the attempt to arrive at party discipline (thereby risking uniformity and homogeneity) should not be viewed primarily as a cause for the Socialist Party's failure, that is, as a cause for its lack of power. Rather, it would be better to view the attempt as a result of the lack of power. What has kept the coalitions of the Democratic and Republican Parties together is just this ability to control power, and, with it, jobs, prestige, and—more power. As Shannon himself writes, "without the political bonds of patronage, without even the hope of patronage, there were only principles to hold the party together." Power has created its own discipline and unity, a kind of indirect homogeneity that drives major disputants back into the party's arms, even at times of great crisis. Lacking power (from other causes), the Socialists sought to maintain discipline and unity along theoretical and programmatic lines. This, in turn, may have caused them to lose more power—as differing theorists and those who could not follow the program divided and departed. But, originally, the drive for homogeneity—in so far as there was such a drive—was largely a reflection, rather than a cause, of the Party's powerlessness. These observations also indicate that the "constant fractiousness" of Socialist life of which Daniel Bell speaks was not due only to its being an "eschatological movement"—sure of its ends, but dividing over the means. This element played a role. However, if the Socialists had had a greater share of political power, the splits within the radical and Socialist movement likely would have been avoided. By the same token, the absence of "fractiousness" in the two major parties is more a result of their power than a cause of their power.[9]

I believe that the above remarks, in their own way, hold equally true in regard to Shannon's criticism of the Socialist Party (he exempts the early Milwaukee and Oklahoma parties) for not building up a local machine and grass-roots organization. Though this may be a legitimate criticism, it is also true (though this needs more research) that such organization is more a result of power, or at least partial success, than one of the causes of initial success. The farther from power, or even the promise of power, the more difficult it is to build such local organizations which, traditionally, have been kept going by the hope of immediately delivered programs or favors.[10]

Unlike Shannon, who sees these internal failures as only peripheral to the larger forces outside of socialism, Daniel Bell places the burden of radicalism's failure throughout the twentieth century on radicalism itself, and not on outside forces such as the New Deal and the like. His thesis, in *Marxian Socialism in the United States,* is "that a set of ideological blinders prevented the American Socialist Party from understanding the society. To state the paradox most forcefully: the American Socialist Party, though often called reformist or right-wing, was actually too much a Marxist Party." And later he writes: "At one crucial turning point after another, when the socialist movement could have entered more directly into American life . . . it was prevented from doing so by its ideological dogmatism."[11]

Bell's interpretation must be rejected, but not because the socialist movement did not make mistakes of its own or have deficiencies of its own. Certainly it did; but its mistakes are dwarfed by the problems outside the particular party structure or particular socialist ideology. Interpretations that transfer the responsibility for the failures of radicalism largely to the shoulders of radicalism itself ultimately do not confront the tragedy of American radicalism. For the hidden, implicit assumption of such interpretations is that if only radicalism had acted differently, the story of its future and perhaps of American history generally would have been different. Of course it would. But the basic question is: if radicalism had acted differently, would it have been more successful? I am forced, for the thirties at least, to answer "no," to argue that radicalism was caught in dilemmas created by the conditions of the thirties and of American history generally and that whichever way it turned it would have failed; it would have failed differently, of course, but it would have failed—in the sense of building a politically successful movement.

Indeed, as I have argued already, to follow the logic of Bell's position would have meant that Socialists give up their socialism for liberal reform. Bell views the 1930's as creating a potential for significant social changes, but argues that the American people were not prepared to accept rigidly dogmatic approaches; their whole tradition was pragmatic. Thus, if the American Socialist Party had chosen to be less Marxist and more reformist, if it had chosen to deal with the New Deal instead of opposing it, if it had chosen programs instead of theoretical niceties, if it had "entered more directly into American life," it would have had more influence on the shape of American politics and perhaps even have been an important force in subsequent American history. There is little to suggest that the Social Democratic Federation, which chose this strategy, thereby increased its power. Indeed, if anything, Norman Thomas's righteous indignation at New Deal failings may have had more influence than the insipid pro-New Deal editorials of the *New Leader,* if one is going to weigh modest degrees of influence. More important is the simple fact that since the ends of the New Deal were so different from the ends of socialism, it seems difficult to imagine such a strategy amounting to anything but a surrender of socialism to New Dealism. Bernard Johnpoll, who opts also for this strategy of socialism as a flank of the New Deal, cannot seem to understand that the ends of socialism and the New Deal were fundamentally opposed. To suggest a strategy for socialism, as distinct from liberalism, that would have meant supporting the New Deal is tantamount to saying that the Socialists should have ceased to be socialists.[12]

If Bell's "internal" critique of Socialism winds up, in essence, saying that the Socialists were wrong for continuing to be socialists, at least it has the merit of recognizing that the conditions for Marxist radicalism in the 1930's were not loaded with obvious and ecstatic possibilities. Other Old Leftists, in particular the Trotskyists, have shared with Bell a critique of the failures of Socialism that focuses on internal Socialist Party weaknesses. But they have argued from different premises about the thirties, and have reached different conclusions as to where Socialism went wrong. The Trotskyists argue that the 1930's were radical, that people were potentially ready for socialism. The failure, they claim, came from radicalism's not providing the necessary radical—i.e., Trotskyist—leadership. If the leadership of the radical movement in the United States had only come from Trotskyists instead of from the reformist Communist Party of the Popular Front period or the centrist Socialist Party, then this mass potential for radical change would have developed.[13]

What is wrong with this analysis? Briefly, it assumes a high potential for radicalism among the masses in the thirties, a potential that only had to be channeled by correct leadership and correct tactics. My reading of the 1930's is quite different. No one would deny an increase in radicalism among the American people. There was an increase in the "general" feeling of being "fed up" with capitalism. There was a new and widespread interest in Marxist ideas. There was a militancy in labor, in agriculture; there was an outpouring of social criticism focusing on the inequities of society. There was a student movement profoundly discontented with capitalist society. But there exists in the analysis of the thirties as a radical period a confusion between militant means and generalized emotions, on one hand, and radicalism, on the other. For example, many workers were willing to follow (and sometimes lead) the militant tactics of radical leadership in strikes, even to engage in radical verbiage, but only a few followed through to radical ends—to extend the critique of capitalism to the Socialist solution. And that, after all, is what radicalism is ultimately all about.[14]

The Trotskyists could answer, of course, that this was due to a lack of proper leadership. But another reading—more pessimistic as far as Socialism in particular and radicalism in general are concerned—is possible and more tenable: chiefly, that there was no ground swell of potential "socialist" radicalism, that only in isolated instances were masses of people even in the slightest prepared to challenge capitalism ("correct" leadership or incorrect leadership), that their ideas, their culture, their life-style, what they demanded and wanted out of life were restricted within the context of a capitalist culture. This is neither to downgrade the heroism and bravery of the protesters—the strikers, the unemployed, the students—of the thirties, nor to deny that a class struggle went on within specific episodes. It is to affirm that, as Melvin Dubofsky argues in his history of the I.W.W., the masses of men wanted into society, and that the Socialists in the formation of the C.I.O. faced the same basic dilemma of the I.W.W. Refusing to be insensitive to human needs and realizing that socialism was not likely to grow out of utter despair, they struggled to bring a better life to the workers. But the very existence of a better life undercut the radical message. The New Deal helped in this, of course—not by moving the country toward socialism, as Johnpoll seems to think, but by combining a welfare program for the masses and a domesticated unionism with a maintenance of the essential power relations of society. As such, the New Deal functioned, though not always consciously, as an episode in the development of twentieth-century corporate capitalism with a welfare base.[15]

In both Bell's and the Trotskyist position, then, the Socialist Party in the 1930's is held responsible for its failures—either for being too dogmatic and Marxist and not reformist enough or for being too reformist and not Marxist and radical enough. But to have followed the conclusions of either critique, in my more pessimistic reading of the thirties, would have led equally to failure. To have opted for the Trotskyist solution in the face of a "non-radical" culture was ultimately (despite individual successes) to cut oneself off from the direction in which the masses were headed; to have opted, however, for Bell's solution of meeting this "non-radical" culture with a reformist radicalism was hardly designed to be more successful in promoting radicalism. The more reformist the section of the Socialist Party in the American Labor Party became, or the more reformist the Communist Party became, the more they served not their purposes, but the purposes of the New Deal—the more, in short, radicalism became indistiguishable from liberalism. The horns of the Samson-Bingham dilemma were difficult to overcome. The choices for the Socialist Party were hardly pleasant. Those who feel that some different choice than the Socialists made—less ideology, a different kind of labor party, more grass-roots organization—would have been better may be correct, but their correctness is of a limited variety. No large options were opened in the 1930's if one wanted to be both radical *and* successful. The thirties were not the fertile ground for radicalism that historians have imagined. Different alternatives meant different forms of failure. This is the tragic dilemma of Socialism in the thirties; unfortunately the tragedy was not only theirs—it is ours.

PART THREE

Ideology: The Socialist Perspective

VII

Socialists and the New Deal

TO SAY that socialism failed in the 1930's in the sense of coming to power or even to near power is not to say that it failed in every sense, or that to choose the path of failure is necessarily wrong (indeed, when I contemplate some of the "successes" of history, I am a great advocate of failure). More specifically, it is my contention that far from failing entirely, it was very perceptive in analyzing certain events and issues. And it was able to do this because it was a *socialist* movement, i.e., had an angle of vision that was other than capitalist or even other than a reordered capitalist vision.

Only a rather simplistic Marxist would at this late date claim that the Socialist analysis of American society in the thirties was either an adequate description of the society or an adequate tool for the advancement of Socialism. Certainly, too many claims were made for the imminent collapse of capitalism and too few for its recuperative powers. There is, however, another side to the picture, a side that recognizes that the ideology was not an absolutely adequate tool of analysis or technique for change, but insists that it furnished the Socialists with a perspective for judgment which, far from being imperceptive, was able to analyze social situations and perceive dangers in advance of the *ad hoc* pragmatism that

Arthur Schlesinger, Jr., and other devotees of liberalism so greatly admire.

When the New Left critique of liberal corporatism began to develop in the 1960's, it was inevitable that the New Deal would be reexamined. The resulting reexamination was a series of brief articles suggesting that the New Deal was part of the development of twentieth-century liberal corporatism. Much of this critique focused on the failure of the New Deal to change the basic power relations in society. This aspect of the New Left critique brought it into conflict with the consensus in New Deal historiography that had emerged after World War II. This consensus had developed with the collapse of all forms of the 1930's radicalism in the 1940's and 1950's. Whether one argued from the conservative right or from the liberal center, whether one believed that the New Deal had evolved slowly through evolution or rapidly through "revolution," the assumption was that significant changes in the capitalist power relations had resulted from the New Deal. Writing as a liberal, Carl Degler could praise the "guarantor" state created by the New Deal, while the conservative Edgar E. Robinson could worry about the impact of this new federal activity on traditional individualistic values. But both shared a consensus on the meaning of the New Deal: it was liberal, democratic, coming to the aid of the poor and economically bereft.[1]

Despite occasional conservatives like Robinson, it was liberal historians—Degler, Basil Rauch, Arthur M. Schlesinger, Jr., Henry Steele Commager—who dominated the historical writing on the New Deal. And though these writers had significant differences, there was little debate over the ultimate ends of the New Deal—the "broad human objectives" as Schlesinger called them. Because they did not question the liberal ends of the New Deal, there was a tendency in the writings of these historians to treat its illiberal aspects either as exceptions to the liberal rule, as initial stages that were soon transformed in the reformist thrust, or as compromises forced on the New Deal by the conservative forces of the time. Moreover, the assumption behind the liberal interpretation was that the New Deal was a success—not *always* a success, more successful at certain times than others, but, nevertheless, a success.

This optimistic view of the success of the New Deal was part of the postwar optimism about the success of liberal capitalism. To Schlesinger, to Daniel Bell, to Seymour Martin Lipset, and to the other prominent "consensus" liberals, capitalism, modified, tamed, democratized, and transformed by the aggressive liberal reforms of the New Deal, had demonstrated its viability in a totalitarianized world. It is therefore not surprising that a radical critique of the New Deal did not emerge until the injustices in American society again came to the political foreground. The civil rights movement of the late 1950's and the New Left of the 1960's set the stage. But even when the New Left developed its theory of liberal corporatism and attempted with some—though not absolute —success to integrate an interpretation of the New Deal into this theory, it did not rediscover the earlier radical critique of the 1930's. That critique had been forgotten; if anything, it was the Communist Party's support of the New Deal during the Popular Front period that was remembered—and condemned. It is my contention that the earlier Socialist critique of the New Deal bears reexamination. Like the New Left interpretation, it does not answer all questions about the New Deal or explain adequately everything that took place. But, again like the New Left viewpoint, it has the merit of not having to explain away central aspects of the New Deal like A.A.A. or N.R.A. as exceptions to liberalism or as forced on the New Deal by conservative forces (Roosevelt welcomed them) or only as initial blunders before the real liberal reform took over. Significant reform of the tenant farming system, despite the Farm Security Administration, never took place, nor could big business, if that was even the desire, ever be seriously controlled once N.R.A. legitimatized and solidified its power. The New Deal undertook a number of beneficial projects and I have no desire to join in the all-too-fashionable contempt for the material improvements that occurred in the lives of many workers during the thirties (though it should be remembered that not all union struggles were supported by the New Deal). Still, the critical perspective of the Socialists comes closer to an adequate interpretation of the New Deal than that of the consensus liberals. It is to the specifics of the Socialist interpretation that it is now necessary to turn.

Let us clear up a minor matter first: Norman Thomas was not nearly as excited about or sympathetic to the New Deal as Bernard Johnpoll argues. Johnpoll says that Thomas was generally enthusiastic about the early New Deal. It is true that Thomas was more enthusiastic initially, in 1933, than he later became. However, a letter to the progressive businessman, Edward A. Filene, that Johnpoll uses to try to show that Thomas was seriously considering backing Roosevelt really indicates that Thomas believed Roosevelt's aims were not socialistic, that Roosevelt had his own interests and political intentions, which did not lie in the direction of socialism, and that Thomas did not confuse what Roosevelt had done with socialism. It was a discussion of the problem, and not a "serious consideration." In 1933 and 1934, Thomas did credit Roosevelt with energy, enthusiasm, and idealism; he did believe that Roosevelt had done some good things. But he did not, as Johnpoll claims, say that Roosevelt's program "far more nearly resembled the Socialist . . . than his own platform." This passage, from *The Choice Before Us,* is a particularly grievous misuse of a quote that misses Thomas's meaning. Thomas wrote, and it gives a fair indication of his early attitude toward the New Deal:

> To say that the Roosevelt Revolution, in so far as it was a revolution at all, was a revolution from *laissez faire* to state capitalism, is not to deny the magnitude of some of its achievements or the considerable measure of social idealism behind them. In Akron, Ohio, and St. Louis, Missouri, and for all I know in other towns, editors did a pretty competent job in showing that certain features of the Roosevelt program far more nearly resembled the Socialist immediate demands than his own platform. Socialists had demanded the thirty-hour week in industry; the workers got a thirty-five- or forty-hour week in most of the codes—some ran as high as fifty-four hours! Socialists had demanded at least ten billion

dollars for public works and direct unemployment relief; the country all together got some $3,800,000,000 in federal appropriation for this end. Socialists had demanded an end of sweat-shops and child labor; the country got the abolition of the worst of sweat-shop conditions under the codes, and of child labor in factories, if not in the beet sugar and cotton fields and the vending of newspapers. It will be observed that even in immediate demands the Roosevelt Revolution only distantly approximated what Socialists had asked. It is more important to observe that the essential thing about the Socialist platform has always been its purpose and its goal rather than its immediate demands. Socialists ask certain things in order that the workers may have strength to go on to take power away from private owners of productive goods. The Roosevelt program makes concessions to workers in order to keep them quiet a while longer and so stabilize the power of private owners. The essence of the Socialist position is its philosophy, a philosophy of social ownership of the great natural resources, the principal means of production and distribution, and their management according to plan for the use of the whole company of the people, and not for the profit of the few. It was, the President's admirers told us, his virtue that he was not cumbered with a philosophy and therefore he could more easily find out what play would work. These eulogists did not share the Socialist fear that, lacking in philosophy and a sense of direction, the quarter-back might make some bold play only to discover that, as happened in a famous game in California, he had scored his points for the enemy behind the wrong goal line.

This extended quote shows that while Thomas was willing to give Roosevelt some credit, he was well aware of the *partial* nature of his immediate demands in terms of Socialism and the Socialist program. He was well aware that Roosevelt's intentions—to stabilize capitalism through these partial concessions—separated him fundamentally from the Socialists. And he was well aware that the New Deal philosophy, no matter how idealistic and well-intentioned in certain areas, was haphazard and contradictory.[2]

Whatever the degree of Thomas's initial enthusiasm for the New Deal (and I believe it was considerably less than Johnpoll argues), his early attitude contained all the elements that would later develop into a full-scale critique. Thomas was bothered by its inadequacies in agriculture, in housing, in social security; he was bothered by the centralization of power into one man, even though he did not think Roosevelt would deliberately misuse it. He was disturbed by the violations of the N.R.A. codes, by the antilabor overtones in the administration of the N.R.A., despite the initial provisions for labor. There was very little outside of T.V.A. that Thomas welcomed without the gravest reservations and exceptions. And he also feared the overall direction in which the New Deal was moving—toward state capitalism. He did not say that the New Deal was out-and-out fascism, as did the Communists; but he recognized the parallels between the economics of state capitalism and the economics of fascism, and he feared, with good reason, considering the administration of it, that the N.R.A. had potential dangers in a fascist direction.[3]

Thomas's critique of the New Deal on the individual and ideological level suggests the two dimensions of the Socialist critique of the New Deal. On one level, the Socialist critique presented a long record of inadequacies and imbalances and business bias—inadequacies in farm tenantry programs, in public housing, in social security, in unemployment insurance, and in relief; imbalances in income; favoritism to large-scale farming interests in the A.A.A. and large-scale business in the N.R.A. The activities of Thomas and the Socialist Party in helping to form the Southern Tenant Farmers Union, in publicizing the conditions of the sharecroppers and the terror used against them, were motivated by the conditions themselves. But the activity was also motivated by the New Deal inactivity, by Roosevelt's capitulation to Senator Joseph Robinson and the Arkansas cotton planting interests, and by the Agriculture Department's shameful attempt (with Henry Wallace's knowledge) to cover up the facts.[4]

It is true that the Socialists saw opportunities for workers to organize under the N.R.A. Most radicals, with the exception of the Communists, felt that it offered workers such an opportunity. But the Socialists, along with other radical groups, accented what the workers had to do for themselves—they needed to use the tool of the N.R.A. for their own purposes, and not, as Roosevelt wished, to have the unions become appendages of and incorporated into the New Deal. Here, in the incorporation of unions into the structure of government, the Socialists recognized the dangers. And they, with others on the left, helped to publicize the dangers inherent in General Hugh Johnson's antiunion statements and actions which indicated that he foresaw a quiescent government-controlled union movement as the result of the N.R.A. Moreover, the Socialists publicized the violations of the N.R.A. business-oriented codes. They exposed the New Deal's antiunion actions in such forgotten strikes as the Colt Arms strike in Hartford, Connecticut in 1933. "If," Thomas wrote, "under a supposedly friendly administration labor fared no better under N.R.A., think what might have been its fate under a reactionary or a semi-fascist government!" It was the Socialists who, while welcoming the mere fact that Roosevelt dealt with social security, exposed the inadequacies of the Social Security Act. And it was Socialists who reminded the American people, when the Communists had joined in the New Deal applause, that whatever progressive (but inadequate) steps Roosevelt had taken before 1936, there was little to indicate any domestic social concern after that time.[5]

The conclusion from the series of individual critiques of measures was that these problems—unemployment, poverty, maldistribution of wealth—would continue as long as there was capitalism. This leads to the second level of the Socialist critique. The Socialist analysis of the New Deal was based on the impossibility of capitalist planning. Even the Old Guard Socialists, before they made their peace with Roosevelt, had criticized the idea of such planning. Algernon Lee, a leading Old Guard Socialist, wrote that all forms of bourgeois planning were antidemocratic and also impossible, based as they were on the inconsistency between the *social* forms of production and the individual forms of property.[6]

The Socialists portrayed the New Deal as an impossible attempt to save capitalism through "the partnership of government and industry"; temporarily it might fool the masses, but its success would surely be short-lived. This partnership of government and business was part of an emerging state capitalism. The Socialists recognized that the New Deal was not saving the old system as it was; it was creating a new structure in the process of saving capiatlism. State capitalism, a term often vaguely defined, was the general theoretical framework which the Socialists applied to the New Deal. State capitalism meant government intervention on behalf of the prevailing profit system. It was, Thomas wrote, "a degree of government ownership and a much greater degree of government regulation of economic enterprises for the sake of bolstering up the profit system." State capitalism was resisted by die-hard laissez-fairists, but the sophisticated upholder of capitalism recognized the necessity of passing sufficient reforms to quell discontent. These reforms were inadequate, but they at least wedded disparate groups to the system. And, here, the Socialists recognized the duality of Section 7A of N.R.A. and also of the Wagner Act, in that, on one hand, they favored labor and could not be opposed out of hand, but, on the other hand, that their effect would increasingly tie labor to the Democratic Party, and, hence, incorporate labor into the system—with an interest in preserving the system. The Socialist drive for independent political action on the part of labor was, in part, an attempt to divert these tendencies.[7]

How does this Socialist analysis of the New Deal stand up? About one thing, the Socialists were absolutely correct: the New Deal was not Socialism. Its partial incorporation of measures that had often been pioneered by Socialists may have improved conditions slightly, and such measures did help undercut the Socialist appeal. But they were not, even as "immediate demands," the Socialist program. An inadequate "immediate demand" does not fulfill the function of immediate demands by Socialists. It does not solve the problem, as the Socialists' proposals hoped to do; it simply alleviates discontent and lulls the development of the kind of consciousness that Socialists wished to create. Moreover, the Socialists' immediate demands were not isolated programs; they were part of an overall Socialist program.

The New Deal implementation of some of these demands took place within the context of a capitalist structure. And it is the basic structure that will determine how the demands function. Thomas understood this better than some of his later critics when he wrote in 1936: "The New Deal as it was, and any successor to it which President Roosevelt may create, will be expressions not of socialism but of capitalism." He went on to acknowledge its "confidence and boldness" that achieved "a degree of recovery" in the early winter of 1933. But, he continued, "it was a recovery as manifest in the profits of the classes which hate Roosevelt as in the wages of those who support him, and no fundamental issue was solved." And in this he was essentially correct too. For while there is no question that the Socialists underestimated the ability of the New Deal to win continual support from the masses by ameliorating conditions and thus rescuing capitalism, it was the war, and not basically the New Deal, that should be given major credit for rescuing the country from the depression.[8]

If the Socialist ideology failed to measure the success of the New Deal, it was able to perceive much else. Later historical research and analysis have supported the Socialist critique of the inadequacies, imbalances, and biases of the New Deal program. Sidney Fine's *The Automobile under the Blue Eagle* has documented the consistency with which Roosevelt and New Deal officialdom sided with business in any major dispute between labor and capital in the auto industry during the National Recovery Administration period. M. Venkataramani and David Conrad are two scholars among many whose work on agriculture and the sharecropping problem fully supports the Socialists' descriptions of the conditions and their charges against the Agriculture Department and the New Deal. Fred Greenbaum's article on Roosevelt and the federal antilynching bill and Raymond Wolters' *Negroes and the Great Depression* buttress the Socialist critique of the New Deal handling of Blacks and directly challenge the liberal interpretation of the New Deal as genuinely interested in serious reform. David Shannon's work in progress on Roosevelt and Congress between

1934 and 1936 shows the New Deal's concern for the sensibilities and interests of conservatives on a number of important issues. Ellis Hawley's *The New Deal and the Problem of Monopoly,* a study of the New Deal's failure to handle the problem of monopoly, supports a frequent Socialist charge in the 1930's. Gabriel Kolko's work on the continued maldistribution of income documents the Socialist position on this question in the 1930's. This is not the place to discuss the continually nagging question of whether the New Deal could have done "more." The fact is that its programs were inadequate and did not solve the problems of unemployment and poverty. The fact is that many of the most important programs did favor established business interests (N.R.A.) and large-scale farming (A.A.A.)—often at the expense of labor and the tenant farmer.[9]

Many of the historians whose work supports the Socialist critique would, of course, resist the theoretical framework in which the Socialists placed these failures. To them, the inadequacies remain the inadequacies of liberal reform and not examples of state capitalism co-opting (to use the prevalent phrase) dissident elements while preserving the power structure of capitalism. The resistance of many historians to the theory of state capitalism may come from two sources. On the one hand, it may be attributable to their resistance to the New Left theory of liberal corporatism. To admit the reality of liberal corporatism might mean to admit the reality of state capitalism, which is quite similar in its formulation. In this case, it would be a "political" rejection of a concept they refuse—for political reasons—to admit existed or a movement that they presently deplore.

On the other hand, the rejection may be attributable to the naive way in which the New Left has formulated its theory and has related the New Deal to liberal corporatism. Here the resistance would not be political, but historical—i.e., the historical description does not suit the facts. To argue, however, that a theory has been formulated naively is not to argue that it is invalid. It seems to me that with proper qualifications and recognitions of paradoxes, of multimotivations, and distinctions between intent and effect, one can apply the terminology of state capitalism—or even liberal corporatism—to the New Deal. With the N.R.A. this appears relatively easy: basically determined by large business interests to stabilize the economy and to preserve their hegemony and dominant power, the N.R.A. granted an afterthought to labor in Section 7A, an afterthought that while it gave an initial psychological benefit to labor, was ultimately used to enmesh labor in the government structure of business-dominated boards, which in their rulings negated any initial benefits to labor. General Hugh Johnson's remark that strikes under the Blue Eagle were both unnecessary and against the government was the logic of the N.R.A.[10]

It is more difficult to relate a measure like the Wagner Act to the theory of state capitalism. But even here, a recognition that the Wagner Act may not have been intended to co-opt the labor movement, a recognition that it was passed by those desiring liberal reform that would not favor business, and a recognition that labor gained some necessary protection, can be consistent with a recognition that by providing an institutional outlet for labor grievances the Wagner Act oiled the machinery whereby the labor movement did indeed become an integral part of the corporate structure. As one historian has written: "The Wagner Act incorporated the union movement into the New Deal, absorbing unions (including Left led unions) into the corporate structure as they devoted themselves to producing with greater efficiency."[11]

But even if "state capitalism" were not an entirely adequate term to describe the New Deal, it is more accurate than "liberal reform." The Socialists may not have been alone in being aware of this trend toward state capitalism and the various actions of the New Deal which were oriented in the direction of corporate enterprise, so that one cannot claim that their perception was due *only* to their Marxist ideology. The only point is that their ideology furnished them with a perspective that was lacking in the pragmatic give-and-take politics of the New Deal; the latter, accepting only the "given," was either unable or unwilling to question the trend or the actions. Only an ideology that had an alternative vision could raise such fundamental questions.

VIII

Socialists and Communism

Russia

AS SIGNIFICANT as their analysis of the New Deal is the fact that it was the Socialists who first gave us the analysis of the bureaucratization of terror under Stalin. While the conservative press blanched at *the revolution,* while much of the liberal press rationalized Stalinism, while the New Dealers ignored the quality of the revolution, the Socialists documented its betrayal, whether in Spain, at the Moscow trials, or in the developing elite in Russia.

These are generalizations, and, as such, are subject to the inevitable qualifications. There were, of course, liberals who were critical of Russia and who criticized the Moscow trials. These liberals—men like John Dewey, Oswald Garrison Villard, Carl Becker—made cogent criticisms of Russia based on their strong commitment to civil liberties. In so far as civil liberties were an essential part of liberalism, one can say that their liberalism contributed to their critique of Russia and the Moscow trials. The surprising thing, however, is how other aspects of their philosophy —especially the stress on planning—contributed to the sympathy for Russia and the subsequent apologies for her anti-civil libertarian aspects that were common among many liberal intellectuals in the 1930's. The focus on planning, on growth, on activism—all central elements in liberal thought in the thirties—led in most cases to sympathy for Stalin's Russia. Aside from a belief in civil liberties, there was little in liberal thought that could seriously resist the temptation to applaud uncritically Russian planning and growth. Unlike the Socialists' commitment to a workers' state, liberal sympathy did not depend on an ideological principle. The emerging Russian bureaucracy could more easily violate and betray Socialist principles than it could liberal "planism."[1]

This is not to say that the radical critique of Stalinism was the peculiar property of the Socialist Party. Certainly, various anti-Stalinist radicals who were outside the Socialist Party—V. F. Calverton, Max Eastman, Sidney Hook among others—contributed to a radical critique of Russian terror and the radical analysis of the bureaucratic dictatorship over the proletariat. The claim that is made in this chapter, then, is not that Socialist Party membership led to this analysis, but that the kind of Marxist ideology that was found in the Socialist Party led to a perceptive critique of the Soviet system. Elements of this critique were later taken out of their radical framework and popularized by those with no sympathy for socialism. But that is no reason for criticizing or ignoring the validity of the Socialists' original insights.

Therefore, in order to see the role of ideology in the judgment on Russia, it becomes necessary to review briefly the history of the Socialist Party's attitude toward Russia. Initially the Socialist Party welcomed the Russian Revolution. Despite the split between the Socialist Party and the nascent Communist parties in the United States, Socialists, even in the right wing of the Party, were not unsympathetic to the Russian attempt to build socialism. As the twenties progressed, the initial enthusiasm was dampened both by Communist activity within the labor movement and on the political scene in the United States and by the tightening grip of the Russian rulers within the Soviet Union, where many Russian Social Democrats and other non-Bolshevik radicals were imprisoned.[2]

With the coming of the Russian Five-Year Plan and the depression in the United States, many Socialists, especially the

younger ones who had not participated in the internecine wars in
the labor movement, came to look at the Soviet Union with renewed sympathy. Much like the liberals around the *New Republic*
and the *Nation,* the "militants" and the "progressives" within the
Socialist Party felt the impact of the contrast between the height-
ened Russian activity in industrialization and agricultural collectivization and the inactivity and passivity of American capitalism
and its political rulers. The Old Guard Socialists, however, looked
on this sympathy as misplaced idealism, naiveté, and feared it
meant the intrusion of Bolshevik ideas into the Party. More closely
aligned with the Labor and Socialist International and with the
Russian Social Democrats, Old Guard spokesmen like James
Oneal and Algernon Lee focused on the imprisonment of political
prisoners in Russia, its economic failures, and the suffering collectivization entailed. The left-wing Socialists were not entirely
averse to the issue of political prisoners. Indeed, as early as 1925
Norman Thomas had joined others in condemning the continued
imprisonment of political opponents by Stalin. Nor could the Old
Guard deny that right-wing Socialists had at one time been impressed with Russian economic progress: James Maurer, the
veteran Socialist leader from Pennsylvania, traveled to Russia with
a group of economists and social scientists in 1927 and was
favorably impressed with Soviet economic progress.[3]

But the emphasis in discussions of the Russian economy differed
greatly: where the left-wing Socialists saw success and the pains of
the birth of socialism, the Old Guard saw suffering and failure. I
have pointed out earlier how this Old Guard view derived in part
from a theoretical structure of how industrialization and socialism
took place; Stalin was trying to "skip a stage." The consequence of
defying the "inexorable laws" of history according to Oneal was
that the Russian regimen must necessarily be brutal. Part of the
Old Guard's attitude came from a simple moral indignation that
their theoretical laws of history rendered meaningless. For if in
trying to socialize an undeveloped country Stalin could not have
done other than he was doing, then why waste time in moral con-

demnation? The contradiction between their morality and the rigidity of their interpretation of the transition from capitalism to socialism did not stop the Old Guard from their moral criticism. But in addition to these two motives for criticism of Stalin, there was another central aspect of their ideology that pointed in a critical direction: their "workers" ideology. The Old Guard, for all its passivity in action, did have a philosophy of a workers' state. Socialism did not simply mean the elimination of private property; it also meant the democratic control of industry by the workers. And in the growth of Stalin's power and oppressiveness, the Old Guard saw the absence of this democratic control.[4]

The Old Guard opposition to Stalin and its critique of the Soviet Union, then, derived not from its conservatism, as the Militants unfairly charged, but from the one aspect of radicalism in its ideology: its socialist philosophy of democratic control of the state by the workers. As long as it had this philosophy, its critique of the Soviet Union was a socialist critique; the Old Guard could favor the recognition of Russia and the normalization of trade relations at the same time that it documented the terror. As the Old Guard moved away from socialism and toward liberal New Deal reformism in the late thirties, its anti-Soviet Union and anti-Communist attitude became not simply a realistic description of conditions there, but a hysterical attitude that could temporize with the Dies Committee and find merit in almost any kind of anti-Communist critique, whether from a socialist perspective or not.[5]

The sympathetic arguments of the Militants often mirrored the liberal arguments in the *New Republic* and the *Nation;* indeed they often were based on similar sources (the reports of Anna Louise Strong and Albert Rhys Williams and other sympathetic travelers). Bernard Johnpoll is correct in saying that there was a large degree of liberalism, rather than radicalism, in their position. Like the liberals, the Militants separated the economic and political spheres. The former could be progressive, despite political suppression. There were, however, two differences between the liberal attitude and the left-wing Socialists, which make Johnpoll's characterization

of the Militant attitude as really "liberal" not quite fair. Whereas
the liberals' sympathy derived from the "planned" feature of the
Russian economy, the Socialist sympathy, while including a strong
element of this "planism," also derived from their belief that the
Soviet economy was a "workers" economy. Planning, though
important to the Socialists, could not exist simply by itself; its
merit lay in the implementation of the socialist base of the economy.
While this may not have been any more acceptable as a complete
analysis of the Russian economy, it gave their sympathy a less
abstract base than the mere concept of planning. It meant that if
the Militants ever became convinced that the Soviet Union did not
have a workers' economy, the aura of "planning" could not continue to cause them to remain sympathetic.[6]

The second area of difference between liberals and Militant
Socialists was in the political area. Whereas, in their enthusiasm
for Russian planning, the liberals slid easily over the absence of
civil liberties in Russia, the left-wing Socialists, inclined though
they might be on occasion to accept the Russian government's interpretation of events, did criticize the absence of civil liberties in the
Soviet Union. There were, of course, persons within the far-left
Revolutionary Policy Committee who could justify Russian political
oppressiveness; on the other hand, there were left-wing Marxist
Socialists who were every bit as critical as the Old Guard. But
among the main body of Militants—Thomas and his supporters—
there was criticism of Russian politics tempered by sympathy for
the economy.[7]

The Militant position, then, was initially quite sympathetic to
Russia. But it had within its framework a perspective that could
easily become critical from a socialist point of view. The Militants'
opposition to the Russian political bureaucracy, coupled with their
position on Russia as a workers' economy, could lead them toward
a Trotskyist or quasi-Trotskyist critique: a belief that Russia was a
workers' state badly corrupted by a political dictatorship and
bureaucracy. Indeed, Thomas, as he became increasingly critical
of Russia in the mid-thirties, acknowledged that he was impressed

by Trotsky's analysis of the Russian state. Thomas still believed Russia had made economic progress, but more and more he felt that the political system was poisoning the progress. Moreover, among the Militants with a more fully developed Marxist perspective, the critique of Russia was already evident in the early thirties. Once again, it was their ideology—their Marxian *socialism*—that furnished them with this perspective.[8]

The possible implications of the "radical" elements (as distinct from the "liberal" elements) in the Militants' perspective might have led them to an earlier critique of the Soviet Union if this perspective had not become intertwined with "practical" considerations. Between 1929 and the 1932 Socialist Convention at Milwaukee when the Russian issue was compromised, the columns of the *New Leader,* at that time the official party paper, were filled with articles and letters concerning Russia. To a large extent the debate centered around facts: was the Five-Year Plan successful or not? What was the story behind the engineers' trial in Russia? But entering into the debate in the 1930's was a distinct tactical note: the Militants, whatever they thought were the "facts" of this or that episode in Russia, were convinced that a progressive party in the United States could not be built on a harsh anti-Soviet position. Young Militant Socialists like Paul Porter, Arthur McDowell, and Alfred Baker Lewis wrote to the *New Leader* in these years to argue that the Old Guard had placed itself in the camp of the Fishes and Hearsts by its anti-Russian line and anti-Russian articles. The Old Guard was, they said, encouraging the reactionary forces that were economically and militarily threatening the first workers' state. James Oneal and Algernon Lee answered that the left-wingers had not challenged the facts and that the left-wingers should know that many times Socialists, for their own reasons, found themselves opposed to men or philosophies that conservatives and reactionaries also opposed. Had not Marx opposed Bakunin at the same time as the latter was being hunted by the secret police? The implication was that Socialists—for their *own* reasons—must continue to criticize Russia.[9]

These Old Guard arguments, while telling, did not get to the heart of what was concerning the Militants. For the Militants were not prepared to look at Russia strictly in terms of facts nor were they even primarily concerned with acknowledging the validity or invalidity of the right wing's argument about Socialist opposition paralleling conservative opposition only on a superficial level. What concerned them, to a great extent, was the question of building a party. How could they appeal to progressive workers—the workers coming to a realization of socialism—if their party took a consistently hostile attitude toward the largest socialist country in the world? And how could they reach out to those Americans disillusioned by American capitalism, sympathetic to Russia's attempt to build socialism, yet fearful and hesitant about accepting the ultrarevolutionary line of the Communists, if their party's stance toward Russia could, superficially or not, be compared to the conservative hostility? Militants like Alfred Baker Lewis specifically acknowledged these concerns. They were not simply upset by the Old Guard opposition to Russia, but also by its seeming indifference to Russia as an example for workers and progressives in the United States. Morris Hillquit, leader of the Old Guard, had given a series of lectures on Russia in which he had apparently implied that the failure or success of the Russian economy would have little impact on the American worker. The Militants protested this stand, insisting that its impact would be enormous—whether it succeeded or failed; therefore, American Socialists should sympathetically support the Soviet experiment so that it would not fail.[10]

Given this attitude and given the enthusiasm of some Militants for the concept of the "dictatorship of the proletariat," it would have been very easy for them to have ignored entirely the absence of civil liberties or Stalin's use of terror. Many prominent liberals, far less radical in their overall ideoolgy and with no ideological stake in defending the workers' state and the dictatorship of the proletariat, did just that. But the Militants could not do this entirely. Though they temporized, their conception of Socialism— and one of the reasons why they were not Communists—included democratic rights. In this they were encouraged by Norman Thomas. Like them, Thomas was sympathetic to the Russian economy; like them, he was concerned with the effects on party-building if the Party adopted a too-hostile attitude toward Russia. But he could not ignore the political persecution, the dictatorship, the cruelty associated with collectivization. He was not as yet willing to confront seriously the totalitarian nature—the inseparability of the political and economic aspects of governmental control—of the Russian state. The result was a mixed attitude toward Russia that eventually led to compromises such as the resolution at the 1932 Socialist Convention.[11]

It was a mixed attitude, but, as indicated, implicit within the concept of a workers' state (with its assumption that socialization meant workers' control and not simply nationalization) lay the roots of a socialist critique of Russia that in its perceptiveness has given us basic insights into the nature of totalitarianism. The Socialists' precise views on these matters have not always been borne out, but the surprising thing is how accurate they were. The seemingly esoteric debates among radicals in the late thirties over whether Russia was state capitalist or state socialist had as their substantive basis the bureaucratic structure of the "left" total state as a new form of social control from on top. Daniel Bell has rightly worried about how economic modernization has been used to justify new forms of exploitation, and Irving Howe and Lewis Coser in 1955 wrote their seminal article on the "technological" authoritarians. But back in 1936, in an article on the Moscow trials, David Berenberg, an editor of the *American Socialist Monthly,* expressed the same basic point when he wrote:

> Irresponsible dictatorships in the name of the proletariat may do wonders in raising the standard of living of the workers, in preparing national defenses, in making foreign alliances, and in developing industrial resources. They may or may not solve the problems of unemployment and of economic depressions. They may, or may not, foster scientific research. These are debatable questions. One thing is not debatable:

irresponsible dictatorships have never led, and cannot lead
to Socialism, even when they hand down from above ready-
made 'democratic' constitutions.

Historians, quick to chastise the ideology of the Socialists, might
pause to consider whether the stress that Socialist ideology placed
on workers' control had not more than a little to do with such per-
ceptions. Firmly persuaded that freedom meant workers' control,
the Socialists could not accept the easy proposition that economic
development *per se* meant freedom; it was only later that many
non-Socialists arrived at analogous conclusions.[12]

All Socialists, of course, did not simultaneously achieve
Berenberg's insight. Once again, however, it was those who were
most ideological, most Marxist, who were quickest to develop this
insight. It was Thomas and other quasi-Marxists, like Clarence
Senior, who, while they were becoming increasingly critical of
Russia, still struggled to keep economic development as a "progressive" category. I have indicated how, at the time of the first
Moscow trials, Thomas was not anxious to have his criticism of
the trials be read as an across-the-board criticism of the Soviet
state. And he was more cautious than the Clarity in stating that
the trials were gigantic frauds. His basic insistence was that Trotsky
be given asylum; that nothing against Trotsky had been proved;
and that the defendants should have a fair trial. Thomas's disin-
clination to speak out more strongly was due partly to his continued desire not to let the trials become an issue in a new round of
intraparty factionalism. But part of the reason was that he, like
many others, was still struggling to keep the "progressive" image
of Russia that the trials so severely challenged. He was too honest
a person and too good a Socialist to rationalize them away, but, in
1936, there was an ambiguity in his remarks that upset both
Russia's defenders and the trials' critics within the Party. After
his trip to Russia in 1937 and the subsequent trials, Thomas became more outspokenly critical. The note of ambiguity ceased. By
1938 he was collaborating with Joel Seidman in a lengthy critique
of the Russian dictatorship.[13]

Whatever the degree of Thomas's criticism of the Moscow trials in 1936, he did see their importance and he did not try to rationalize them in the manner of the Popular Front liberals. Indeed, it was the anti-Stalinist Left which gave us our initial insights into the trials. Only a few Socialists, like Alfred Baker Lewis, seemed untouched by the trials and advised Thomas not to play them up for Party reasons. And even Lewis qualified his advice in a later letter to Thomas by explaining that the lesson to be learned from the trials was for Socialists to avoid all forms of Communist—Stalinist or Trotskyist—dictatorship. The typical American response to the Moscow trials, on the other hand, was that they were over "there." They were viewed as having little importance for Americans. Louis Adamic, who became a member of the Trotsky Defense Committee, admitted that his first inclination was that it was all a distant family feud between Stalin and Trotsky. It was largely the Socialists, along with the Trotskyists, independent radicals, and some liberals, who forced the public's attention on the trials, in so far as the public ever became aware of them and their implications. It is one of the ironies of history that the trials now serve as a key weapon in the arsenal of those historians anxious to chastise all ideology, Socialist as well as Communist. Certainly the Socialists deserve a better fate. For all the loose talk about "bogus democracy" in Socialist circles, it was the Socialists (of various persuasions) who realized that something momentous was going on in the Moscow trials in relation to democratic rights and civil liberties, and they did more to clarify the relation of civil liberties to political power than the "non-ideological, pragmatic" Roosevelt, who temporized with Martin Dies and refused to break with Frank Hague.[14]

The trials broke the last vestige of any lingering sympathy for Russia in the Socialist Party. No longer could she be considered even a workers' state, corrupted by a political dictatorship. Socialists were led in the direction of viewing her as either a variety of state capitalism or state socialism, both of which were incompatible with democratic socialism and workers' control. But even before most Socialists began working out these theories of the Russian state, they had come to the realization that the progress of democratic socialism and the progress of the Russian state were going in opposite directions.[15]

In order to avoid crediting Socialist ideology with some role in the battles surrounding the question of the nature of totalitarianism, historians have had to ignore that ideology in practice. Schlesinger writes that Lenin's famous "who-whom" question is "the fundamental issue of politics." Applying it to Russia, he concludes:

> Who whom? This is the question which the democratic left, through the years, has had to put with increasing insistence to the Soviet Union. For a generation, it had allowed itself to be turned away with evasions. . . . Today the answer is clear. Who?—the Communist bureaucracy. Whom?—the workers, peasants, intellectuals, all the human beings outside the ruling clique. Rosa Luxemburg, Karl Kautsky and others knew this from the start. . . . With the full comprehension of Lenin's conundrum—Who whom?—comes the rebirth of the democratic left—the rise, in the popular phrase, of the non-Communist left.

It is safe to praise Luxemburg's and Kautsky's answers, for they are long dead and, since they were European, Schlesinger does not have to confront the fact that their answers depended on *their* ideology. But Schlesinger conveniently forgets that a generation of the Socialist Left in the United States had answered the question, had been the first in the United States to center the critique of Russia on her bureaucracy. Who whom? Forgotten Marxist ideologues like Haim Kantorovitch and David Berenberg answered the question long before most "pragmatic" liberals confronted it. And why was that? Basically, because their ideology held workers' control central to true democracy, while the "pragmatic" liberals were more concerned with the simple existence of "planning"—not with "who" was planning and for "whom." Indeed, the very type of liberal that Schlesinger labels "doughface" was, in the thirties, not an ideologue, but a pragmatist accenting the role of planning, the relativity of civil liberties, and the process of industrialization as progress. He was, in short, a student of Dewey's who had forgotten Dewey's stress on theory and who had, as Randolph Bourne realized Dewey had in World War I, become enmeshed in the "means."[16]

But perhaps Schlesinger should not be taken too seriously in all this: he posits that Reinhold Niebuhr "with his tragic sense of the predicament of man" stands as one of the "prophets . . . who refused to swallow the fantastic hypocrisies involved in the defense of totalitarianism." And his ideal in politics is a kind of Niebuhr-cum-Roosevelt "pessimistic pragmatism." I have no wish to label Niebuhr a defender of totalitarianism in the thirties; he was not (though he worked with Communists in Popular Front organizations as one of the few Socialists who subscribed to "collective security"). But let it be recorded that when Niebuhr questioned the Moscow trials, he characterized as "very fair" Waldo Frank's proposal for an investigation of the trials by the executive organs of the American and British Socialist and Communist Parties, a proposal that had been coupled with the usual ridicule of the Dewey Commission's possible fairness in arriving at a just verdict because it was "controlled" by "Trotskyists." At the same time, Niebuhr spoke of Stalin's policy as "immeasurably superior" to Trotsky's because it was "a responsible policy" and he analyzed Stalin's motives as a matter of mistaken judgment. With all the insights that Niebuhr's tragic pessimism is supposed to give, it was not Niebuhr, but the supposedly shallow, optimistic Marxists like David Berenberg who knew that, whatever Trotsky's policy was, Stalin's was certainly not "responsible," and it was they who first saw that the horror of the trials was more than a matter of mistaken judgment.[17]

The Popular Front

Schlesinger's inability to perceive how ideology could easily point toward anti-Stalinism and how an absence of ideology could easily lead toward rationalizations for suppression suggests how badly he misreads the whole question of the Popular Front, where he assumes a correlation between ideological commitment and participation in the Popular Front. For the liberal who entered into the Popular Front, it was not a matter of liberal ideologue meeting Communist ideologue, but of a deracinated pragmatic liberalism searching for ideology and explanation. As I have argued elsewhere, it was not ideology, but the lack of ideology, that caused the Popular Front. Equally true was the fact that Popular Frontism among Socialists was not a matter of "doctrinaire ideology." Schlesinger attributes Popular Frontism among Socialists in France and Italy to their being "more doctrinaire" than in Western countries. Significantly, he does not mention the United States, where rejection of the Popular Front by Socialists was most evident among the Socialists who were clearly wedded to a Marxist approach to history. Equivocal and sometimes tentative support for a Popular Front was more apt to come from the "flexible" Socialists, parts of the post-1936 Militant faction, who, while insisting on their Marxism, felt that the Marxism of their Socialist colleagues was too rigid and formal—in brief, too "doctrinaire." Such a rigid interpretation of Marx, they argued, was not suitable to the United States and the existing conditions. Suitable or not, it furnished a perspective that was the key in rejecting the Popular Front.[18]

Even the earlier issue of the United Front, which should not be confused with the Popular Front, did not win its adherents basically for ideological reasons. It was the failure of German Social Democracy, the fear of fascism, and the splintered Left in the United States that caused Norman Thomas and his Militant allies to consider a United Front with the Communists. There were organizational reasons too; the historical reasons had increased the pressures for unity on the left, and Thomas and the Militants were afraid that the Party would lose many of its younger members if it rejected the opportunity for at least attempting united action on specific issues. The theory of a United Front, unlike that of the Popular Front, was of *interradical* cooperation, with each radical party maintaining its organic structure and its right to criticize others' theories. But they were to cooperate in different organizations and specific actions.[19]

Since cooperation would be interradical, the United Front did not raise the kind of ideological objections from Marxist radicals that the later Popular Front, which entailed cooperation with bourgeois parties and groups, did. The Old Guard, with its deep hostility to the Communist Party, objected strongly, of course. And it was one of the key issues—if not *the* key issue—which brought about the final split. Other left-wing radicals were also suspicious of the Communist role in United Front activities, and Norman Thomas shared this suspicion. He had seen the role the Communists had played in organizations like the Terzani Defense Committee, and he was not about to plunge thoughtlessly into a general United Front. In fact, Gus Tyler, one young left-wing Militant, published a pamphlet documenting the Communists' divisive role in previous United Front activities. But few in the left wing of the Socialist Party were prepared to raise theoretical objections to a United Front. That was done by the Old Guard, which, in addition to tactical objections, believed that the basic incompatibility between Communism and Socialism made United Front activities wrong in principle.[20]

The objections of Thomas and the Militants were largely tactical: the Communists tried to run all United Front activities; they used these activities to "raid" rival radical parties and groups; they continued bitterly to attack the Socialist Party in nonfraternal terms, while at the same time urging a United Front. Given this situation, there were very few in the Socialist Party prepared to endorse wholeheartedly a general United Front, and certainly not an organic unity of parties, which Browder began talking about in 1935. At best, the Militants and Thomas were ready to discuss the possibilities of joint actions and to cooperate on specific issues, like civil-rights cases, unemployed protests, or political rallies. Thomas and the Militants welcomed any sign that the Communists were prepared to cooperate genuinely in these activities. Thomas believed the Socialists had to be receptive to cooperation if the disastrous splintering on the left was to be overcome. But he and the Militants were far from wanting to commit the Party to any general United Front—a fact that the Old Guard could not believe. The Old Guard was certain that the Thomas-Browder 1935 Madison Square Garden debate was the prelude to, if not an actual beginning of, a general United Front. Thomas, for his part, saw the debate as an opportunity for discussing frankly the issues dividing the parties in order to see if there was room for any kind of United Front. And he took the opportunity to state openly the impediments that the Communists placed in the way of United Front activities, and why any activities needed to be limited to specific cases. Despite his care in defining differences and impediments, all the Old Guard saw in the debate was a "love feast."[21]

When the Communists switched from the third period to the Popular Front line in the summer of 1935, the possibilities for cooperation seemed to open up. The switch meant the cessation of the "social fascist" line that had been a barrier to cooperation, and it meant dropping the rhetoric of violent revolution. But at the same time that it seemed to open up possibilities, it also created new problems. While the new position on the manner of social change might be preferable, the new position on foreign policy and war ran counter to the traditional Socialist position. With its treaty with capitalist France and its entrance into the League, Russia had turned to "collective security." The whole theory of collective security, for Socialists, created a situation where there could be "good" imperialist wars and "bad" ones. In his debate with Browder, Thomas saw this new Communist position on foreign policy as creating problems that would negate some of the positive elements in the new position.[22]

Moreover, by 1936 the Communist Party had begun to readjust itself to Roosevelt and the New Deal. It was not quite yet prepared to cozy up as far as it would by 1937 and 1938, but the direction was indicated. Thomas and the Socialist Party were more convinced than ever that the New Deal was not the answer to capitalism's economic ills or the dangers of fascism. The Communists were tacitly supporting Roosevelt by focusing all of their energies on the fascist dangers that would derive from a Landon victory. But the Socialists were determined to run an independent *socialist* campaign. They recognized the difficulties facing them in the 1936 election, but they felt it was important that they run a campaign on the issue of capitalism versus socialism, especially since the Communists had diluted the issue to a vague "democracy versus fascism." Bernard Johnpoll claims Thomas only ran as a way to help bring about a national Farmer-Labor Party. No doubt he wished this; but there is also no reason to doubt his statement that it was important to conduct a *socialist* campaign for educational reasons. It was not the only time in his life that Thomas would run, despite his personal wishes and impossible conditions, in order to attempt to educate the public on an issue.[23]

The Communist rapprochement with the New Deal ended all hope for any general Popular Front cooperation between the Communist and Socialist Parties. The Communist Party was following a pro-collective security, pro-New Deal, pro-liberal reformist line; the Socialist Party was opposed to collective security, the New Deal, and simple reformism. Still, there remained the problem of Socialist work in mass organizations—unions, obviously, but also the Workers' Alliance and the American Student Union. The history of these latter two organizations deserves more scholarly attention than it has yet received. But here, the main point is that the Socialists were to work in mass organizations, but they were to work for the Socialist position. Both David Lasser in the Workers' Alliance and Joseph Lash in the American Student Union pursued policies—pro-New Deal and collective security—that were too close to the Communists to suit the Socialist Party. And, eventually, both were expelled from the Party. In each of these cases, it was the left wing of the Socialist Party, the Clarity Group, that was most opposed to Popular Frontism and most eager for discipline to be applied to Lasser and Lash. And they were the most Marxist and revolutionary in their ideology (not counting the Trotskyists, who, by 1937, were on their way out of the Socialist Party). Clarity viewed the Popular Front as a brand of liberal capitalist reformism, designed to mute the class struggle and prevent the coming of socialism. It felt the Popular Front was self-defeating, since capitalism, as the breeder of fascism, could not check fascism no matter how liberal capitalism became. Only a socialist revolution could prevent fascism.[24]

On the other hand, less ideological former Militants like Paul Porter in Wisconsin and Alfred Baker Lewis in Massachusetts were more eager to try to work with Communists, less responsive to the Clarity and Trotskyist critique of Stalinism and the Popular Front. In his 1937 pamphlet, *Which Way for the Socialist Party?*, Porter came closest to adopting a clearly pro-Popular Front position. Porter argued that a Marxist perspective, far from meaning a parroting of rigid revolutionary phrases, required an analysis of the social and economic forces at work in the United States. These forces demonstrated that the next stage on the road to socialism would be a national farmer-labor party. This party would not be committed to socialism, but it would be the vehicle through which Socialists should work in educating the workers to the necessity of socialism. A revolutionary crisis was not at hand; workers would not spontaneously rise up in revolt in answer to "a revolutionary line." What was required was that Socialists work through mass organizations—through the Wisconsin Farmer-Labor Progressive Federation, the Minnesota Farmer-Labor Party, the American Labor Party, the Workers' Alliance, the American Student Union—in a disciplined manner in order to further their educational task.[25]

Porter's strategy meant dropping Socialist electoral activity. Maintenance of a strong Socialist Party was necessary, but the developing farmer-labor parties should be the electoral vehicle for the foreseeable future. In one instance (Florida), where the Democratic Party was the only party on the ballot, Porter said that Socialists might have to work as a left-wing group within the Democratic Party. Porter's strategy also meant cooperating with other left-wing groups: Communists, Old Guard Socialists, Pro-gressive Farmer-Laborites. The pamphlet was obviously aimed at the Trotskyists and their ideological allies within the Socialist Party. Its sharpest barbs were directed at the Trotskyists and their "sectarian" politics. The pamphlet spoke optimistically about cooperation with the Communists. It did not endorse their pro-New Deal domestic policy, but, in general, it subscribed to a brand of People's Frontism. It placed great emphasis on reaching out to the middle class. Most important, it endorsed an international People's Front as the way to prevent war. It criticized the neutrality legislation and suggested a boycott of arms to aggressor nations and aid to the victims of aggression. It minimized the role, accented by the Trotskyists and the Clarity, that a workers' boycott could play in preventing war. And, in general, Porter adopted the collective-security language of the Popular Front of keeping "war out of the world."[26]

Thomas liked Porter's stress on the need to work with indigenous farmer-labor parties and his critique of the ultra-revolutionary sectarians in the Party. He welcomed Porter's remarks as they aided him in the battle with Trotskyists in the Party; Porter, since the early thirties, had been one of the people whose advice he respected most. However, Porter's language and his foreign policy position were too close to the Communist Popular Front line. He warned Porter of the need to differentiate his position from the Communists' and suggested that his too ready acceptance of their phraseology resulted from the Wisconsin situation, where the Communists were weaker than they were in New York.[27]

As a general rule, then, the more one was a reformist in ideology, the more likely one was not to reject the Popular Front *in toto*. This applies to Porter, who insisted on his Marxism, but who came closest in 1937 to accepting the Popular Front, and to Thomas, who was frankly an eclectic Marxist, and was more critical of it than Porter. Though Thomas rejected the Popular Front in the United States, he was willing to give it critical support abroad. But the main point is that, in terms of socialist ideology at the time, Thomas's and Porter's perspective was more reformist —willing to accept cooperation in reformist parties and criticizing the revolutionary line of the Clarity. On the other hand, the more "doctrinaire" one was in his Marxism, the more likely one was to reject the Popular Front completely. It was the Clarity and, while they were in the Party, the Trotskyists, who took the severely critical position toward the Popular Front governments of France and Spain. It was Thomas and the Militants who supported, though they believed them inadequate to the necessary tasks of defeating fascism and creating socialism, these same Popular Front governments. This point leads us directly to the Spanish situation.[28]

The Spanish Civil War

Crediting today's Niebuhrian pessimism with the basic insights is, of course, related to the view that the Marxist vision of the thirties lacked a sense of the complexities of history. Yet it was the Socialists, both Marxists and quasi-Marxists, who, along with other anti-Stalinist radicals, were the first to grasp the complexities of the Spanish tragedy. Amid the reactionary red-baiting of the conservatives, the Popular Front clichés of most of the liberal journals, and the irresponsible policy of the Roosevelt administration, it was the Socialists who recognized the tragic burden: to defend the Loyalist cause, while acknowledging that the cause had been severely compromised. It is ironic that Bell should pick out the Socialist policy on Spain as peculiarly symptomatic of the Party's ineffectuality. Bell writes: "When the Loyalists in Spain demanded arms, for example, the Socialist party could only respond with a feeble policy of 'workers aid,' not (capitalist) government aid; but to the Spaniard, arms, not theoretical niceties, were the need of the moment." First of all, the Socialists did urge the New Deal to lift the embargo, which would have provided "capitalist arms," a move that the "pragmatic" Roosevelt, accepting the "premises" of his society, refused to follow. One of the reasons Thomas was so critical of Sam Baron, in fact, was that he felt that Baron's testimony would jeopardize the movement to lift the embargo.[29]

Second, Bell assumes that the Party's policy of "workers aid" was simply a matter of "theoretical niceties." Certainly it was that; but it was also a nicety that was connected with history and capitalist policy. The capitalist governments were the ones who had shown their ineffectuality in meeting the Spaniards' "need of the moment." It was the capitalist governments of England and France that participated in the mockery and hypocrisy of the nonintervention agreement; it was the Roosevelt administration that requested Congress to extend the neutrality legislation to cover the Spanish Civil War. Realizing that all one could do on that score was urge Roosevelt to repeal the embargo, the Socialists still had to offer a substitute policy. To ridicule "workers aid" as a "feeble policy" is all very well (as well as very fashionable), but, in the context of capitalist hypocrisy and inaction, it made a great deal more sense; compared to Roosevelt's and Hull's "feeble policy," it was a tower of political responsibility.[30]

These are general remarks, but they do not tell the full agonizing story of the Socialist Party and Spain, a story that is tied in with almost every other issue: the Popular Front, party building, Russia, ideology. It would seem that the Spanish issue should have been one on which the Party could have achieved unity, and in one sense, it did: all parts of the Socialist Party were committed to the defeat of fascism; all were opposed to the purge of the anti-Stalinist left; all believed that progress in the Spanish social and economic revolution should not cease during the war. Beyond this, however, there were difficulties. The official Socialist position, supported by Thomas, endorsed the Caballero government in Spain and the Blum government in France. Both governments, led by Socialists, were Popular Front governments. Thomas, who rejected the Popular Front in the United States, argued that despite some disappointments with Blum's program, both governments were justified under the circumstances of immediate fascist danger. Moreover, since they were headed by Socialists, he was inclined

to be sympathetic and generous in his evaluation of both governments. Both the Trotskyists and the Clarity opposed the Popular
Front from a revolutionary viewpoint. They argued that a Popular
Front government was involved in buttressing up capitalism, and
that since capitalism bred fascism, this was self-defeating. Only a
socialist revolution could prevent fascism. It was the Trotskyist
critique of the Popular Front governments which, to a large degree,
created much of the Trotskyists' original trouble with party discipline, which eventually led to their ouster. The Clarity's criticism
of foreign Popular Fronts was temperate only by comparison to
the Trotskyists'. It too viewed them as impediments to, if not
betrayers of, the workers' revolution. The Clarity's was a left-wing
critique that could easily emerge as persuasive if a controversial
issue developed.[31]

Before that issue—the Barcelona uprising and the subsequent
purges—the Socialist Party had become involved in cooperation
with the North American Committee to Aid Spanish Democracy.
Like the Workers' Alliance and the American Student Union, this
was largely Communist-controlled, but, like them, it was considered a mass organization where Socialists should work. Moreover,
it was the leading committee to aid Spain. And the Socialists were
determined to aid Spain. Indeed, the New York local split the
party in an unusual direction when it announced it was attempting
to raise a Eugene V. Debs Brigade to fight in Spain under the
slogan of "arms for Spain." The National Office was embarrassed
by this unilateral action, which was taken without prior consulta-
tion with the National Executive Committee. But it went along
with it, partly urged by Thomas's argument that it was necessary
for the Socialist Party to pursue its own aid course and not have
all credit fall to the Communists and other organizations. But the
pacifists within the Socialist Party, like John Haynes Holmes,
Winston Dancis, and Jessie Wallace Hughan, raised serious objections, accusing Thomas of deserting his World War I pacifism.
Thomas, who was able to eliminate the slogan of "arms for Spain,"
defended himself by pointing out that he was no longer an absolute

pacifist; that he wished he could believe there was another way to defeat Franco except by arms, but that he could not; and that the brigade was only accepting fully informed volunteers. Eventually, he was able to persuade the pacifists to remain in the party. The Debs Brigade enterprise proved a flop, and today it is likely to look a little silly, especially when compared to the more successful Abraham Lincoln Brigade. Given the needs of the Spanish Loyalists and the New Deal's inaction, a more generous reading of the attempt is called for.[32]

Except for the Socialist pacifists, most of the Party could unite on the Debs Brigade issue. But events were happening in Spain that would cause the Party trouble. Already, it was obvious that the social revolution was being slowed down; that the slogan of "win the war first, make the revolution later" was to be the policy. Thomas and the Socialists more sympathetic to the Popular Front believed that all social change should not be set aside for the duration. But they were more patient with the orientation of the government's policy. The Clarity kept sniping away at both the French and Spanish Popular Fronts for not moving toward socialism. The Trotskyists, on their way out of the Party, accused the government of having betrayed the revolution and the Socialist Party of having abetted the betrayal by its defense of the class-collaborationist Popular Front government.[33]

The Barcelona uprising in May, 1937, provided the dramatic event that elicited further internal controversy. Thomas, much as he objected to the purges that followed, much as he felt there were legitimate grievances, believed the uprising was wrong, damaging to the government's cause. It came, he believed, from a small Anarchist minority, and it came in the midst of war against fascism. The left-wing Clarity looked on the uprising with much more sympathy. It, along with the Trotskyists, saw the crushing of the uprising as part of a betrayal of the revolution. And this analysis derived again from their more doctrinaire Marxism, their greater impatience with and opposition to mere Popular Front reformism.[34]

The defense of the Barcelona uprising was a left-wing position. Even the rabidly anti-Stalinist Old Guard *New Leader* condemned the insurgents as disloyal; writing from a New Deal reform perspective now, it had little sympathy for the left-wing POUM and the Anarchists. It is interesting that the *New Leader,* so quick to publish any unfavorable article on Russia and the domestic Communists, was slower in revealing the anti-Stalinist purges in Spain, though eventually it did. But as a supporter of the right-wing Spanish Socialists, Negrín and Prieto, it never acknowledged their role in the purges or confessed its own support for the right-wing Socialists who cooperated with the Communists in purging the anti-Stalinist Left in Spain.[35]

Thomas was not silent on the purges. He published columns indicating the dangerous tendencies of what was taking place in Spain. He wrote to the Spanish Ambassador in Washington, Ferdinand de los Rios, urging fair treatment. His letters reveal he was becoming increasingly disturbed by reports coming out of Spain and the growing intolerance he saw in the Loyalist government. Caballero's ouster and his replacement with Negrín and Prieto may have freed him to be more critical, though even here he was hesitant to specifically criticize foreign Socialists. Certainly, the ouster of Caballero convinced the Clarity that the Spanish cause had been seriously damaged, and it had a similar effect on Thomas. He was, then, deeply disturbed. But he was also convinced that while Socialists could not remain silent, they had to be careful not to hurt the Spanish cause. While there was still a possibility of lifting the embargo, he was eager that criticisms remain within certain bounds. This, as we have seen, was why he was so upset by Sam Baron's testimony. Thomas felt it was exaggerated and that it conflicted with reports from James Loeb, the chairman of the Socialist Party's Committee on Spain. Both Thomas and Loeb saw signs that the purges were moderating, that the trials in 1938 had been conducted more fairly. Both were still deeply disturbed by events, but they interpreted the picture less bleakly than Baron and the Clarity. The prime motive for this less pessimistic reading, however, was not really the facts of the case, but the damage Baron's testimony might do to the Socialist Party and the Spanish cause. Thomas went so far as to threaten resignation unless disciplinary action was taken against Baron. The Clarity felt that Baron should not have testified, but was more inclined toward sympathy with his case, arguing that if the Socialist Party had been more receptive to his evidence, the whole episode might have been avoided.[36]

The Baron matter faded into the background as the war in Spain moved toward its tragic ending. Thomas urged new attempts at lifting the embargo; Congress did not respond. The Party continued to give aid and to work through the North American Committee to Aid Spain, even though it increasingly distrusted the committee as reports of political discrimination in dispensing aid filtered in. Franco triumphed; the Loyalist government surrendered. Refugees flocked into France, where the Socialist Party tried to aid them. No matter which faction of the Socialist Party one had been in—the Clarity with its left-wing critique of the Spanish Popular Front and the anti-Stalinist purges, or the Thomas group, who continued to back the government even as they urged upon it toleration and the need to continue reform—no matter which faction one was in, the position, aside from that of other anti-Stalinist radicals, was the only honorable one. What I have said at the beginning of this section bears repeating. It was the Socialists who recognized the tragic burden: to defend the Loyalist cause, while acknowledging that the cause had been severely compromised. It was the capitalist New Deal that was "feeble" in Spain, and in the end its feebleness was criminal for the Spanish masses. Roosevelt is supposed to have remarked to Ambassador Claude Bowers, after Loyalist Spain had been defeated, that Bowers had been right all along, that the embargo should have been lifted (as the Socialists, contrary to Bell, had consistently urged). If so, his remark was "too little, too late" —like so much of the New Deal.[37]

IX

Socialists and World War II

I HAVE argued that the angle of vision furnished by socialism enabled the Socialist Party to have basic insights into the New Deal, the Soviet Union, the Moscow trials, the events in Spain: where members did not have these insights it was generally the result of a non-Marxian perspective or because they allowed concerns about party building to interfere with their basic judgment. It might seem that it would be difficult to argue that the angle of vision furnished by socialism provided the Socialists with a better perspective on World War II than that of non-Socialists. No Socialist policy of the thirties has been subjected to harsher criticism than the Party's policy on World War II, and no evaluations of Norman Thomas have been more critical than those of his views of the United States foreign policy between 1938 and December 7, 1941. Bernard Johnpoll has said Thomas's "assumptions were erroneous, his rationale faulty, and his conclusions ludicrous." Is it possible, at this late date, to come to another conclusion?[1]

I believe that it is. I do not support the policy of the American Socialist Party in the years immediately preceding World War II, nor Thomas's opposition to aid to the Allies, but I think that the substance of the policy had more validity than the illusions that were common among supporters of such aid. A few words are necessary as to the policy and its effect upon the Socialist Party.

158

The Socialist Party organized the Keep America Out of War Congress in early 1938. The Congress conducted general antiwar propaganda, including warnings against the repeal of the neutrality legislation and against moves by the New Deal to build up armaments. As war approached, prominent members like Alfred Baker Lewis, Paul Porter, and Jack Altman urged the Party to modify its position on collective security. With the outbreak of the European war, they urged the modification of the neutrality legislation to permit aid to the Allies. The fall of France increased the pressure for more aid to the Allies. More and more Socialists were supporting moves like Lend-Lease or Roosevelt's destroyer deal. Each step toward government aid to the Allies was opposed by Thomas and rejected by the Party. The end result was a steady and persistent decimation of the Party. Members either resigned, were expelled (like Altman), or became inactive. Alfred Baker Lewis and Jack Altman left before the 1940 election. During the next year, they were joined by members from all groups in the Party: Paul Porter, Frank Crosswaithe, Leonard Woodcock, Arthur McDowell, Gus Tyler, Frank Trager.[2]

In theory, the Socialist position was based on the belief that capitalism bred imperialism, and that modern international warfare was imperialist warfare. The function of Socialists in such circumstances was not to support either imperialist side, but to use the opportunity to build socialism. The revolutionary rhetoric of the Declaration of Principles of 1934, with its threat of a general strike and widespread Socialist resistance to war, had little meaning by 1939, although the threat of a "general strike" in case of war was repeated in the 1938 National Convention's Resolution on War. But the theory of Socialist opposition to capitalist war prevailed. Moreover, taking off from the Declaration of Principles' statement on war, the Clarity had, between 1936 and 1938, developed a critique of collective security and the need for a socialist revolution to prevent war. Gus Tyler, Herbert Zam, and other Clarity spokesmen had consistently warned workers against being entrapped into capitalist wars through the instrumentalities of collective security and the whole Popular Front line. There were no "good" imperialist wars; World War I should have brought that lesson home to the workers. Only a socialist revolution could end modern imperialist war, and it was to this task that Tyler and Zam encouraged the workers to bend their efforts. By 1939, the rhetoric of revolution seemed inapplicable; the general strike, much less revolution, seemed years away. But the Clarity had been able to win the Party's acceptance for its main foreign policy position. When the European war began in September, the Party condemned it as another imperialist war. When the Russo-Finnish war broke out, the Party took the stand that Socialists should only aid the Finnish workers, and that the Party should not support American aid to Finland. It is true that, at the time, the Party also brushed aside those voices calling for a policy of "revolutionary defeatism" by the Finnish workers, voices that might have received a greater hearing two years earlier. But the heart of the statement on the Finnish war was to reassert the essential Clarity position: workers should not rely on capitalist governments to end war.[3]

In addition to the Clarity viewpoint, the Party contained a significant proportion of pacifists and quasi-pacifists like Thomas. Theory—revolutionary or pacifist—, however, was not the only motivating force behind the Socialist opposition to collective security. There were very practical arguments: the European nations had demonstrated little interest in genuine collective security during the thirties; moreover, there was a real practical question of whether collective security could succeed. Finally, there were the deep remembrances of World War I—its hypocrisies about the "war to make the world safe for democracy," the violations of civil liberties, the persecution of radicals, the imprisonment of Debs. Some Socialists, like Thomas (whose brother had been imprisoned for conscientious objection during the war), had harsh personal remembrances of Wilsonian "liberalism" in wartime. Many of the radicals and Socialists who, in the late thirties, came to support aid to the Allies had earlier in the 1930's believed that if the United States went to war, fascism would be the result domestically. Indeed, the strength of the Socialist antiwar sentiment is shown by the fact that very few "interventionist" Socialists were prepared when the European war broke out to advocate American entrance into the war. As they departed from the Socialist position, they insisted that theirs was an antiwar position. Aid to England would prevent American entrance.[4]

It is wrong to label the Socialist position as isolationist unless one qualifies that term. There were, within the Party, those whose opposition to war derived from a revolutionary socialism that placed its faith only in the international working class. Thomas was inclined to feel these people were romantic. He had little faith in capitalist governments' keeping peace, but he was willing to use such devices as the neutrality legislation to check the war tide. While he placed much importance on workers' aid, especially in the case of Czechoslovakia and Finland, and people's boycotts, he did not rely on the rhetoric of revolutionary socialism. His rhetoric was antiwar and, in a sense, isolationist. But one must be precise, here, as Manfred Jonas has attempted to be, in designating types of isolationism. Thomas's isolationism resulted from a radical perspective that believed that the American entrance into war would lessen the chances of the advance of meaningful social change in the United States and the advance of democratic socialism throughout the world. He believed that civil liberties would be destroyed if the country went to war, and that fascism was likely to result. He never put the matter in absolutes: that staying out of war involved no risks. He was opposed to fascism and distinguished the "new" imperialism of the fascist nations from the "old" imperialism of traditional capitalism. But he argued that if the United States became involved, the end result would be a totalitarianized world. The United States could not maintain democracy while it sought to defeat fascism by entering the war. Total mobilization would follow; the United States would be engulfed in the totalitarian tide. As long as she maintained her aloofness, however, her sanctuary of sanity in a world gone mad, there was some small hope of avoiding a totalitarianized world.[5]

Again, in his arguments for a negotiated peace before Pearl Harbor, Thomas did not put the issue in terms of absolutes. Any course ran risks. But a victorious Germany, or even a victorious Allied cause, boded more ill for the world than a negotiated peace. Some of the more revolutionary Socialists talked of the workers in the respective countries negotiating the peace, but Thomas was less optimistic. He talked about putting pressure on the American government, but was rather vague about how it would be done and about whether the European governments could be trusted to negotiate an acceptable peace. All he was certain of was that a total victory for either side would lead to a new Versailles and to the breeding of the same conditions that had produced Hitler. This possibility reinforced his belief that while the "new" imperialism was worse, radicals and liberals should have no illusions and place little faith in the "old" imperialism. Morally it might be better, though its record was shameful. And as an answer to the world's problems it was completely inadequate. He saw, especially in the Far East, that the United States was pursuing the kind of imperialist course that the old world powers had followed. He was especially critical of our policy toward Japan, whose imperialist adventures in China he also condemned. In our rivalry with Japan, he said, we were supplying her with war goods, while we continued to insult her. This paradoxical action, he predicted, could only lead to disaster.[6]

More than on any other issue, Norman Thomas was, on the war question, the Socialist Party. The left-wing Socialists wanted a greater labor accent in his antiwar campaign (quite correctly), but they were in no position to conduct a more radical antiwar line than Thomas was prepared to set forth. And so it is really Norman Thomas's position on the war that one evaluates when one evaluates the Socialist Party position. Many of the evaluations apply to the rest of the Party, but increasingly in 1939–40 Thomas was the voice of the Party on the war.[7]

Let me dispose of three things first. The fundamental weakness in Thomas's argument, from a socialist perspective, was its failure to face the effect of a Nazi victory on the European labor movement. Even the revolutionary Socialists acknowledged that it was romantic to talk of an uprising such as Lenin had envisaged in a war-wracked Europe. Given this fact, how could the labor movement best be preserved? Alfred Baker Lewis, who was not right in all points of his long-running exchange of letters with Thomas, argued that, in the end, the thing that pushed him toward aid to the Allies was the consequences of a Nazi victory for the European working class. This was a hard question for a Socialist to answer, and one that Thomas never satisfactorily confronted.[8]

Second, Thomas was wrong to cooperate with the America First Committee. In 1941, trying desperately to stem the war sentiment, he agreed to appear on speaking platforms with members of that committee. The Committee, as Wayne Cole has shown, was not entirely a conservative or reactionary organization; it had liberal members too. But, especially on a local level, it was difficult to control the reactionary, anti-Semitic joiners. Thomas was absolutely right to point out that the issue between interventionists and antiwar people was not one between liberals and conservatives, that the William Allen White Committee and the leading interventionists represented not basically progressives, but what today we would call the "eastern Establishment." And, as Mark Chadwin's *The Hawks of World War II* demonstrates, both liberals and conservatives were among the most vociferous proponents of the war.[9]

Thomas tried to check the conservative elements in the America First Committee by gentle prodding, and he never became a member. However, it was hardly the ideal platform for a socialist. He justified himself by analogies to the Socialist position on work in mass organizations. Socialists worked in unions, in unemployed groups, in antiwar organizations, not because everyone agreed with them, but in order to win the masses of people to their point of view. The America First Committee, he said, was where the most people were; he would have preferred them to be with the Socialist-organized Keep America Out of War Congress, but they were not. Therefore, the opportunity to speak to an America First audience,

Thomas argued, gave him a chance to reach people with the Socialist message—and, with it, a repudiation of any racism—that otherwise he would not have had. The problem, however, was more
difficult than this. For while it was true that he might have a chance
to combat other speakers' conservatism and racism, he was also
being used as a kind of "liberal" showpiece. As the organization
developed, its earlier liberal support began to drop off—never entirely, but significantly. Thomas, then, was a testament to the
Committee's bipartisanship and toleration. But, as a nonmember,
he had no voice on policy. All he could do was to gently chastise
its excesses. The much publicized incident of Lindbergh's famous
anti-Semitic speech simply dramatized the predicament. The Socialist Party and Thomas could repudiate the remarks, but they could
not control the situation. They would have done better to conduct
a more narrowly socialist, if smaller, antiwar campaign.[10]

Third, Thomas's fears that fascism would come to the United
States if war broke out were exaggerated. As mentioned, these were
commonly shared fears in the 1930's. "The day war is declared,"
Sidney Hook wrote in 1936, the "fascist emblem will flutter over
the nation's capital—be it France, England, or our own United
States." One can partially defend Thomas by arguing that without
men like Thomas calling attention to the dangers of fascism, the drift
toward fascism inherent in total mobilization, conscription, and a
war emergency would have been accented. But, granting the truth
of this observation, it also remains true that while there was a great
deal to fear, the fears of fascism itself were exaggerated.[11]

The weaknesses in Thomas's antiwar position were paralleled
by severe weaknesses in the arguments he was trying to combat—
the argument for all-out aid to the Allies. There was a case to be
made for American aid to the Allies, but it was a case that was
made poorly, with all kinds of exaggerations and distortions that
would later reap their bitter harvest. The *New Leader,* in its enthusiasm for all-out aid, forgot its earlier comments on Marx and
Bakunin—that Socialists oppose policies for their *own* reasons
and that if reactionaries also criticize the same policies, the two

are not similar. Scandalously, the editors linked all opponents of the war, and accused Thomas of playing the "fascist" game. With little concern that their own rhetoric was doing much to aid a totalitarian mentality, they perfected a "guilt by association" technique. The *New Leader's* attitude is understandable, if not excusable; it was writing in the heat of emotion. The attitude of later historians is not. There still remains a temptation for those who endorse American participation in World War II to uncritically applaud those intellectuals who supported all-out aid to the Allies between 1939 and 1941 and to put down those who opposed American involvement in Europe. The latter are lumped together as "professional pacifists, political opportunists, philosophic isolationists, narrow-minded legalists, thinly-veiled pro-Nazis, self-appointed peacemakers, glamorous military experts, totalitarian apologists, idealist reformers, passionate President-haters, thoughtless academics and university students . . . devout Quakers and reverend clergy, unprincipled journalists, and washed-up novelists" to quote a review by a "thoughtful" academic. This conjoining of men with vastly different motives and perspectives makes it impossible to understand the perspective of the radical and Socialist intellectuals who opposed American aid to the Allies.[12]

Moreover, it seems to me both unfair to those leftist intellectuals and more than fair to their critics. Their critics operated, as one writer has put it, on "grand abstractions and dubious assumptions" and they contributed as much confusion and dangerous simplicities to the debate as did their opponents. Their Socialist opponents, with all their faults, were often asking the right questions, while the theories of the pro-Allied enthusiasts have contributed to much that is wrong in American intellectual culture in the postwar period. Archibald MacLeish's attack upon the "irresponsible" intellectuals for contributing to the failure to check the growth of totalitarianism is simply the best known example. MacLeish's theory, a dangerously simplistic history, had even worse implications for the future, for he expressed a theory that would make intellectuals and artists adjuncts to the state and applauders of the healthy side of

American life. And this was what happened in postwar America during the 1950's—"the Age of Conformity." MacLeish was not guilty of the charges he leveled at the irresponsibles, but he had helped create a cultural theory and climate that grew inevitably from the "rediscovery of America" that began to occur among intellectuals in the immediate prewar years.[13]

To understand the problem more thoroughly, one needs to examine briefly the writings of two of the leading prowar intellectuals: Lewis Mumford and Waldo Frank. In *Men Must Act* (1939), Mumford urged an aggressive policy of nonintercourse against the fascist nations. The next year, in *Faith for Living,* he advocated a policy of all-out aid for the Allies against fascism, and by 1941 he was criticizing Roosevelt and the State Department for holding back on entering the war. Waldo Frank's *A Chart for Rough Waters* expressed a similar philosophy. Both books were greeted enthusiastically by advocates of collective security. Reinhold Niebuhr applauded Mumford's critique of liberals who wanted to use only reason and not force, and he praised Frank's critique of the isolationists. Niebuhr used these books to counter the shallowness and weaknesses of rationalistic, optimistic liberalism with its unawareness of the "depths" of human personality and its inability to understand "the malevolence to which human conduct may sink."[14]

There were "two sides" to the thought of Mumford and Frank. On the one hand, they asserted that the battle was between Western civilization—with its virtues of human freedom, liberty, and justice—and fascism; the Allies, in this view, were the bastion and hope of Western civilization. On the other hand, fascism was a disease that was found in Western civilization; the seeds were present in the United States, and the United States had many imperfections that might develop into fascism. This latter view was in actuality not very different from what many of their opponents were saying about the danger of fascism within the United States—only their conclusion was different: in order to defeat fascism in the United States, Mumford argued, it was necessary to defeat it in Germany; in order to defeat fascism in the United States, his opponents said, it was necessary to avoid war and re-make the United States.[15]

In this second view, Mumford's and Frank's argument might point toward a policy of "critical support" of the war. In fact, there were many individual statements in their writings that pointed toward this: Mumford's plea that he did not want to fight for British and French or American imperialism (it is difficult to see where his plea changed the facts) and Frank's critique of the capitalist system and plea for radical change. However, where the logic of this part of their argument might point to a tentative, detached, highly self-critical support of aid to the Allies and later support of the war—a position similar to the one the Socialist Party adopted during the war—the first side of their argument (the half focusing on the dichotomy between Western civilization and its ideals and fascism) pointed toward a new crusade that posited the United States as representing the "free world" in a fight against totalitarianism. In December, 1940, Mumford wrote the following in answer to the question of the reason for fighting:

> What, then, are the minimum goals that we must set our-selves? Let me begin with the negative conditions. First: We cannot live in a world that is part totalitarian and part free. There is no possibility of security in such a world. There is no possibility of co-operation in such a world. Two systems of ideas are now at war; they are fighting for the right to organize the world, as the armies of the Christians and the Saracens when they met on the battlefield of Tours were struggling for the narrower right to organize Europe.
>
> This is a knock-down fight between these two ideas. If the totalitarian states win, the nations of the world will, one by one, be enslaved and looted for the benefit of their barbarian conquerors. . . . If the English-speaking democracies win our task will be . . . nothing less than the establishment of a democratic world society in which each nation and region will play a co-operative part.
>
> Nothing short of a world union will justify the losses and the sacrifices of the present war, and no effective world union

> can be envisaged except one between peoples who speak the
> same political language and practice the same kind of loyalty
> to moral right and objective truth. . . .
>
> We cannot continue to view with tolerance or indifference the
> continuation of obsolete systems of government, the preval-
> ence of barbaric ideas of public order and right; and we
> cannot admit the possibility of active collaboration with
> governments that do not rest on the free consent of the
> governed.[16]

We all know this particular kind of language in the postwar
period: it is the language of the cold warrior and Pax Americana.
Its grievous fault is certainly not its justified outrage at totalitarianism, but rather its arrogance about the good intentions and essential
healthiness of the Western democracies (the second side of Mumford's argument should have warned against attributing these
qualities to the West). In short, the balance of his own thinking in
1939 could, in less subtle hands (and his own hands became less
subtle), be easily transformed into the stark dichotomies and
puerile clichés about the free world versus totalitarianism which
would have such a detrimental effect in the postwar period. Just as
MacLeish's theoretical formulations became reduced to the Luce
publications' postwar pleas for writers to uphold the "American
way of life," so Mumford's and Frank's joining the "West" with
"Western civilization" and human freedom could easily lead to the
self-righteous assumption that the United States was really the
free world.[17]

Yet this was precisely what the supporters of all-out aid to the
Allies posited. With no attention to the United States' imperial
needs, with little attention to the imperial needs of Great Britain,
with little interest in enlarging concrete freedom in the United
States, they proposed a new holy crusade in which any ambiguity
about support was dismissed. We cannot escape the "tempest," the
New Leader wrote in October, 1941; the President must make this
clearer. He had the "power, prestige, and authority." But he could
not do it by "proclamations, however desirable, calling people to

give some thought to the problem at their leisure," but only through "a fiery crusade that will set this nation afire from one end to the other with the urge to unsheath its mighty sword in defense of freedom and civilization and carry that sword to the ends of the earth, if need be, to track down and destroy the enemies of America and of mankind." And what might happen to those who had doubts or questions or might want to protect the rights that we were supposedly fighting for? Well, the *New Leader* had already put those rights to sleep for the duration back in January, 1941. In an editorial entitled "Silly? or Worse?" the nominally Social Democratic paper criticized the American Civil Liberties Union for worrying about Congress's legislation against Communists and Bundists. It accused the A.C.L.U. of being motivated by an "actual hatred of democracy and actual leanings toward dictatorship." Ignoring its own undemocratic philosophy, it wrote that "when Europe is ablaze and flames are being blown in our direction, the A.C.L.U. deems it a fit moment for insisting that the fire brigade observe traffic rules and for obstructing any round-up of known pyromaniacs."[18]

The *New Leader* might occasionally give some verbal support to democratic rights, as in a brief protest against the prosecution of the Minneapolis Trotskyists. But everything indicated that the paper, which now published a broad spectrum of liberal-left support of the war, was unconcerned, was willing to rally round the leaders and the flag in a festival of national unity. "No democratic people," it wrote in December, 1940, "ever lost their liberties by loyally supporting in a moment of crisis men to whom by their votes they had given authority to act for them."[19]

The philosophy was unanalytical, uncritical, undemocratic, and, at bottom, hypocritical. It led into the kind of hypocrisy that assumed the four freedoms were the goals of the war and that "The House I Live In" was some kind of accurate description of American reality. We are all, I hope, familiar with the most dramatic paradox: the portrayal of the United States as the champion of freedom, democracy, and the dignity of man in contrast with the reality of the black man in America. At least we know it in postwar America and are beginning to look at it in wartime America. But historians have treated with remarkable complacency the general cultural climate that developed in the war years, when, to use a Mumford-like phrase, the "moral health" of the nation was in terrible shape. And they have chastised severely the left-wing intellectuals who opposed the war in the years immediately preceding American participation. To many in the postwar years, Mumford's critique of Randolph Bourne displaced Bourne's stark pessimism as the realistic attitude that intellectuals should take on the subject of war.[20]

Yet what were these left-wing, largely Socialist, intellectuals—the recipients of the Mumford-Frank-MacLeish-*New Leader* critique—really saying? At their most extreme, which they admittedly often were, they were saying that if the United States went to war, fascism would come to the United States; the total mobilization necessary to defend democracy would eliminate democracy. Since fascism did not come to the United States, the Socialists, as I have indicated, exaggerated the dangers—though they were right to point them out. But it is surprising how much of the rest of their critique and predictions have held. For, minus the hyperboles regarding the fascist takeover in the United States, the basic ingredients of the argument were very perceptive.

Thomas and the antiwar Socialists warned of the dangers of an "armament economics." They perceived correctly that the New Deal had not solved the basic economic problems of capitalism, that poverty, unemployment, a maldistribution of income still existed. And they saw the New Deal increasingly turning to defense spending. They may have exaggerated the relationship: that the New Deal's war policy was motivated solely by economics. But they perceived correctly that the New Deal, bankrupt in ideas and drive, was coming increasingly to rely on defense spending. Moreover, they foresaw the permanency of this trend, that, once established, a reliance on armament economics would become a permanent feature of a capitalist economy. The continued reliance on just that in the postwar economy, the emergence of the military-industrial complex—sadly, Thomas and the antiwar Socialists foresaw it.[21]

Thomas and the antiwar Socialists opposed the draft as an oppressive and totalitarian device. They predicted that once a draft was established, it would be hard to eliminate it. In the midst of public support for World War II and the Cold War during the 1950's, the issue Thomas had raised was forgotten. The draft was accepted; few protested its antidemocratic nature. Only with the Vietnam war and thousands of deaths later, were steps taken to change the draft.[22]

Thomas and the antiwar Socialists warned of the increasing reliance on one man, on presidential power, in foreign affairs. They had supported the Ludlow Amendment in 1937 on the ground that the people should decide on anything as momentous as war. The Ludlow Amendment, its provisions for a referendum, and its supporters have been castigated ever since by historians. But was the Ludlow Amendment so silly, so hampering to the conduct of foreign affairs? It did not require a referendum in case of attack. It may not have been practicable, but at least the antiwar Socialists perceived that the real danger in foreign affairs came not from Congress and the people, but from the centralization of power in one man and a small group of advisors, no matter how "well-intentioned." They knew the tendency to take foreign affairs out of the hands of Congress, to keep secrets from the American people, was dangerous and destructive to democracy. The liberals and prowar Socialists who, because they trusted Roosevelt, enthusiastically supported presidential discretion and dismissed fears for democracy in this kind of decision-making, did not serve the cause of democracy. It took the Vetnam war twenty-five years later to wake them up; Thomas and the antiwar Socialists sadly had foreseen this pattern too.[23]

And were the prowar liberals and Socialists right to trust Roosevelt? Genuinely moved by the German destruction of the Jewish people, these people placed their faith in Roosevelt and the New Deal. In 1942, Israel Knox, editor of the Workmen's Circle

Call paper, wrote Thomas that Roosevelt was a great "humanitarian." Perhaps. But from what we know today of the New Deal and the refugee problem, of the New Deal and the fate of the Jews, the word seems overblown, to say the least. Thomas and antiwar Socialists worked to aid beleaguered refugees in Europe; if all of them did not advocate opening the door to all refugees, at least they proposed opening it up more adequately. Ironically, it was some of the prowar Socialists and liberals (who placed all their faith in Roosevelt) who advised against any general campaign to enlarge immigration. Fearful that it would play into the hands of the nativists, willing to trust Roosevelt to handle individual cases, they played the game of the art of the possible and got little reward for their efforts.[24]

Thomas and the antiwar Socialists had said that all reform would end during the war and that civil liberties would be jeopardized. And were not their forebodings born out? New Deal reform, ambiguous at its best and already in retreat, was further dismantled as dollar-a-year men assumed increased responsibilities and agencies like the Natural Resources Planning Board, the National Youth Administration, and the Farm Security Administration were sacrificed or rendered impotent for the war effort. A labor draft was narrowly averted, and it is interesting that the President of the largest democracy in the fight with fascism should have even considered this totalitarian device, if his philosophy and goals were what his left-liberal supporters proclaimed. Over 100,000 Japanese-Americans were herded into concentration camps under the shabbiest of excuses, with little protest from the left-liberal supporters of the war. Occasionally they criticized the conditions in the concentration camps. But few challenged the basic assumptions. And one, James Oneal, wrote letters to his friends on the East Coast about the majority of disloyal "Japs" and the bleeding-hearts who protested. To men like Oneal, the concern of Thomas and the small band who protested was probably like "insisting that the fire brigade observe traffic rules."[25]

Most historians are now willing to admit this shameful story in our history, but go on to argue that civil liberties survived World War II much better than World War I. No one would deny this, but too many historians forget that the basic reason was not the enlightenment of the government, but the minimum of dissent on the war. Moreover, the Smith Act *was* applied to the Trotskyists in Minneapolis during the European war, and sixteen men went to jail for very little reason. German Bundists were tried on vague charges, with very little protest, and some applause, from prowar Socialists and liberals. The government policy during the war was not enlightened on civil liberties; there was simply not much opposition to the war. It certainly was not enlightened on other domestic issues, where Southern-oriented advisors ignored mounting black-white tensions, and the New Deal responded inadequately to a series of race wars.[26]

Thomas and the antiwar Socialists had said that the end results throughout the world would not be an increase of democracy; more likely, they said, if the Allies won, Russian and British imperialism, with the United States attaching itself to British imperialism and taking over its prominent role, would be the result. As the war progressed, Thomas foresaw the eventual division of Europe between rival powers, and he recognized that he had been right in arguing that the war would not automatically assure democracy. Thomas and the antiwar Socialists had been frightened by the prospect of the United States emerging as an imperial power. They believed that she had followed this course in Asia, and was increasingly directing her attention to South America. The war did increase the role of the United States in Asia; it did increase American hegemony in the Western Hemisphere; it did divide the world into new rival Russian and American imperialist blocs. Once more, Thomas had foreseen these consequences.[27]

At the end of the war, the atom bomb was dropped. Already the moral distance between the Allies and the Axis had been diminished by the fire bombings of Dresden. And who protested the atomic holocaust? Not the prowar Socialists and liberals. Some were concerned that the bomb be used now for peaceful purposes;

some were concerned with international control of the bomb; the old Popular Front liberals around the *Nation* and *New Republic* were anxious that Russia be included in the nuclear sharing and control. But they did not address themselves to the moral question. Only the few antiwar radicals and the Thomas "critical supporters" knew that something terrifying and dreadful had been performed in the name of freedom.[28]

Writing in 1947—when it was clear that the four freedoms were a hollow echo throughout the world—Dwight MacDonald wrote: "However realistic it may have appeared at the time to back an Allied victory as 'better than Hitler,' it now looks like pure romanticism to have expected from the military defeat of Germany by the Allies anything more than the military defeat of Germany by the Allies." This was not enough for MacDonald; in retrospect it is still, after everything is said, enough for me. But I stand with the earlier MacDonald for raising the correct issues. For he was writing immediately after Truman had instituted a Loyalty Board where the accused could not confront his accuser, and where the accused were to lose their jobs for connections with groups whose identity they were not told. And he labeled this move correctly as "Nazi-Stalinist jurisprudence," an injection of totalitarian tactics into American life that mushroomed in the succeeding McCarthy period, where liberals competed with reactionaries to prove their toughness, where the rhetoric of the Cold War affected Reinhold Niebuhr and John Foster Dulles alike.[29]

The Cold War period is under reexamination today. What seems necessary—in addition to reappraisals of American diplomacy—is to examine the roots of the intellectual complacency and self-righteousness that characterized American life during these years. The roots, I believe, trace back to the war years, and, beyond them, to the years preceding the war, when the intellectual advocates of aid to the Allies began to drop their radical politics and "idealize" American democracy. I have no desire to accuse Mumford and Frank of being a new set of "irresponsibles"; not even the *New Leader*. Intellectual history is more complex than Mac-

Leish's theory imagined. Certainly the postwar careers of Mumford and Frank do not associate them with the prevalent mood. Yet there was a tendency in the uncritical side of their writing to raise the ante, to make the United States more than she was, to find in her—perhaps somewhat tarnished—all that was good in Western civilization, to lose sight of the critical side—the "guilt" of the United States—in their "call to arms." Ironically, it was Socialists like Norman Thomas who fought the "call to arms" and only *critically* supported the war, who did more than anyone else to put concrete meaning into the vague generalities of the prowar enthusiasts. It is tragic that they were not listened to more.

X

Socialists and "Utopian" Politics

I HAVE argued that socialism provided a perceptive angle of
vision on many issues of the 1930's. I have no wish to claim
it was perceptive on every issue. Its traditional class analysis of
racism and race relations did not penetrate to the depths of the
problem, though it was not completely wrong. Still, I believe that
on individual issues—Spain, the New Deal, the Moscow trials, the
Popular Front, the Stalinist bureaucracy, parts of the war question
—the record of the Socialists' "ideology" stands up well under
critical scrutiny. But there is another dimension to their ideology
that transcends the immediate issues and events: its supposedly
"utopian" nature. For example, the faith that many Socialists
placed in "workers' aid" in foreign policy or in "workers' control"
in industry is now seen by most critics as part of their indefatigible
utopian optimism. And, indeed, Socialists were optimistic and
utopian—not simply about the long-range perspective of history,
but about what the triumph of socialism would mean in the *quality*
of life. "Not only in the structure of the state, not only in the
operation of industry, but in a thousand subtle psychological responses, will socialism liberate human personalities from bondage,"
wrote Devere Allen in 1935. The modern postwar world, with its
sense of the absurdity in all life and its acceptance of a more
restricted concept of politics, finds such observations lacking in
depth. And certainly there is nothing in the history of many

"socialist" countries that would lead one to be optimistic about the freeing of the human personality. But there is another angle from which one can judge such remarks: the very problems that bother many in society today—the feeling of economic and social impotence; the impersonality of modern life and the consequent search for direct human contacts; the bureaucratization, whether in government or industry, that seems to destroy the immediate and spontaneous—all these, and more, are connected with a restricted concept of politics that has developed the present environment and rationalized it. In this light, the Socialist ideal of "liberating human personalities" was not simply an optimistic statement about the future benefits of socialism, but a deep statement about the goals of any meaningful politics.[1]

The question of Socialist "utopianism" in the 1930's can be approached through the famous exchange between Norman Thomas and Reinhold Niebuhr in 1944. One of Thomas's early biographers, Murray Seidler, felt that it laid "bare the differences on issues and approaches to politics that separated Thomas then and in years to come from ardent liberals and socialists who had become New Dealers." This is correct, but can also be carried backward into the 1930's. Bernard Johnpoll argues that Niebuhr's reply to Thomas is "devastating" and "one of the most effective and accurate critiques of Norman Thomas ever written." That remains to be seen. But certainly it brings into focus Thomas's "utopian" politics and the Niebuhrian creed of politics as "the art of the possible," a creed Johnpoll heartily subscribes to. The full exchange is important and meaningful. On July 25, 1944 Norman Thomas wrote an Open Letter to Reinhold Niebuhr:

> I write this open letter to you because you stand for—yes, and lead—many men and women of unquestioned sincerity and good-will who, through the Political Action Committee, the Union for Democratic Action or otherwise, are now supporting the Democratic ticket, although by conviction they are democratic socialists. I ask why, this year of all years, you are supporting the Democrats.

I could have understood it far more easily in 1936; I did understand it, despite my own disagreement, in 1940. But NOW! . . .

Is it on the platform? That I can hardly believe. The Democratic platform is virtually interchangeable with the Republican. Indeed, the latter is slightly more liberal, for instance, in dealing with the vital matter of action to promote race equality.

However, Roosevelt and Dewey could exchange platforms and the voters would be none the wiser. The Republicans are not more emphatic than the Democrats in asserting their faith in "competitive enterprise." And they will be as little sincere and effective in making such an economic order work after its abysmal failure.

How often have you yourself argued that there can neither be full employment nor abundance without plan and without the social control of the commanding heights of our economic order! You have shared my conviction that such control CAN be democratic and can indeed increase the amount of true freedom in the world. Have you changed your mind now that the undesirability and impossibility of restoring the dominance of the profit system has been proved by depression and war and the miracle of war time production under planning?

I shall not insult you by assuming that you support the Democratic ticket because of its planks, which are virtually identical with the Republican. They contain no application of ethical principles you have so eloquently preached, and no formula for avoiding that Third World War of whose probability you have warned us. They are based on the fallacy that machinery for the enforcement of peace makes the nature of the peace to be enforced unimportant and that a Quadruple—really a Triple—Alliance masked behind phoney internationalism will succeed when all similar alliances have failed. That fallacy lies at the heart of the President's Great Design.

If not the platform, is it the man, Roosevelt, whom you are supporting? Granting his real accomplishments, especially in his first term, will you not admit these facts:

Roosevelt has pushed no major progressive legislation since 1937.

Before the war he had not conquered unemployment but had stabilized it and subsidized unemployment at a level of about 23 per cent of the workers.

Today most of his former progressive associates constitute the New Deal Government-in-Exile. His reconverters are the capitalist Bernard Baruch and the cotton broker Will Clayton.

Roosevelt advocated total conscription of human beings in war and gives signs of supporting permanent military conscription of our youth in peace.

He has no program adequate to the conquest of poverty, and his underwriting of white supremacy in the Far East and the Balkanization of Europe between Moscow and London is an invitation to new war.

Finally, on the basis of one of your own favorite quotations, "power corrupts and absolute power corrupts absolutely," there is a very real argument against the fourth term. That agreement may be outweighed by the case against Governor Dewey, but we Socialists offer you an alternative to both. (And that alternative is not support of this New York 'Liberal Party,' which broke with the Communist-dominated American Labor Party only to support the same candidate as it and the Democrats are supporting!)

There is, or was before the defeat of Mr. Wallace, one more possibility: namely, that your group thought to overcome all these disadvantages by forcing through the Democratic convention the renomination of a genuine, if somewhat erratic, liberal for Vice-President. It would at best have been a poor consolation. BUT EVEN THAT FAILED.

Roosevelt was too sure of you and your liberal and labor colleagues. He had to appease Hague and Bilbo. So the Democrats, with Roosevelt's blessing, gave us as a Vice-Presidential candidate and possible future President one of Convict Boss Prendergast's protégés, whose record is not adequately redeemed by the fact that he has been chairman of a useful Senatorial Committee.

Roosevelt told us that Dr. New Deal died. The convention proceeded to jump on his grave.

You left us because of honest differences over an interventionist policy before Pearl Harbor. We got war. It—
especially the European war—is almost won. Now, *HOW
ABOUT WINNING THE PEACE?* How about insisting that
the demand for unconditional surrender be replaced by terms
which may hasten a constructive people's revolution in Germany?

What party but the Socialist Party is demanding that?

You may reply that the kind of peace we want is impossible
now. Very likely. But to work for it is the only self-respecting
thing to do; the effort may have greater influence than you
think: and the struggle need not stop in the postwar years.

The larger the Socialist vote, the greater and more immediate the pressure for a decent peace and for freedom and
plenty with which the cause of peace is bound up.

The larger the Socialist vote, the greater the inspiration
toward the kind of political realignment which our friends in
Canada are auspiciously achieving.

*IN THE LIGHT OF THESE FACTS, I THINK YOU
AND THOUSANDS OF MEN AND WOMEN OF LIKE
OPINION WILL BE VERY UNHAPPY IF YOU THROW
AWAY YOUR VOTE BY VOTING FOR WHAT YOU
DON'T WANT, AND GETTING IT—AS YOU WILL IF
EITHER ROOSEVELT OR DEWEY WINS. IT IS NOT
TOO LATE. YOU WILL BE WELCOMED WITH OPEN
ARMS TO THE COMPANY OF THOSE WHO FIGHT
UNDER THE BANNER OF DEMOCRATIC SOCIALISM
—FOR PLENTY, PEACE, AND FREEDOM.*

On September 8, 1944, Niebuhr replied:

As chairman of the Union for Democratic Action, allow
me to answer your open letter asking the U.D.A. to justify
its support of President Roosevelt in the coming presidential
election.

Let me say at once the members of the Union for Democratic Action long ago abandoned the 'Utopia or bust' position in politics. You suggest that because the foreign policy
of the Roosevelt Administration will not lead us at once into
a genuine world society, we should renounce the possibility
inherent in it of forging a world organization on the basis of

continued cooperation of the United Nations. We reject this doctrine. One of the most interesting ironies of this time lies in the spectacle of American Socialists talking of the necessity of 'winning the peace'; if America and the democratic world had listened to those Socialists who before Pearl Harbor were telling us that our capitalist society was not pure enough in heart to take up arms against fascist aggression, Hitler would be making the peace today.

You suggest that because the present Administration no longer manifests its earlier New Deal militancy, American progressives should abandon their efforts to make the Democratic Party the liberal party and should cast in their lot with the Socialists. But we believe with Vice-President Wallace that the New Deal must be revived and strengthened. You use the defeat of Wallace as an argument—but you are not seriously concerned with that defeat, nor were you in the battle to win his re-nomination. If Wallace had won, your position would be the same, and another argument would serve instead.

Indeed, although you profess many progressive ideals and support many progressive measures, there is an exasperating quality of irresponsibility about the whole Socialist position, and it is difficult to take seriously your criticisms. This irresponsibility, which led to the folly of your pre-Pearl Harbor isolationism, stems from your inability to conceive of politics as the act of choosing among possible alternatives. This blindness makes it impossible for you correctly to gauge the political climate of the country.

America, in the years immediately ahead, may be the scene of basic political realignments. But Americans will not, in the foreseeable future, be called on to make a choice between Socialism and reaction. A sizeable Socialist vote in November will prove nothing and influence no one. The realistic, actual choice before Americans is that of reverting to the period of Harding-Coolidge normalcy, of trying again, under the Dewey-Bricker banner, the laissez-faire formula which failed before and ended in depression or of moving militantly forward in the determination to make the last four years of the Roosevelt era a period of social reconstruction and reform, courageously using whatever resources of government are needed to achieve full employment and social security.

We are convinced that Americans will not choose another depression.

Have No Illusions

We do not pretend to be pleased or heartened by many tendencies which have characterized the Roosevelt Administration in recent years. We are not defenders of the Northern machine bosses and Southern poll-taxers who still dominate the Democratic Party. We have no illusions regarding the difficulty of pushing them from the seats of power. But we are aware that for the first time in party history, these men were openly challenged at the Democratic Convention in Chicago. The lines are drawn.

I remind you once again that the battles ahead will not be contests between unmitigated evil and absolute good, and that a true perspective of the struggles of our time cannot be had from the Olympian heights of Socialist dogma.

If you are contemptuous of the differences between a Roosevelt and a Dewey, between a Congressman who voted against, and one who voted for, the fortification of Guam, between a Senator who opposed subsidies and one who supported them, between men who wanted a federal ballot for the soldier vote, between men who, whatever their limitations, have some grasp of the big issues and forces of the modern world, and men who have no ideas, no plans, only a longing for 'normalcy'; in short, you shun the daily skirmishes and belittle the modest gains which are the staff of politics, then you—not we—are 'throwing away your vote' on those decisions affecting the course of the war and the nature of the peace.

The Union for Democratic Action contends that Americans cannot afford the luxury of a gesture toward a perfect program, while real issues are being decided on a much more modest level. We refuse to sulk in our tents or to flaunt our ideological superiority in the faces of men and women in all countries who are fighting.

I reiterate that the course we have chosen represents a fighting chance for a sick society. Since the American people, in the years immediately ahead, must not return to the mad Republican cycle of doom and depression, and since they will not advance to a Socialist Commonwealth, the realistic choice is a continuation of the present Administration in office, with a determination to push it forward along the paths of domestic reform and of genuine international organization.[2]

Far from being "devastating," and "one of the most effective and accurate critiques of Norman Thomas ever written," Niebuhr's answer to Thomas is remarkable for its political naiveté and ineffectiveness. The assumption that the Democratic Party would respond to pressure from those it was surest of—the liberal intellectuals and the labor movement—has proved one of the most "utopian" assumptions ever made. The great breakthrough for the labor movement came when the Democratic Party was *not* certain of labor leaders' support; the alliance of the labor movement with the Democratic Party achieved the Taft-Hartley Bill and a twenty-year stagnation in the labor movement. And the liberal intellectuals who thought that somehow they would reform the Democratic Party from within—this proved one of the greatest illusions of the postwar years. If the Democratic Party has begun to make gestures toward reform, it has not been in response to today's Socialist Party, with its strategy of rebuilding the Democratic Party around a liberal-labor coalition. Rather, the Democratic Party has responded to fears of disaffection—fears of groups building outside of the Party; fears of losing groups that have been in their coalition. Niebuhr's strategy led directly to a situation where the Democratic Party could depend on its intellectual allies; in the usual relationship of masters and dependents, the masters knew all that was necessary was occasional gestures to keep the support of the dependents.

No more disastrous strategy for radicals *and* liberals was ever designed than Niebuhr's strategy that those who wanted radical change in society, those who were convinced society was "sick," should play the "inside" game of "immediate ends." For what Niebuhr apparently failed to recognize was that those who stood outside were not simply "flaunting their ideological superiority," but (ironically, to be sure) furnishing the liberal "insiders" with their only pressure for social reform. As Hal Draper wrote back in 1962: "Organized liberalism is in the sad state we see here *because* there is no aggressive American socialism and radicalism to press them on the flank. Its spine stiffens only when it gets cuffed from the left. It can stand up to the right only when it can point with alarm to a threat on the other side of it. A radical political program is the only effective answer to the ultra-right—if only because its very first effect is to stir the liberals to life in order to denature it."[3]

Certainly there is nothing from the experience of the thirties and the New Deal to refute this perspective. Louis Hartz has written perceptively that because Roosevelt did not have a threat on the left, he could be flexible, moving left in the crisis, while professing his orthodoxy. There is a great deal of insight here into the weak condition of the Left in the thirties. But it is not quite accurate to see much of Roosevelt's flexibility as "left" flexibility; the N.R.A. and A.A.A.—his two key programs—certainly were not. The weakened Left may have, in Hartz's scheme, left Roosevelt free from the "liberal" ideological scruples of European liberalism. However, though the Left was weak, there was always a *potential* Left—a Left that while it often played ball with the New Deal could not be counted on with complete assurance; a labor movement which, at least in its early days, could threaten to become an autonomous force outside the Democratic Party. It is not unfair to read whatever left-liberal measures there were in the New Deal in terms of responses to forces outside the Democratic Party. James MacGregor Burns has argued that it was the desertion of the right, rather than the growth of the movements of the disaffected, that pushed Roosevelt left. Perhaps, though one suspects that the desertion by itself would only have contributed to a static situation; it took outside pressure to get the liberal measures. Clearly this is true with the meager steps toward aiding the tenant farmers. The measures were far too few and not designed to correct basic problems. But in so far as they were instigated, this resulted from the outside pressure of Norman Thomas, the Socialist Party, and the Southern Tenant Farmers Union. These finally "stiffened the spine" of a supposedly liberal administration, temporarily forcing it to stand up to the big cotton owners. But in order to get even these inadequate measures, it was necessary that there exist a politics which transcended the art of the possible.[4]

This leads directly into another of the weaknesses in Niebuhr's analysis: its tendency to accept the "given" in terms of political reality. It is one thing to declare, as Niebuhr did, that the American people were a long way from socialism; nothing should have been more obvious. But to deny a prerevolutionary situation, much less a revolutionary situation, is quite different from accepting the existing political forces in the country as a definition of what can be worked with and struggled with. Certainly, anybody analyzing the existing political forces in the United States in 1934 would not have predicted that one of the largest degrees of Socialist success would have come among the depressed cotton sharecroppers of Arkansas. Nor would a "realistic" reading of the political and economic climate have predicted the end results of the auto workers' sit-down strikes. Twenty years later, a "realistic" reading of the political climate would have warned Martin Luther King against leading a bus boycott in Montgomery, Alabama; it certainly would have told Mrs. Rosa Parks to sit at the back of the bus. It was "realistic" Niebuhrian liberals who told the peace movement to keep quiet in 1964–65; it was "realistic" liberal, labor, and civil-rights leaders who were cautious about declaring their opposition to the war in Vietnam. And what did it get them? War—and more war.

Thomas knew the kind of peace he and Niebuhr wanted was "impossible now." But he also knew that nothing approximating it would come about without a struggle outside the bounds of conventional two-party politics. He sensed the continuing truth of what Randolph Bourne had written in 1917 about those who adjust their political sights only to the immediate and the "given": "If your policy as a publicist reformer is to take what you can get, you are likely to find that you get something less than you should be willing to take. . . . Vision must constantly outshoot technique, opportunist efforts usually achieve less even than what seemed obviously possible. An impossibilitist élan that appeals to desire will often carry further. A philosophy of adjustment will not even make for adjustment. If you try merely to 'meet' situations as they come, you will not even meet them. Instead you will only pile up behind you deficits and arrears that will some day bankrupt you."[5]

Bourne's defense of "utopian" politics years later found an echo in the moving words of the exiled Polish philosopher, Leszek Kolakowski. In suggesting the continual necessity of utopian left-wing politics, Kolakowski has written: "Yet why is a utopia a condition of all revolutionary movements? Because much historical experience, more or less buried in the social consciousness, tells us that goals unattainable now will never be reached unless they are articulated when they are still unattainable. It may well be that the impossible at a given moment can become possible only by being stated at a time when it is impossible. . . . *The existence of a utopia as a utopia is the necessary prerequisite for its eventually ceasing to be a utopia.*" Kolakowski's words remind us that the problem of utopian versus realistic politics is a problem that transcends the American environment. But it would be foolish to assume that it only has meaning in countries where a corrupted brand of state socialism has forced the dissenters to raise "utopian" demands.[6]

For most liberal intellectuals in the United States during the post-World War II period, the kind of vision Bourne urged and the kind of utopianism Kolakowski expresses held little meaning. Liberals prided themselves on their hard-headed realism, their ability to address *immediate* problems, their willingness to make "pragmatic" compromises with "reality." The irony was that the politics they applauded often turned out to be completely unrealistic.

Nothing should be clearer than the fact that, whatever its individual accomplishments on specific measures, the general philosophy of Niebuhrian liberalism buttressed a politics—the Democratic Party politics—of the postwar years that ultimately brought bankruptcy to the general philosophy. And one of the reasons for this is clearly expressed in Niebuhr's original statement: the assumption that the battle between the Democratic Party and the Republican Party was, in 1944 (it was not even in 1932, 1936, and 1940), a battle between "the laissez faire formula" and a party that might be dedicated to "social reconstruction and reform." Both parties had long ago—by the early 1900's—abandoned the "laissez faire formula," whatever the ideological statements of supporters and publicists. Nor has the Democratic Party been, in the least, dedicated to "social reconstruction"; the "industrial state" described by Galbraith and others grows out of the Republican and Democratic Parties alike. There have been various policy differences between the two parties, in 1944 and in the 1930's, but the Niebuhrian language, in order to give meaning to the daily political skirmishes, exalted the battle into a fundamental ideological battle between the two parties. The language says little about reality nor adds anything to a comprehension of the political and economic forces and decisions that shaped American capitalism in the twentieth century.[7]

Perhaps the fatal fault for Socialists in Niebuhr's philosophy was that it led to an absorption with "tactical" considerations. Clearly, tactics are important; any sensible radical has to deal with them. Nor can tactics be separated from ethics; the old ends-and-means question is not irrelevant. But the constant absorption with tactics and strategy has led radicals, as well as liberals, away from the first order of business: the protest of injustice and inequity. In 1894, a delegation from the striking Pullman Company workers went to the convention of the newly formed American Railway Union. Eugene Debs, as president of the union, knew that supporting the strike would run terrible risks. Every practical argument was against it: a newly formed and still relatively weak union (not representing all the railway workers) would have to confront a powerful established company backed by the Railroads' General

Managers Association. Yet the American Railway Union Convention would not turn its back on the pleas of the Pullman strikers. Reluctantly, after unsuccessful efforts to get Pullman to compromise failed, Debs agreed. But he did not agree to support the strike for practical reasons; he had to for essentially "ethical" reasons: the claims of the Pullman workers and the desires of his union could not be ignored. The strike eventually failed, the railway union was broken, and Debs went to jail. Hopes for building the one big union of railway workers vanished.[8]

From a "practical" viewpoint, Debs had made a mistake. One could argue that in terms of building long-range morale in the labor movement, Debs took a strategically practical step. But he did not take it for this long-range reason; he took it because the demands of justice for the Pullman workers overrode any strategically practical considerations. And he was right to have responded in this fashion: it was the meaningful and relevant response to inequity and injustice; to have set aside these ethical considerations because of the tactical risks involved would have forfeited the reasons for building the union in the first place.[9]

Norman Thomas, as I have suggested, was constantly concerned with practical questions of building the Socialist Party in the 1930's. He was constantly concerned that rival radical parties, like the Communists, not gain a tactical advantage over the Socialists in the work among the unemployed, labor, students, and in antiwar activity. He was hardly averse to the Socialists getting publicity out of episodes like his protest over Jersey City Mayor Frank Hague's anti-free speech ban. But what led him to protest Hague's rule, what led him into the onion fields of Ohio, into the mining country of Illinois, into the textile mills of North Carolina, to the sharecroppers of Arkansas, was not practical considerations. Johnpoll recognizes this; he recognizes Thomas's ethical impulse. But he badly misreads its meaning. For it was this that made Thomas a great political leader. Norman Thomas knew that, in the end, a radical politics must respond to ethical claims, that it loses its meaning and its purpose when it becomes obsessed with narrow practical strategies. The liberals, radicals, and ex-radicals who were unwilling to protest the imprisonment of the Japanese-Americans because it might break the wartime "unity," who, in the name of realism, did not object to the violation of the rights of Communists during the McCarthy period, let practical strategic matters overcome ethical claims; they had forfeited the purposes that originally had brought them to radicalism and liberalism.[10]

Socialism: A Final Word

In the end, the critic of Socialism in the thirties might admit the possibility that it was useful, if impractical, to have a group calling us to our ethical responsibilities. He might even admit the possibility that Socialist ideology, in some instances, might provide a perceptive angle of vision. But the critic would insist, as he has insisted, that this does not deal with the most serious charge. That is, it could be granted that the Socialists were right on certain particular issues and that there even may have been some connection between their ideology and their position, but the root critique would still exist: that like all ideologues who placed their faith in history in reaching their millennial dream, they would sacrifice man's present to man's future, and that it is this ethos of sacrifice, with Stalin as the archetypal practitioner, which is the horrifying experience of the twentieth century. Schlesinger writes of the Communist who "has no hesitation in sacrificing life to history." And Bell quotes Alexander Herzen's eloquent remark: "An end that is infinitely remote is not an end, but, if you like, a trap; an end must be nearer. . . . Each age, each generation, each life has its own fullness. . . ." The risks are certainly there (though one wonders if any politics does not do this *partially*); the absence of political outlets plus technology plus "wait for the future" equals totalitarianism.

But what is the historian to say about the history of American Socialism on this question? Was it the early Socialists working for industrial unionism who sacrificed the present for the future, or was it Theodore Roosevelt, who counteracted militant unionism with a highly abstract concept of "general welfare"? Was it Eugene Debs fighting for the right of free speech in the *present* during World War I who sacrificed the present for the future, or was it Woodrow Wilson (like Roosevelt, a "give-and-take" politician until the issue of the ratification of the Treaty of Versailles), sacrificing civil liberties for the duration of the war, who set aside the present for the future under the claims of national security and a future safe for democracy? Was it the Socialists who helped lead the drive for industrial unionism in the 1930's who sacrificed the present for the future, or was it Franklin Roosevelt, who agreed to a union-busting dual unionism in the name of a common good until his hand was forced? Was it Norman Thomas, H. L. Mitchell, and Howard Kester working to build up the Southern Tenant Farmers Union or Franklin Roosevelt working with the Democratic politicians to break it? Was it Norman Thomas protesting the imprisonment of the Japanese-Americans during World War II, or was it the liberals who were afraid to raise their voices because of the "practical" needs of wartime consensus? Was it the David McReynolds Socialists who urged immediate withdrawal from Vietnam in the mid-sixties, or the liberals and McReynolds' fellow "pragmatic" Socialists who said that it was an impossible strategy? Just who has sacrificed whom for the future?[11]

I do not mean these questions only rhetorically; I admit the answers are—or can be at times—complex. But, at a minimum, they point to the conclusion that the Theodore Roosevelt give-and-take tradition, while perhaps free from sacrificing life to history (though it has done that too), has sacrificed life—and by this I mean the *fullness* of the present—to some abstract "public interest." And that is the final point: the real issue is not that of history-ridden ideologues versus pragmatic compromisers; the question is whether life is being sacrificed to *any* spurious abstraction. On that score, the Socialist tradition, including the Socialist Party during the 1930's, stands up better than the "give-and-take" tradition of American politics.

Appendix

Declaration of Principles of
the Socialist Party

As Adopted in Convention at Detroit and Approved by Referendum, 1934

The Socialist Party is the party of the workers, regardless of race, color or creed. In mill and mine, shop and farm, office and school, the workers can assert their united power, and through the Socialist Party establish a cooperative commonwealth forever free from human exploitation and class rule.

If the workers delay and drift, they will prolong the period of their enslavement to a decadent capitalism. This uncreative, wasteful and brutally oppressive social system takes jobs away and turns millions of would-be producers into the streets with no assurance that ever again they may become employed—financiers, for their own selfish gain, control markets and prices and autocratically regulate the extension or withdrawal of credit. Those who utilize the profit motive for their own advantage restrict the workers' standard of living save where labor has aggressively organized and struggled energetically for its rights—and even then deny to the working class the abundance which the modern productive process is technically capable of bestowing upon those willing to labor for the common good. Capitalism invades the peace of farming areas with the all-pervasive danger of insecurity and in many regions with bitter destitution. Throughout the land it attacks the American home and brands countless children with the pinch of want.

The privileged minority who benefit from exploitation of the multitude are not content with owning the mechanisms of production and distribution, which perpetuates their property power; they control the press, radio, and motion picture; they starve and poison the educational system; they dominate our courts, our municipalities, our state legislative assemblies, and our national government; for the extension of their economic domain they expose to the appalling menace of new imperialist wars the innocent youth in our own and other countries, on whom they will lay the ruthless clutch of conscription and send to fight those wars. To confuse the voting masses and retain their authority, they maintain great political parties whose appeal fluctuates between frank reaction and fictitious liberalism, neither of which offers to the workers any substantial or enduring program for the acquisition of their birthright.

Only those who labor with hand and brain, in their concerted might, can overthrow this monstrous system and replace it with a Socialist order. Whenever they will, they can transfer to the people the ownership of industry, land, finance and natural resources including water power, and operate these possessions of the Socialist commonwealth for the material and cultural enrichment of all—beginning with the large scale industries of a public character such as banking, insurance, mining, transportation, communication, and the trustified industries, and extending the process rapidly to the point where rent, interest, and profit are abolished.

The Socialization of industry as Socialists conceive it, however, means more than simple government ownership— it involves the opposite of irresponsible bureaucracy, and includes democratic administration through the elected and responsible representatives of the workers in the respective industries and of the workers as a whole.

The Socialist Party advocates the establishment of a system of co-operative and publicly owned and managed warehouses, markets and credits, to promote direct dealing between farmers and city consumers at the cost of the service in their mutual interests, thus reducing the cost of living, assuring farmers a just compensation for their labor, and enabling them to escape from the twin curses of tenantry and mortgaged serfdom.

Workers of town and country must be strongly organized on economic as well as on political lines. The ceaseless struggle of the labor unions and farm organizations, and the constructive work of bona fide cooperative societies, are necessary, not only for the immediate defense and betterment of the condition of the producing class, but also to equip producers with the understanding and self-discipline required for the efficient administration of the industries of which they are to win control.

It is the duty of every Socialist wage worker to be a loyal and active member of the union in his industry or trade, and to strive for the strengthening and solidifying of the trade union movement. It is the duty and privilege of the Socialist press to aid the unions in their struggles for better wages, increased leisure, and better conditions of employment.

The Socialist Party, while standing for the interests of the American people, recognizes that the well-being of any one nation is inextricably interwoven with that of every other. To divisive capitalist nationalism it opposes international workers' solidarity; to the Socialist parties of other countries it extends full support in their struggles, uniting with them in the common effort to build a world-wide federation of Socialist republics.

The Socialist Party is opposed to militarism, imperialism, and war. It proposes to eradicate the perpetual economic warfare of capitalism the fruit of which is international conflict. War cannot be tolerated by Socialists, or preparedness for war. They will unitedly seek to develop trustworthy working class instruments for the peaceable settlement of international disputes and conflicts. They will seek to eliminate military training from schools, colleges and camps. They will oppose military reviews, displays and expenditures, whether for direct war prepared-ness or for militaristic propaganda, both in wartime and in peacetime. They will loyally support, in the tragic event of war, any of their comrades who for anti-war activities not in contravention of Socialist principles, or for refusal to perform war service, come into conflict with public opinion or the law. Moreover, recognizing the suicidal nature of modern combat and the incalculable train of wars' consequences which rest most heavily upon the working class, they will refuse collectively to sanction or support any international war: they will, on the contrary, by agitation and opposition do their best not to be broken up by the war, but to break up the war. They will meet war and the detailed plans for war already mapped out by the war-making arms of the government, by massed war resistance, organized so far as practicable in a general strike of labor unions and professional groups in a united effort to make the waging of war a practical impossibility and to convert the capitalist war crisis into a victory for Socialism.

In its struggle for a new society, the Socialist Party seeks to attain its objective by peaceful and orderly means. Recognizing the increasing resort by a crumbling capitalist order to Fascism to preserve its integrity and dominance, the Socialist Party intends not to be de-ceived by Fascist propaganda nor overwhelmed by Fascist force. It will do all in its power to fight Fascism of every kind all the time and everywhere in the world, until Fascism is dead. It will rely on the organization of a disciplined labor movement. Its methods may include a recourse to a general strike which will not merely serve as a defense against Fascist counter-revolution but will carry the revolutionary struggle into the camp of the enemy.

The Socialist Party proclaims anew its faith in economic and political democracy. It unhesitatingly applies itself to the task of replacing the bogus democracy of capitalist parliamentarism by a genuine workers' democracy. Capitalism is doomed. If it can be superseded by majority vote, the Socialist Party will rejoice. If the crisis comes through the denial of majority rights after the electorate has given us a mandate we shall not hesitate to crush by our labor solidarity the reckless forces of reaction and to consolidate the Socialist state. If the capitalist system should collapse in a general chaos and confusion, which cannot permit of orderly procedure, the Socialist Party, whether or not in such a case it is a majority, will not shrink from the responsibility of organizing and maintaining a government under the rule of the producing masses. True democracy is a worthy means to progress; but true democracy must be created by the workers of the world.

Note on Sources

I have relied most heavily on the Norman Thomas Papers in the New York Public Library and the Socialist Party Papers, the Social Democratic Federation Papers, the Algernon Lee Papers, the James Oneal Papers, the B. C. Vladeck Papers, and the Morris Hillquit Papers at Tamiment Library, New York University. I have also used the Socialist Party Papers in the William R. Perkins Collection at Duke University. The Wisconsin Historical Society supplied me with relevant material from the Morris Hillquit Papers located there and from its collection of radical pamphlets. I made extensive use of the collection of radical pamphlets at Tamiment Library. A list of the periodicals and newspapers most frequently cited in the notes is found at the beginning of the note section. Of these, the *Socialist Call,* the *New Leader,* and the *American Socialist Quarterly* (later the *American Socialist Monthly* and, still later, the *Socialist Review*) were the most important. In addition, I consulted a number of radical periodicals of the 1930's *(Challenge, International Review, Labor Age, Labor Bulletin, Militant, New Frontiers, New Militant, One Big Union Advocate, Our America, Revolt, Revolutionary Age, Student Outlook, Workers' Age)* that do not appear in the notes.

As for books, those that were most important for the study are cited so frequently that it seems superfluous to list them again. Those which I consulted, but did not cite in the notes, were so marginal to the study that to list them would be pretentious. The following is a list of the more important pamphlets I used. Most of them are located in the Tamiment Library.

Adler, Friedrich. *Democracy and Revolution* (New York, 1934).
————. *The Witchcraft Trial in Moscow* (New York, 1937).
Altman, Jack. *A Reply to the Open Letter of Dr. Hendin* (New York, n.d.).
Ameringer, Oscar. *The Yankee Primer* (Oklahoma City, 1933).
Berenberg, David. *A Workers' World* (New York, 1931).
Browder, Earl. *The Meaning of Social-Fascism* (New York, n.d.).
Burnham, James. *Let the People Vote on War* (New York, n.d.).

————. *The People's Front* (New York, 1937).

Cahan, Abraham, ed. *Hear The Other Side* (New York, 1934).

Casey, James. *The Crisis in the Communist Party* (New York, n.d.).

Claessens, August. *Essentials of Socialism* (New York, 1933).

————. *What Organized Labor Wants* (New York, 1937).

Coleman, McAlister. *Symbols of 1936* (1936).

Draper, Hal. *Are You Ready for War?* (New York, n.d.).

————. *Out of Their Own Mouths* (New York, n.d.).

Deutsch, Julius. *The Civil War in Austria* (Chicago, 1934).

Eastman, Max. *A Letter to Americans* (New York, 1941).

Foster, William Z. *The Crisis in the Socialist Party* (New York, 1936).

Goldman, Albert. *From Communism to Socialism* (1935).

————. *What Is Socialism?* (New York, 1938).

————. *Why We Defend the Soviet Union* (New York, 1940).

Hamilton, Albert and Churchill, Edmund. *Building a New World Through the Socialist Party* (Chicago, 1936).

Hamilton, Albert. *Students Against War* (1937).

Herberg, Will. *The N.R.A. and American Labor* (New York, 1933).

Hillquit, Morris. *The Practical Accomplishments of Socialism* (Girard, Kansas, 1931).

———— and Woll, Matthew. *Should the American Workers Form a Political Party of Their Own?* (New York, 1932).

Hughan, Jessie Wallace. *If We Should Be Invaded* (New York, 1941).

————. *What About Spain?* (New York, 1937).

Kantorovitch, Haim. *Problems of Revolutionary Socialism* (New York, 1936).

————. *The Socialist Party at the Crossroads* (New York, 1934).

Krzycki, Leo. *The Unions and the Socialists* (Chicago, 1935).

Laidler, Harry W. *America in the Depression* (New York, 1935).

————. *An Appeal to White Collar Workers and the Professions* (New York, n.d.).

————. *The Federal Government and Functional Democracy* (New York, 1940).

————. *The New Capitalism and the Socialist* (New York, 1931).

————. *Putting the Constitution to Work* (New York, 1936).

————. *Toward a Farmer-Labor Party* (New York, 1938).

————. *Unemployment and Its Remedies* (New York, 1931).

Levenstein, Aaron. *A Letter to a Comrade* (New York, 1937).

————. *Make Freedom Constitutional* (New York, n.d.).

Lewis, Alfred Baker. *Do We Have a Stake in This War?* (New York, n.d.).

_____. *Labor, Machines and the Depression* (New York, 1939).

_____. *Why the C.I.O.* (New York, 1937).

Lippmann, Walter. *National Unity for Defense* (New York, 1940).

Lovestone, Jay. *New Frontiers for Labor* (New York, n.d.).

_____. *People's Front Illusions* (New York, n.d.).

_____. *What Next for American Labor* (New York, 1934).

Morrow, Felix. *The Civil War in Spain* (New York, 1936).

_____. *Revolution and Counter-Revolution in Spain* (New York, 1938).

Muste, A. J. *The A.F.L. in 1931* (New York, 1932).

_____. *Which Party for the American Worker?* (New York, 1935).

_____. *Why a Labor Party* (New York, 1929).

Nearing, Scott, Thomas, Norman, and Lescohier, Don D. *Which Offers More for the Future? Communism, Socialism, Capitalism.* (Chicago, 1932).

Oneal, James. *An American Labor Party* (New York, 1936).

_____. *The Austrian Civil War* (New York, n.d.).

_____. *Socialism versus Bolshevism* (New York, 1935).

_____. *Some Pages of Party History* (New York, n.d.).

Page, Kirby. *How to Keep America Out of War* (1939).

_____. *National Defense* (New York, 1931).

_____, Sayre, John Nevin, and Muste, A. J. *Pacifism and Aggression* (New York, n.d.).

Panken, Jacob. *Socialism for America* (New York, n.d.).

Porter, Paul. *America for All: The Commonwealth Plan* (Chicago, 1934).

_____ and Biemiller, Andrew. *Memorandum on an Economic Program* (n.d.).

_____. *Which Way for the Socialist Party?* (Milwaukee, 1937).

Schactman, Max. *Behind the Moscow Trial* (New York, 1936).

Seidman, Joel. *Introduction to Labor Problems* (New York, 1935).

_____. *A Labor Party for America?* (Katonah, 1936).

_____. *The Labor Movement Today* (Katonah, 1934).

_____. *Shall Strikes Be Outlawed?* (New York, 1938).

_____. *Sit-down* (New York, 1937).

_____. *The Wagner Act and the Automobile Worker* (1937).

Souchy, Augustin. *Spain* (New York, 1936).

_____. *The Tragic Week in May* (Barcelona, 1937).

Sullivan, John F., Biemiller, Andrew J., and Krueger, Maynard C. *The National Industrial Recovery Act* (Chicago, 1933).

Symes, Lillian. *Communism—World Revolution to Red Imperialism* (Chicago, n.d.).

Thomas, Norman. *Collective Security Means War* (1938).

————. *Democracy and Japanese Americans* (New York, 1942).

————. *Democracy versus Dictatorship* (New York, 1937).

————. *Emancipate Youth from Work—Old Age from Fear* (1936).

————. *Is the New Deal Socialism?* (1936).

————. *The Plight of the Sharecropper* (New York, 1934).

———— and Seidman, Joel. *Russia—Democracy or Dictatorship?* (New York, 1939).

————. *The Socialist Cure for a Sick Society* (New York, 1932).

————. *Shall Labor Support Roosevelt?* (New York, 1936).

————. *A Socialist Looks at the New Deal* (New York, 1933).

————. *The Socialists Mean Business* (New York, 1934).

————. *Stop the Draft!* (1940).

————. *War as a Socialist Sees It* (New York, n.d.).

————. *What Socialism Is and Is Not* (1932).

———— and Browder, Earl. *Which Road for American Workers: Socialist or Communist?* (New York, 1936).

————. *Why Did NRA Go Wrong?* (Chicago, n.d.).

————. *Why I Am a Socialist* (New York, n.d.).

Tyler, Gus. *The Elements of Revolutionary Socialism* (New York, n.d.).

————. *The United Front* (New York, 1933).

————. *Youth Fights War!* (New York, n.d.).

Yvon, M. *What Has Become of the Russian Revolution?* (New York, 1937).

Notes

The following abbreviations have been used for periodicals and manuscript collections:

Periodicals

American Socialist Monthly	*ASM*
American Socialist Quarterly	*ASQ*
Harper's Magazine	*H*
Hammer and Tongs	*HT*
International Council Correspondence	*ICC*
Modern Monthly	*MM*
Modern Quarterly	*MQ*
Nation	*N*
New Leader	*NL*
New Republic	*NR*
Proletarian Outlook	*PO*
Revolutionary Socialist Review	*RSR*
Socialist Appeal	*SA*
Socialist Call	*SC*
Socialist Review	*SR*
World Tomorrow	*WT*

Manuscript Collections

Algernon Lee Papers	AL Papers
B. C. Vladeck Papers	BCV Papers
James Oneal Papers	JO Papers
Morris Hillquit Papers, Tamiment	MH Papers, Tamiment
Morris Hillquit Papers, Wisconsin Historical	MH Papers, Wisconsin
Norman Thomas Papers	NT Papers
Oral History Collection, Columbia	OH Columbia
Social Democratic Federation Papers, Tamiment	SDF Papers, Tamiment
Socialist Party Papers, Duke	SP Papers, Duke
Socialist Party Papers, Tamiment	SP Papers, Tamiment

Introduction

1. Devere Allen, "The Conquest of Democracy," *ASQ* (March, 1935), p. 4.

2. David Shannon, *The Socialist Party of America* (New York, 1967), pp. 258–260; Arthur M. Schlesinger, Jr., *The Vital Center* (Boston, 1962), p. 165; Daniel Bell, *The End of Ideology* (New York, 1962), p. 121.

3. Harry Fleischman, *Norman Thomas* (New York, 1964), p. 245; Murray B. Seidler, *Norman Thomas: Respectable Radical* (Syracuse, 1961), pp. 295–296; Bernard Johnpoll, *Pacifist's Progress* (Chicago, 1970), pp. 177, 286–293.

Chapter I The Realist Critique Examined

1. Shannon, *The Socialist Party of America,* pp. 182–256.

2. Bell, *The End of Ideology,* pp. 279–282; Schlesinger, *The Vital Center, passim;* Arthur M. Schlesinger, Jr., *A Thousand Days* (New York, 1967), pp. 679–680; Johnpoll, pp. 250, 289. I am not concerned here with whether Bell has misinterpreted Max Weber's meaning and position in order to develop his thesis. A cogent criticism of Bell's use of Weber has been made by Stephen W. Rousseas and James Farganis in "American Politics and the End of Ideology," in Chaim I. Waxman, ed., *The End of Ideology Debate* (New York, 1968), pp. 209–212.

3. I believe that Bell exaggerates the chiliastic overtones in modern American Socialism. Part of this is a result of his equating chiliasm with ideology, an equation that requires more criticism than it has been given. See Ludwig Mahler, "Ideology and History," *New Politics* (Fall, 1961), pp. 133–134. In my work, I have tried to meet Bell on his own terms.

4. William McLoughlin, "Pietism and the American Character," *American Quarterly* (Summer, 1965), p. 176.

5. Quoted in Jacob Cohen, "Schlesinger and the New Deal," *Dissent* (Autumn, 1961), p. 467; Arthur M. Schlesinger, Jr., *The Politics of Upheaval* (Boston, 1960), p. 155. In criticizing *ad hoc* liberal reformism, Dewey wrote: "But 'reforms' that deal now with this abuse and now with that without having a social goal based upon an inclusive plan, differ entirely from effort at re-forming, in its literal sense, the institutional scheme of things." See John Dewey, *Liberalism and Social Action* (New York, 1963), p. 62.

6. David Potter, *People of Plenty* (Chicago, 1954), p. 122.

7. In *Why Is There No Socialism in the United States,* Werner Som-

bart wrote of the American worker and socialism: "On the reefs of roast beef and apple-pie socialistic Utopias of every sort are sent to their doom." Quoted in Goetz A. Briefs, *The Proletariat* (New York, 1937), p. 193; Johnpoll, p. 290; Oneal to Comrade Lewis, November 30, 1940 (in JO Papers); Oneal to Algernon Lee, March 15, 1940; Oneal to Lee, March 27, 1940; Oneal to Lee, April 16, 1940 (in AL Papers).

8. Johnpoll, p. 82.

9. Louis Waldman to Thomas, June 9, 1934; Louis Hendin to National Executive Committee, June, 1934; James Oneal to Harold Kelso, July 7, 1934; Herbert M. Merrill, Minutes of Joint Meeting of State Executive and New York City Members of the State Committee, September 18, 1934; Sarah Limbach to Thomas, December 8, 1934; Oneal to Clarence Senior, March 4, 1935 (in NT Papers); *The Crisis in the Socialist Party* (New York, 1934), pp. 3–8 (in SDF Papers, Tamiment); Robert Hoffman to Sam Friedman, May 14, 1936 (in SP Papers, Duke); David Shub, "Why Socialists Are against a United Front with the Communists," *NL* (November 23, 1935), pp. 9–12; *NL* (November 30, 1935), pp. 4, 6; Oneal, *NL* (November 17, 1934), p. 5; Oneal, *NL* (April 6, 1935), p. 9; Oneal, *NL* (April 20, 1935), p. 6; Oneal, *NL* (July 13, 1935), p. 7; Thomas to Socialist Party Meeting, September 6, 1934; Thomas, draft of a letter for Max Delson and Amicus Most, September 17, 1934; Thomas to Don Sweetland, December 12, 1934; to Dr. Anderson, January 11, 1935; to *Herald Tribune*, March 26, 1935; to Florence Bowers, August 9, 1934; to National Executive Committee, October 22, 1934; Thomas, Memorandum on Problem before N.E.C., 1934; Thomas to Members of the New York State Committee, November 7, 1934; to Daniel, Hapgood, Hoan, Hoopes, Krueger, Krzycki, August 17, 1934; to Francis Henson, December 6, 1934; to J. B. Matthews, December 14, 1934; to Dan Hoan, January 21, 1935; to Mary [Fox] and Harry [Laidler], November 21, 1934; Thomas, Memorandum on the RPC, December, 1934; Thomas to Richard B. Whitten, January 24, 1935; to Robert Hoffman, January 26, 1935, to Ernest Baumann, January 30, 1935, to Francis Henson, October 24, 1934, to Senior, January 22, 1935 (in NT Papers): Thomas, "What Happened in Detroit," *WT* (June 28, 1934), pp. 320–323; Thomas, *After the New Deal, What?* (New York, 1936), pp. 217–221. The phrases "romantic parliamentarism" and "romantic revolutionism" were Reinhold Niebuhr's. See Niebuhr to Thomas, December 11, 1934 (in NT Papers).

10. For Thomas's strong criticism of the Revolutionary Policy Committee, see Thomas, Memorandum on the RPC, December, 1934 (in NT Papers): Thomas, *NL* (January 27, 1934), p. 8. For Thomas's posi-

tion on the Browder-Thomas Madison Square Garden Debate, see Thomas to Julius Gerber, October 8, 1935, to *Jewish Daily Forward,* November, 1935 (in NT Papers). For Militant pressure for "no compromise" with the Old Guard and speedier N.E.C. action against the Old Guard, see Paul Porter to Thomas, 1934; Amicus Most to Thomas, 1934; Max Delson to Thomas, May 29, 1935; Aaron Levenstein to Thomas, May 29, 1935; Levi Tonks to Thomas, June 8, 1935 (in NT Papers); Jack Altman to John B. Wheelwright, February 14, 1936 (in SP Papers, Duke). For Old Guard personal backbiting against Thomas, see Hillquit to Oneal, July 10, 1931 (in JO Papers); James Maurer to Algernon Lee, January 9, 1936; William Feigenbaum to Lee, March 24, 1936; to Lee, 1936 (in AL Papers).

11. Daniel Bell, *Marxian Socialism in the United States* (Princeton, 1967), p. 189; Johnpoll, pp. 77, 126, 130, 177, 292. In analyzing why Thomas supported the Declaration of Principles, Johnpoll attributes this largely to his "commitments to the young intellectuals, who he feared would abandon the party if the Socialists did not 'revolutionize.' " He had to prove to them that the Party hadn't become "too flabby." Johnpoll, p. 126; Florence Bowers to Edward J. Meeman, August 8, 1934 (in NT Papers). Clearly Thomas was fearful of losing young radicals if the Socialist Party did not develop a militant approach. However, to say that he supported the Declaration largely because of this fear misses the fact that there was nothing in the Declaration to which, in the critical world situation of 1934, Thomas could not subscribe. Johnpoll sees much of the Declaration as parroting the "bombastic pseudo-revolutionary rhetoric of the Militants and the Revolutionary Policy Committee" (p. 126). But, as James Weinstein has pointed out, the Declaration was milder than what Hillquit had written before and during World War I. See James Weinstein, *The Decline of Socialism in America* (New York, 1967), p. 338. In 1921, Hillquit had written of democracy under capitalism in much the same way as the Militants, who condemned it as "bogus democracy." Hillquit wrote: "In a capitalist regime the whole machinery of democracy operates to keep the ruling-class minority in power through the suffrage of the working-class majority, and when the bourgeois government feels itself endangered by democratic institutions, such institutions are often crushed without compunction. . . . Democracy does not secure 'equal rights and a share in all political rights for everybody, to whatever class or party he may belong.' It only allows free political and legal play for the existing economic inequalities. The democracy of every social regime is adjusted to the purpose of maintaining the regime. Democracy under capitalism

is thus not general, abstract democracy, but specific *bourgeois democracy,* a democracy within the bourgeoisie or as Lenin terms it—democracy for the bourgeoisie." See Morris Hillquit, *From Marx to Lenin* (New York, 1921), pp. 58–59. The rhetoric of the Declaration is explained more by the depression and the rise of fascism than by Thomas's needs for keeping his admiring youth. For Thomas's discussions with young radicals, see Biemiller to Thomas, September 12, 1933; Thomas to Biemiller, September 14, 1933; Most to J. B. Matthews, September 21, 1933; to Thomas, September 30, 1933; Thomas to Most, October 5, 1933; Porter to Thomas, January 28, 1934; Thomas to Porter, January 30, 1934 (in NT Papers).

12. Johnpoll, p. 77. For Thomas's position on an "inclusive" party, see, e.g., Thomas to *Jewish Daily Forward,* November 19, 1935 (in NT Papers). The issue of an "inclusive" party would continue into the latter half of the 1930's, where it would largely revolve around the question of the Trotskyist faction within the Socialist Party. See Thomas to Glen Trimble, January 21, 1937 (in NT Papers).

13. Louis Sadoff to Thomas, February 26, 1941 (in NT Papers). Sadoff, along with Mary Hunter and Jack Sullivan, were "Centrists" in the inner party struggle. But they were loyal supporters of Thomas. See Mary [Hunter] to Senior, January, 1935; Mary [Hunter] to Clarence [Senior], June, 1935; Jack Sullivan to Senior, Krueger, Biemiller, and Paul Porter, November 25, 1935 (in SP Papers, Duke). For Socialist criticisms of German Social Democracy, see, e.g., Haim Kantorovitch, "The German Tragedy," *ASQ* (Summer, 1933), pp. 3–13; David Berenberg, review of Calvin Hoover's *Germany Enters the Third Reich, ASQ* (Summer, 1933), pp. 62–64; Thomas to Kenneth Gordon, December 6, 1933 (in NT Papers); Thomas, "Along the Class-Struggle Front," *WT* (September 28, 1933), pp. 537–538. For the Revolutionary Policy Committee's positions on issues, see Revolutionary Policy Committee, *An Appeal to the Membership of the Socialist Party* (April, 1934), pp. 1–12; "Vote 'Yes'," pp. 1–5 (in SP Papers, Tamiment); Bulletin of the Revolutionary Policy Committee, September 20, 1934; Resolution in Favor of the United Front, August 23–25, 1935; Hal Draper, "Statement to State Committee of New York State," October 22, 1934; Statement of RPC, Buffalo Local of the Socialist Party, January 14, 1935 (in NT Papers); "Why the RSR?" *RSR* (November, 1934), pp. 3–4; "On the N.E.C." *RSR* (Summer, 1935), pp. 5–6. For Thomas's conception of the Declaration as a warning, see, e.g., Thomas to Dr. Anderson, January 11, 1935 (in NT Papers); Thomas, *After the New Deal, What?* p. 221. Thomas emphasized that the nonparliamentary

aspects of the Declaration only applied to a situation of complete collapse. And he stressed that the nonparliamentary aspects should not receive the main emphasis in discussing possible means of "transferring power." See, e.g., Thomas to Eric Ross, July 26, 1934 (in NT Papers).

14. Louis Hendin to National Executive Committee, June, 1934 (in NT Papers). For Old Guard defenses of the German Social Democrats, see S. Lipschitz to *NL* (February 11, 1933), p. 10; *NL* (May 6, 1933), p. 10; Oneal, *NL* (June 9, 1934), p. 5. For criticisms of the German Communists, see, e.g., Herman Kobbé, "The Role Played in the Crisis by the German Communists," *NL* (March 11, 1933), p. 3.

15. The debate over the Declaration can be followed weekly in the *New Leader* between June and October, 1934. In addition, for the Militant support of the war sections of the Declaration, see David Berenberg, "Socialism and War," *ASQ* (Autumn, 1934), pp. 43–52; Devere Allen, "Why the Declaration Must Pass," *WT* (June 28, 1934); pp. 323–326. For the Old Guard fears about the war sections, see, e.g., *The Crisis in the Socialist Party* (New York, 1934), pp. 4–5 (in SDF Papers, Tamiment).

16. *The Crisis in the Socialist Party*, pp. 5–8 (in SDF Papers, Tamiment); Oneal, *NL* (July 7, 1934), p. 7; Oneal, *NL* (August 4, 1934), p. 7; Andrew Biemiller, "Socialism and Democracy," *ASQ* (Spring, 1934), pp. 20–28; Thomas, "What Happened in Detroit," *WT* (June 28, 1934), p. 12; Thomas, *NL* (July 7, 1934), p. 12; Thomas to George Mahela, July 10, 1934; to *New York Times,* November 2, 1934 (in NT Papers); Haim Kantorovitch, "Is This Militancy?" *ASQ* (April, 1932), pp. 37–43.

17. For the Old Guard's belief that the Declaration would further alienate labor from the Socialist Party, see, e.g., Louis Hendin to N.E.C., June, 1934; B. C. Vladeck to Thomas, June 14, 1934 (in NT Papers). For Thomas's disillusionment with the New York Old Guard leadership, largely as a result of its actions—or inactions—in the labor movement, see, e.g., Thomas to George Steinhardt, July 21, 1933 (in NT Papers).

Chapter II The Socialist Party and the Labor Unions

1. Shannon, pp. 173–181, 210, 261–262. For Socialist criticism of the role of the A. F. of L. in the 1924 campaign, see the remarks of Hillquit in *Should the Workers Form a Political Party of Their Own?* (New York, 1932), p. 25.

2. On the "third period" dual-union policy of the Communists, see

Irving Howe and Lewis Coser, *The American Communist Party* (New York, 1957), pp. 236–272.

3. Johnpoll, pp. 74–75; *NL* (January 12, 1929), p. 1; *NL* (January 19, 1929), p. 1; Thomas, *NL* (January 26, 1929), p. 8; Hillquit, "A. F. of L. Incredibly Reactionary," *NL* (March 9, 1929), p. 3; A. J. Muste, "Socialism and Progressive Trade Unionism," *NL* (April 6, 1929), p. 4; A. J. Muste and Louis Stanley, "C.P.L.A. Before Two Labor Bodies," *NL* (July 20, 1929), p. 3; Oneal, "Socialism and Progressive Unionism," *NL* (June 14, 1930), p. 4.

4. Oneal, "The Case for a Labor Party Here," *NL* (August 17, 1929), p. 4; Hillquit, "The Paradox of American Labor," *NL* (July 25, 1931), p. 8; *NL* (July 30, 1932), p. 1; Louis Waldman, "Socialist Party Support Goes to Labor Everywhere," *NL* (September 3, 1932), p. 5; *NL* (November 26, 1932), p. 3; Hillquit, "American Labor on the March," *NL* (November 26, 1932), p. 3.

5. James Oneal, "The American Trade Union Movement," *ASQ* (Winter, 1933), pp. 12–22; *NL* (May 3, 1930), pp. 1, 7; *NL* (July 9, 1932), p. 5.

6. Oneal, "The American Trade Union Movement," pp. 14–16.

7. *NL* (January 3, 1931), pp. 1–2; Oneal, "The American Trade Union Movement," pp. 12–22; Oneal to *NL* (December 3, 1932), p. 10; Oneal to *NL* (October 8, 1932), p. 10.

8. Oneal, "The American Trade Union Movement," pp. 20–22.

9. *NL* (July 30, 1932), p. 1; *NL* (September 10, 1932), p. 2; Oneal to *NL* (December 3, 1932), p. 10; *NL* (December 3, 1932), pp. 1, 7; Hillquit, "American Labor on the March," *NL* (November 26, 1932), p. 3; Oneal, *NL* (September 22, 1934), p. 5; Oneal, "Industrial Form of Unions Is Needed," *NL* (September 29, 1934), pp. 1, 8; *NL* (October 21, 1933), p. 3.

10. Powers Hapgood, "The Socialist Party and the Labor Movement," *ASQ* (Summer, 1933), pp. 37–44; Jack Altman, "Socialists in the Trade Unions," *ASQ* (March, 1935), pp. 14–25; *NL* (January 3, 1931), pp. 1–2; Murray Gross to the *NL* (June 6, 1931), p. 8; Paul Porter to *NL* (October 8, 1932), p. 10; Murray Baron to *NL* (December 3, 1932), p. 10; Thomas, *NL* (October 21, 1933), p. 8.

11. *NL* (May 3, 1930), pp. 1, 7; *NL* (January 3, 1931), pp. 1–2; Hapgood, "The Socialist Party and the Labor Movement," pp. 37–44; Altman, "Socialists in the Trade Unions," pp. 14–25; Haim Kantorovitch, "The Socialist Party and the Trade Unions," *ASQ* (November, 1935), pp. 34–44.

12. Julius Gerber to *NL* (February 20, 1932), p. 6; Kantorovitch, "The Socialist Party and the Trade Unions," pp. 39–40, 42.

13. Kantorovitch, "The Socialist Party and the Trade Unions," pp. 40–44.

14. Thomas to Julius Gerber, September 29, 1933, to B. C. Vladeck, January 10, 1935 (in NT Papers). See also Thomas to Nathan Ratner, October 31, 1934 (in NT Papers).

15. Thomas to *NL* (October 24, 1931), p. 8, to Senior, November 14, 1933, to Labor Committee, New York Local, May 9, 1934 (in NT Papers). For Thomas's criticism of the Old Guard role in the fur industry, see, e.g., *Memorandum on the Situation in the Fur Industry,* June 14, 1933; Thomas to George Steinhardt, July 21, 1933; to Labor Committee, New York Local, September 11, 1933; to Secretaries of Branches, September 7, 1933; to David Kaplan, September 21, 1933 (in NT Papers); Thomas, *NL* (December 2, 1933), p. 12; Thomas, *NL* (December 23, 1933), p. 8. For Thomas's complaints on the Old Guard's inaction investigating charges against Hyman Nemser, a Socialist accused of union racketeering, see Thomas to Irwin Nussbaum, September 24, 1935, to Nussbaum, October 8, 1935 (in NT Papers).

16. Thomas, *NL* (September 5, 1931), p. 1; Thomas, *NL* (October 7, 1933), p. 8; Thomas, *NL* (October 21, 1933), p. 8; Thomas, *NL* (September 29, 1934), p. 8; Thomas, *NL* (October 6, 1934), p. 12; Thomas, *NL* (July 28, 1934), p. 12; Thomas, *NL* (July 30, 1932), p. 12; Thomas, *NL* (December 3, 1932), p. 16; Thomas, *NL* (September 23, 1933), p. 8; Thomas to Alton Lawrence, October 23, 1934 (in NT Papers); Thomas, *America's Way Out* (New York, 1931), pp. 263–277; Thomas, *The Choice Before Us* (New York, 1934), pp. 131–141. For Thomas's criticism of the Old Guard's "blind support" of the A.F. of L. leaders, see Thomas to George Steinhardt, July 21, 1933 (in NT Papers).

17. The Socialist Party has adopted a policy of placating the A.F. of L.-C.I.O. officialdom. The efforts can be followed in *New America* over the past eight years. Frequent socialist criticism of labor's officialdom can be found in *New Politics* over the past twelve years.

18. Johnpoll, p. 154.

19. Thomas to Labor Committee, New York Local Socialist Party, May 9, 1934 (in NT Papers). Thomas was opposed on "principle" to one union group using an injunction against another group. But he was also concerned about its negative impact (as in the Furrier's Union

case) on the development of the Socialist movement. See Thomas to
George Steinhardt, July 21, 1933 (in NT Papers).

Chapter III The Moral and the Practical

1. Thomas to E. Marshall Bush, June 18, 1934, to James H. Bailey,
August 9, 1934. Thomas connected his fight against the Old Guard
with the need to develop the kind of dynamic Socialist Party that could
take advantage of the possibility of a national Farmer-Labor Party—a
possibility that Thomas hoped for, but did not foresee before the 1936
presidential election. See Thomas to Dan Hoan, October 30, 1935, to
Alfred Baker Lewis, December 14, 1935 (in NT Papers). On Thomas's
feeling, after the 1938 elections, that the role of the Socialist Party in
the future would be educational in mass organizations, rather than
electoral, see Thomas, "Our Party's Future," *SC* (December 24, 1938),
p. 4; Thomas to Elliott Herman, November 26, 1938, to William Hollister, November 30, 1938 (in NT Papers).

2. For left-wing criticism of an all-inclusive party, see Haim Kantorovitch, "Some Notes on an All-Inclusive Party," *ASM* (December,
1936), pp. 14–16; Lillian Symes, "The Socialist Party Faces the
Future," *ASM* (February, 1937), pp. 11–15. For Thomas's desire for
an inclusive party, see Thomas to *Jewish Daily Forward,* November 19,
1935 (in NT Papers). For Thomas's fears of Trotskyist sectarianism in
an inclusive party, see Thomas to Lillian Symes, February 3, 1937 (in
NT Papers). On the Commonwealth Plan, see Paul Porter, *America for
All: The Commonwealth Plan* (Chicago, 1934), pp. 1–29; Thomas to
Porter, August 28, 1934 (in NT Papers). On the Washington Bureau,
see Thomas to Mary Fox, December 27, 1934; to Clarence Senior,
December 4, 1936; to Porter, January 21, 1937 (in NT Papers). On
the Workers Rights Amendment, see "Thomas Challenges Opponents
on Constitutional Amendment," *SC* (September 19, 1936), p. 2.
Thomas also urged Socialist Party delegates to stress the Workers
Rights Amendment in the abortive Communist-organized Workers
Rights Congress. See Thomas to Senior, March 2, 1936 (in NT
Papers). On the Non-Partisan Labor Defense Committee and the Work-
ers' Defense League, see "Provisional Committee for Non-Partisan
Labor Defense," 1934; Thomas to Herbert Solow, May 5, 1934; Report
of the Sub-Committee on the Workers' Defense League to the N.E.C.,
July 12, 1936; Thomas to Maynard Krueger, August 3, 1936 (in NT
Papers). On Upton Sinclair, see Thomas to Sinclair, September 27,

1933, to Sinclair, May 1, 1934; Sam White to Senior, September 17, 1934 (in NT Papers). Thomas also feared that Socialist support of Sinclair would set a precedent for similar actions in other states. The Socialist Party then would be caught in a fatal crossfire from the Right, by those who wanted to imitate Sinclair's tactics, and from the Left, by the Communists "who at least stick by their guns." See Thomas to A. Alan Clark, September 13, 1934 (in NT Papers).

3. Oneal to *NL* (October 8, 1932), p. 10; *NL* (January 3, 1931), pp. 1–2; Oneal to Jack, July 21, 1931 (in JO Papers); Shannon, p. 210; Harry Fleischman, *Norman Thomas* (New York, 1964), pp. 167–168; Norman Thomas, Memorandum, 1936 (in NT Papers).

4. Johnpoll, pp. 79–80. For a selection of Thomas's views on Russia, both sympathetic and critical, see Thomas, *NL* (January 11, 1930), p. 1; Thomas, *NL* (November 22, 1930), p. 1; Thomas, *NL* (November 29, 1930), p. 8; Thomas, *NL* (December 13, 1930), p. 1; Thomas, *NL* (December 20, 1930), p. 1; Thomas, *NL* (September 5, 1931), p. 1; Thomas, *NL* (December 15, 1934), p. 8; *NL* (February 7, 1931), pp. 1–2; Thomas to J. Bornstein, June 29, 1934; to Robert Potter, December 19, 1934; to John E. Geary, January 4, 1935; to William Raoul, January 10, 1935 (in NT Papers); Thomas, *America's Way Out* (New York, 1931), pp. 70–96; Thomas, *The Choice Before Us* (New York, 1934), pp. 67–68. On Thomas's fears that a too hostile attitude toward Russia would alienate those whom the Socialists were trying to reach and thus hurt the Party, see Thomas, *NL* (March 5, 1932), p. 16; Thomas to *NL* (April 9, 1932), p. 6. For a similar fear that a rejection of his debate with Browder would hurt the Party in the eyes of its younger members, see Thomas to Julius Gerber, October 8, 1935 (in NT Papers). On the other hand, Thomas also felt that a too indulgent Socialist expression of sympathy for Russia would alienate the "average man." See Thomas to Senior, November 24, 1933 (in NT Papers).

5. For Thomas's views on the Moscow Trials, see Thomas to Leon Despres, August 28, 1936; to Harry M. Wynn, September 2, 1936; to L. Kruhe, September 1, 1936; to Aaron Levenstein, September 1, 1936; to Inquiring Comrades, September 3, 1936; to Hildegard Smith, September 23, 1936; to Dagobert D. Runes, November 18, 1936; to Comrade Joslin, December 4, 1936; Socialist Party Office Release, January 21, 1937 (in NT Papers); Thomas, *SC* (August 22, 1936), p. 2; Thomas, *SC* (August 29, 1936), p. 6; Thomas, *SC* (September 5, 1936), p. 9; Thomas, *SC* (January 30, 1937), p. 12; Thomas, *SC* (February 6, 1937), p. 12; Thomas, *SC* (February 13, 1937), p. 7. On Thomas's feeling that Trotsky's criticism of the Stalin bureaucracy

was increasingly valid, see Thomas to William Raoul, January 10, 1935 (in NT Papers). For Thomas's criticism of Eastman, see Thomas to George Novack, December 18, 1936; to Felix Morrow, January 27, 1937; to Robert G. Spivak, February 2, 1937 (in NT Papers). For criticism of Thomas by those who were convinced of the defendants' innocence, see Gus Tyler to Thomas, August 28, 1936; Harry M. Wynn to Thomas, August 27, 1936; Rae Spiegel to Thomas, August 29, 1936; David T. Burbank to Thomas, September 1, 1936 (in NT Papers). For stronger printed views than Thomas's, see *SC* (September 5, 1936), p. 4; Gus Tyler, "Soviet-American Diplomacy behind the New Soviet Trials," *SC* (January 30, 1937), pp. 2, 8; Jack Altman, "People's Front and the Moscow Trials," *SC* (January 30, 1937), p. 4; Herbert Zam, "World Socialism: the Moscow Trial," *SC* (February 6, 1937), p. 5. For Lewis's and Senior's views, see Lewis to Thomas, January 27, 1937; Lewis to Thomas, 1937; Senior, "Memorandum on Trotskyites in the Socialist Party," January 25, 1937 (in NT Papers). Senior demanded that Max Schactman be expelled from the Socialist Party for his pamphlet, *Behind the Moscow Trials*. Senior said it called for assassination of Soviet leaders.

6. Alfred Baker Lewis to *NL* (January 31, 1931), p. 8; Algernon Lee to *NL* (February 21, 1931), p. 8; Hillquit to *NL* (December 6, 1930), p. 8; Oneal, *Socialism versus Bolshevism* (New York, 1935), pp. 5–18; Oneal, "The Economics of Bolshevism," *NL* (June 20, 1931), p. 4; Karl Kautsky, "The Bolshevik Dromedary," *NL* (October 24, 1931) p. 4; (October 31, 1931), p. 4; Bela Low, "Socialism and the Russian Bolshevik Government," *NL* (February 14, 1931), p. 4; Low, "Can Bolshevism Bring about Socialism?" *NL* (February 21, 1931), p. 4. In the early 1920's Hillquit had not been so certain that Russia couldn't "leap" an historical phase. In *From Marx to Lenin* (New York, 1921), p. 124, he noted the "precarious nature" of any such "leap," and wrote that the Russians had paid a "heavy penalty" for its "youthful enthusiasm." Now, he continued, it was making a new and more difficult start "at more realistic beginnings." However, despite portraying the difficulties of the task, Hillquit did not treat the leap as foredoomed to failure. Indeed, the front cover of the book contained Lenin's quote before the Second Congress of the Communist International: "We must abandon scientific prejudices that each country must absolutely pass through capitalist exploitation."

7. Paul Porter to *NL* (February 21, 1931), p. 8; Paul Blanshard to *NL* (September 19, 1931), p. 4; Theodore Shapiro, "The 'Militant' Point of View," *ASQ* (April 15, 1932), pp. 29–37; Algernon Lee to

NL (September 26, 1931), p. 4; Louis Hendin to N.E.C., June, 1934 (in NT Papers).

8. For Trotskyist and Clarity criticisms of the Spanish Popular Front government and/or the Socialist Party's Spanish policy, see George M. Whiteside to Thomas, September 16, 1936; to Dear Comrade, November 6, 1936 (in NT Papers); John Newton Thurber, "People's Front Tried and Found Wanting," *ASM* (October, 1936), pp. 19–23; Ernest Erber, "Spain: New Outpost of World Revolution," *ASM* (December, 1936), pp. 17–20; Max Schactman, "Towards a Revolutionary Socialist Party," *ASM* (May, 1937), pp. 13–18. For Thomas's "mixed" attitude toward the Spanish Popular Front, see Thomas, *Socialism on the Defensive* (New York, 1938), pp. 119–145. For Thomas's desire not to let attitudes toward the Spanish question determine basic Socialist policy in the United States, see Thomas to St. Louis Local, July 27, 1937 (in NT Papers). For Thomas's discouragement with trends in Spain, see Thomas, *SC* (January 30, 1937), p. 12; Thomas to Friedrich Adler, November 29, 1937 (in NT Papers).

9. Thomas, *SC* (June 12, 1937), p. 3; Thomas, *SC* (June 19, 1937), p. 8; Thomas, *Socialism on the Defensive,* pp. 136–142; Thomas to Fernando de los Rios, November 8, 1937; to Fernando de los Rios, November 18, 1937 (in NT Papers). On Thomas's desire not to have the American Socialist Party get involved in the internecine fights between Spanish anti-Fascists, see Thomas to N.E.C., June 25, 1937 (in NT Papers).

10. Thomas to Hon. Fernando de los Rios, November 8, 1937; Louis de Brouckère to Señor Juan Negrin, November 12, 1937; Sam Baron to the Socialist Party of the United States (two letters), November 19, 1938 (in NT Papers). Baron and Liston Oak published a series of articles on the Stalinist purges in Spain in the *SC* during 1938. Loeb resigned from the editorial board of the *Socialist Review* in protest over its printing an article by Baron. See James Loeb to Herbert Zam, November 8, 1938 (in NT Papers). For Zam's reply, see Zam to Roy Burt, November 9, 1938 (in NT Papers). For Clarity's view of the Baron affair, see Travers Clement to Thomas, December 2, 1938 (in NT Papers). For Thomas's views, see Thomas, *SC* (December 3, 1938), p. 4; Thomas to Roy Burt, November 29, 1938; to Central Committee, Local, New York, November 28, 1938; to Lillian Symes, December 19, 1938; to the Members of the Grievance Committee, Local New York, November 25, 1938; to Burt, November 25, 1938 (in NT Papers). For protests against the Party's repudiation of Baron's facts, see Charles C. Schleicher to Thomas, November 25, 1938; to

Thomas, December 9, 1938 (in NT Papers). For Thomas's reply, see Thomas to Schleicher, November 30, 1938; to Schleicher, December 13, 1938 (in NT Papers).

11. Thomas to the Central Committee, Local, New York (December 28, 1938); to Roy Burt, November 29, 1938; Liston Oak to Sam Baron, November 26, 1938 (in NT Papers). Thomas liked Oak's letter. See Thomas to Oak, November 28, 1938 (in NT Papers). The *SC* also criticized Baron's decision to testify. See *SC* (December 3, 1938), p. 4. The Spanish ambassador had been disturbed by Baron's remarks after he was freed from prison. See Fernando de los Rios to Thomas, November 16, 1937 (in NT Papers). For Thomas's reply, see Thomas to Fernando de los Rios, November 18, 1937 (in NT Papers).

12. For the Popular Front liberals' attitude toward the anti-Stalinist purges in Spain, see Frank A. Warren, *Liberals and Communism* (Bloomington, Ind., 1966), pp. 131–142. Thomas to Hon. Fernando de los Rios, November 8, 1937; to Sr. Ramon Gonzales Pena, 1938 (in NT Papers); Thomas, *Socialism on the Defensive,* pp. 138–139; Thomas, *SC* (November 26, 1937), p. 4.

13. Bell, *The End of Ideology,* pp. 287–288.

14. Ibid., pp. 278–279, 292.

15. Ibid., p. 121.

16. Ibid., pp. 121, 292; Woodrow Wilson, *The New Freedom* (Englewood Cliffs, New Jersey, 1961), p. 109.

Chapter IV Theoretical Strategies

1. Norman Pollack, *The Populist Response to Industrial America* (New York, 1962), *passim;* Ludwig Mahler, "Ideology and History," *New Politics* (Fall, 1961), p. 134. James Loeb, a former Socialist, became the first executive secretary of the Union for Democratic Action. Among the other former Socialist Party members of the Executive and Sponsoring Committee of the U.D.A. were Jack Altman, Albert Sprague Coolidge, Franz Daniel, Francis Henson, Alfred Baker Lewis, Paul Porter, Reinhold Niebuhr, Murray Gross, Lazar Becker, Daniel Bell, Andrew Biemiller, Frank Crosswaith, Arthur G. Mc-Dowell, H. L. Mitchell, Rose Stien, and Monroe Sweetland. See James Loeb to Thomas, September 18, 1941 (in NT Papers).

2. Thomas's main works in the 1930's were *America's Way Out* (New York, 1931), *The Choice Before Us* (New York, 1934), *After the New Deal, What?* (New York, 1936), and *Socialism on the Defensive* (New York, 1938). Corey's two large works are *The Decline*

of American Capitalism (New York, 1934) and *The Crisis of the Middle Class* (New York, 1935).

3. Alfred Bingham, *Insurgent America* (New York, 1935), *passim.*

4. Ibid., pp. 11–43.

5. Ibid., pp. 47–64.

6. Ibid., pp. 65–77.

7. One of the more persistent demands to Americanize Marx was made in the mid-thirties by the independent radical, V. F. Calverton. See Calverton, "The Wind Before the Storm," *MM* (February, 1935), pp. 709–711; Calverton, "Father Coughlin: The Silver Messiah," *MM* (March, 1935), pp. 5–12, 18; Calverton, "In the Name of Marxism," *MM* (April, 1935), pp. 69–70; Calverton, "It Can Happen Here," *MM* (December, 1935), pp. 374–375. In these articles Calverton discussed, in a suggestive manner, the lower middle-class psychology of Americans and the strength of the "Populist" tradition. However, his analysis remained rudimentary. And in another article, a year earlier, Calverton concluded that farm-dominated movements must inevitably turn toward fascism. Workers might make concessions to the farmers, but workers had to lead any radical movement. See Calverton, "The Farmer Cocks His Rifle," *MM* (January, 1934), pp. 726–731. Norman Thomas had been concerned, since the twenties, that the Socialist Party "speak the American language" and "deal with the American situation." But his analysis of what this entailed did not go much beyond warnings against depending on foreign socialist movements and against sectarianism. See Thomas, *NL* (November 14, 1925), pp. 1, 3; Thomas, *NL* (November 21, 1925), pp. 1–2; Thomas, *NL* (November 28, 1925), pp. 1–2.

8. Leon Samson, *The American Mind* (New York, 1932), passim.

9. Ibid., pp. 5–8.

10. Ibid., pp. 22, 161–162, 167.

11. Ibid., pp. 26, 211, 297–298, 301, 325–328.

12. Ibid., pp. vii, 281–284. In an article written in 1931, Morris Hillquit dealt briefly with Samson's paradox—the full development of the capitalist economy and the backwardness of the labor movement. Like Samson, he accepted the idea that the American economy was the most advanced capitalist economy. However, he attributed the weaknesses of the labor movement to the rapidity and recentness of this development; the working class had not yet had time to develop a class-conscious outlook. But, like most radicals in the depression-ridden 1930's, he felt that it was quickly developing one. Samson, however, did not see the recentness of the development as the main

problem; more time would not necessarily lead to greater class consciousness (though Samson did share with other radicals the belief that the eventual collapse of capitalism would force class consciousness onto the worker). See Hillquit, "The Paradox of American Labor," *NL* (July 25, 1931), p. 8. On the elitism of Albert Jay Nock, see Michael Wreszin, *The Superfluous Anarchist* (Providence, R.I., 1972), pp. 118–120.

13. Leon Samson, *Toward a United Front: A Philosophy for American Workers* (New York, 1934), pp. ix–xii, 3–103.

14. Ibid., pp. 1–15.

15. Ibid., p. 16.

16. Ibid., pp. 16–17.

17. Ibid., pp. 17–18.

18. Ibid., pp. 18–19.

19. Ibid., p. 21.

20. Ibid., p. 23.

21. Ibid., pp. 68–69.

22. Ibid., pp. 40–48, 55–56, 73–103, 168–184, 201–211.

23. Bingham, *Insurgent America,* pp. 78–81, 97; Samson, *The American Mind,* p. 54. Samson wrote: "Guaranteeism—one of the definitions of socialism—here takes on the form of family insurance."

24. Bingham, *Insurgent America,* pp. 104–105, 125, 177–179, 194–201.

25. Ibid., pp. 202–228; Samson, *Toward a United Front,* p. 211.

26. Samson, *Toward a United Front,* pp. 214, 244–245, 259.

27. Ibid., pp. 256–276.

Chapter V Parties

1. Norman Thomas was one of the organizers of the League for Independent Political Action in 1928—an organization of liberals and radicals which looked forward to becoming a third party. James Maurer was a vice-chairman of the L.I.P.A. And Devere Allen, Reinhold Niebuhr, Harry W. Laidler, and Thomas were executive members. See Johnpoll, p. 70; Shannon, *The Socialist Party of America,* p. 208. B. C. Vladeck was probably the most persistent spokesman in the Socialist Party for the formation of a third party. See *NL* (October 10, 1931), p. 4. For a statement in favor of Socialist cooperation with reform coalitions (but only if the Socialist Party was able to keep its organization intact), see Murray E. King, "Should Socialists Join a Reform Coalition?" *NL* (March 25, 1933), p. 4.

2. Thomas to Thomas Amlie, April 22, 1935, to James H. Bailey, August 1, 1934 (in NT Papers); Thomas, *America's Way Out,* pp. 287–291; Thomas, *The Choice Before Us,* pp. 229–232.

3. Johnpoll, pp. 70–73; B. C. Vladeck to Hillquit, June 24, 1932 (in BCV Papers); Murray Seidler, *Norman Thomas,* pp. 105–106; *NL* (January 3, 1931), pp. 1, 4; Oneal, *Some Pages from Party History* (New York, 1934), p. 10; *NL* (January 3, 1931), p. 2. For Thomas's own disagreements with the L.I.P.A., see Thomas to Hilda Busick, February 28, 1933; to Henry Weihofen, December 7, 1933 (in NT Papers).

4. For the Old Guard's earlier support of a labor party, see Oneal "The Case for a Labor Party Here," *NL* (August 17, 1929), p. 4. For Hillquit's belief that a labor party might not be necessary in the United States, see *NL* (October 10, 1931), p. 4. In a debate in 1932 with Matthew Woll, Hillquit argued that "the workers of America will be effective in their struggles for justice and liberty only if they are organized economically in an all-embracing and powerful union and politically in a party of their own, a Socialist party or a labor party, which is the same thing." See *Should the American Workers Form a Political Party of Their Own?* (New York, 1932), p. 18. For Old Guard and Militant criticism of "middle-class" radicalism that manifested itself in such groups as the L.I.P.A., see *NL* (January 3, 1931), p. 2. For a Marxist critique of the reformist trends in the Socialist Party, see Haim Kantorovitch, "The New Capitalism—and After," *ASQ* (January, 1932), pp. 17–32. Some of the Militants' stress on discipline was the result of a belief that party members should concentrate on building the Party. See Amicus Most to J. B. Matthews, September 21, 1933 (in NT Papers). Most wrote that a revolutionary movement required a political vehicle and that the Socialist Party could "through our effort become that vehicle in the near future." When the Conference for Progressive Labor Action moved to form a new third party, its Socialist members resigned. See *NL* (November 14, 1931), p. 3; *NL* (December 19, 1931), p. 2.

5. Daniel Hoan, George Hampel, Al Benson, and Andrew Biemiller to Thomas, April 10, 1934; Vladeck to Hoan, December 28, 1933; to Hoan, April 20, 1934; Minutes of the National Executive Committee, Socialist Party, Boston, Massachusetts, November 30-December 2, 1934 (in NT Papers); *NL* (October 10, 1931), p. 4; Hoan to Vladeck, April 27, 1934; Tom Duncan to Vladeck, March 4, 1934; to Vladeck, December 4, 1934; to Vladeck, August 7, 1935; Vladeck to Duncan, August 12, 1935 (in BCV Papers).

6. Vladeck to Hoan, December 28, 1933; to Hoan, April 20, 1934; Hoan, Hampel, Benson, and Biemiller to Thomas, April 10, 1934 (in NT Papers). Vladeck felt that his analysis had been borne out by the results of the 1934 Wisconsin elections, where the Progressives elected Phil LaFollette governor and the Socialists did not do well. See Vladeck to Hoan, September 26, 1934 (in BCV Papers).

7. Thomas to Vladeck, December 29, 1933, to Andy [Biemiller], March 14, 1934 (in NT Papers).

8. On the origins of the Wisconsin Farmer-Labor Progressive Federation and the Socialist participation in it, see Harry Laidler, *Toward a Farmer-Labor Party* (New York, 1938), pp. 25–30; Hoan and George Hampel to Dear Comrades, October, 1935; Hoan to N.E.C., May 14, 1936, to Thomas, October 2, 1936 (in NT Papers). The Socialists did run a candidate against Governor Phil LaFollette in 1938. See *SC* (August 6, 1938), p. 3. For Socialist criticism of Hoan in the 1940's, see Frank Zeidler to Al Hamilton, June 13, 1942. On Hoan's career after 1940, see Hoan to Thomas, September 3, 1940; Paul Porter to Thomas, September 4, 1940 (in NT Papers); Travers Clement, "Statement on Naming Hoan to Defense Board," *SC* (September 21, 1940), p. 5; Edward Kerstein, *Milwaukee's All-American Mayor* (Englewood Cliffs, New Jersey, 1966), pp. 200–205.

9. Thomas and Blanshard, *What's the Matter with New York,* (New York, 1932), *passim;* Oneal to Algernon Lee, June 26, 1931 (in JO Papers); Blanshard to Coleman B. Cheney, November 21, 1933 (in SP Papers, Duke); Thomas to the Editor, September 14, 1935 (in NT Papers); Thomas, "Along the Class-Struggle Front," *WT* (September 28, 1933), pp. 537–538. See also *WT* (September 28, 1933), pp. 531–532. Thomas was especially hurt by Blanshard's action. See Thomas to Blanshard, September 14, 1933, to Andrew Biemiller, September 14, 1933 (in NT Papers). For Thomas's request that other Socialists working for LaGuardia resign from the Party, see Thomas, Memorandum to Rosner, White, and Maslow, December 19, 1933 (in NT Papers).

10. P. W. Henderson to Thomas, September 17, 1934; E. Backus to Thomas, September 7, 1934; Jerry Voorhis to Thomas, April 2, 1934; Extracts from a letter of Katherine Cline, 1934; Anna H. Dalley to Cameron H. King, June 20, 1934 (in NT Papers).

11. Thomas to Sinclair, September 14, 1933; to Sinclair, September 27, 1933; to Sinclair, May 1, 1934; to *Christian Century* (October 1, 1934); to Jerry Voorhis, April 19, 1934; H. R. to Thomas, September 13, 1933 (in NT Papers); Thomas, *NL* (September 30, 1933), p. 8;

Thomas, *NL* (July 14, 1934), p. 8; Thomas, *NL* (September 29, 1934), p. 8; Thomas, *NL* (October 27, 1934), p. 8.

12. Oneal, *NL* (September 29, 1934), p. 5; Oneal, *NL* (October 6, 1934), p. 9; Oneal, *NL* (October 27, 1934), p. 5; Oneal, *Some Pages of Party History* (New York, 1935), pp. 3–5, 14–16; M. Shadid to Comrade Krzycki, November 14, 1934; Senior to Shadid, November 17, 1934; Shadid to Senior, November, 1934; Senior to Shadid, December 8, 1934; Siegfried Ameringer to Senior, December 10, 1934; Shadid to Senior, December 10, 1934; Senior to Shadid, December 15, 1934; Shadid to Senior, December 31, 1934; Senior to Shadid and Ameringer, January 3, 1935; Senior to Shadid, January 4, 1935 (in SP Papers, Duke); Senior to Thomas, October 9, 1934, to Thomas, October 17, 1934; Maynard Krueger to Thomas, October 25, 1934; Sam White to Senior, September 17, 1934; Executive Secretary, Local Buffalo, New York to National Executive Committee, October 30, 1934; Thomas to Ameringer, November 2, 1934; Ameringer to Thomas, November 3, 1934; Thomas to Ameringer, November 8, 1934; Ameringer to Thomas, November 19, 1934; Thomas to Ameringer, November 22, 1934; Ameringer to Thomas, December 7, 1934; Thomas to Ameringer, December 11, 1934; Ameringer to Thomas, December 16, 1934; Thomas to Ameringer, December 26, 1934; Ameringer to Thomas, December 27, 1934; Thomas to Ameringer, January 2, 1935 (in NT Papers). During his long correspondence with Ameringer, Thomas modified his original demand for Shadid's resignation because of the damage Ameringer said that a resignation would do to the Oklahoma Socialist Party. Thomas was willing to settle for an apology. However, Thomas never brought any pressure to bear on fellow members of the N.E.C., which meant that Shadid's resignation would be demanded. It is not impossible that Thomas really welcomed Shadid's resignation because his close friend, Devere Allen, would take the vacated place on the N.E.C., and that knowing his resignation was assured, Thomas decided to placate the Ameringers by modifying his personal position on the issue. This, however, must remain an undocumented supposition.

13. Thomas to the Meeting in Support of the Declaration of Principles, September 6, 1934; Ameringer to Thomas, November 3, 1934; Dempster to Senior, November 27, 1934; Thomas to Dempster, September 12, 1934 (in NT Papers). Thomas's letter to Dempster was confidential. Publicly, he wrote to Dempster and the California S.E.C. giving all the reasons for opposing Sinclair and running a Socialist candidate. See Thomas to Dempster and the State Executive Committee

of California, September 11, 1934 (in NT Papers). Dempster did not withdraw and destroyed Thomas's confidential letter. See Dempster to Thomas, September 17, 1934; Sam White to Senior, September 17, 1934 (in NT Papers).

14. On the origins of the American Labor Party, see Laidler, *Toward a Farmer-Labor Party,* pp. 36–39. On the Old Guard's reaction to the formation of the American Labor Party, see *NL* (July 18, 1936), pp. 1, 3; *NL* (July 25, 1936), pp. 1, 6; *NL* (August 8, 1936), pp. 1, 6. On the Old Guard's feeling that Thomas was turning the Party into a "liberal-reform" party, see, e.g., Oneal to Algernon Lee, July 17, 1931 (in MH Papers, Tamiment). On earlier Old Guard criticism of the New Deal, see, e.g., *NL* (March 24, 1934), p. 3-L; Aleck Miller, "Waldman Flays Richberg's Views on NRA," *NL* (February 24, 1934), p. 4A.

15. On the Social Democratic Federation's post-1936 support of the New Deal, see, e.g., Oneal, "Why Socialists in This Campaign Support President Roosevelt," *NL* (October 31, 1936), p. 5; Louis Goldberg, "The Road to Socialism: A Criticism of our Critics," *NL* (November 7, 1936), p. 5; *NL* (November 7, 1936), p. 8; Alexander Kahn, "Hillquit's Lifelong Struggle—Bears Fruit in New Deal Laws," *NL* (July 8, 1939), pp. 3, 7.

16. Thomas, *SC* (February 8, 1936), p. 12; *SC* (April 18, 1936), p. 4; *SC* (April 18, 1936), p. 6. See also Senior to Friedrich Adler, August 28, 1936; Thomas, "Why Labor Should Support the Socialist Party," *ASM* (July, 1936), pp. 3–7. Thomas wrote Daniel Hoan asking him to make clear in the campaign the difference between what the Wisconsin Socialists were doing in relation to the Wisconsin Farmer-Labor Progressive Federation and what the Old Guard Socialists were doing in New York by going into the A.L.P. and supporting Roosevelt. See Thomas to Hoan, September 23, 1936 (in NT Papers).

17. In addition to the Wisconsin Farmer-Labor Progressive Federation and the older Minnesota Farmer-Labor Party, there were incipient farmer-labor parties in Illinois, Iowa, and a number of other states. See Laidler, *Toward a Farmer-Labor Party,* pp. 19–30, 33–36. Moreover, the Communists were calling for a national farmer-labor party in the spring of 1936. See Howe and Coser, *The American Communist Party,* p. 329. Norman Thomas believed that any Communist lead in the formation of a hastily formed national farmer-labor party would only delay the emergence of a "real party." See Thomas, Memorandum to Paul Porter, January, 1936; to Spencer Kennard, April 22, 1936 (in NT Papers). For the position of Thomas and the Socialist Party on a

farmer-labor party in 1936, see Thomas, "May Day, 1936," *SC* (May 2, 1936), p. 24; Thomas, "Main Issue in the Campaign Is Capitalism or Socialism," *SC* (July 18, 1936), p. 12; Daniel Hoan, "Time Not Ripe for Farmer-Labor Party—Build Socialist Party in 1936 to Achieve Goal," *SC* (May 30, 1936), p. 8; *SC* (June 6, 1936), p. 2. For the left-wing Socialist and Trotskyist critique of farmer-labor and labor parties, see George M. Whiteside to Dear Comrade, November 6, 1936 (in NT Papers); James Burnham, "For a Revolutionary Socialist Party," *SA* (September, 1936), pp. 5–8; Carl Pemble, "On the Labor Party," *SA* (November 1, 1936), pp. 7–8; Gardner S. Wells, "California and the Farmer-Labor Party," *SA* (November 1, 1936), p. 8.

18. Thomas, "May Day, 1936," *SC* (May 2, 1936), p. 24.

19. Ibid.; *SC* (June 6, 1936), p. 2.

20. Thomas, "Main Issue in the Campaign Is Capitalism or Socialism," *SC* (July 18, 1936), p. 12.

21. *SC* (July 25, 1936), p. 4.

22. Thomas, "Speech on Labor's Non-Partisan League," *SC* (September 12, 1936), pp. 6–7; John Ball, "The Roosevelt 'Labor Party,' " *SC* (August 8, 1936), p. 7; *SC* (September 5, 1936), pp. 6–7.

23. *SC* (September 5, 1936), pp. 6–7.

24. Bell, *Marxian Socialism in the United States,* pp. 171–172; Paul Porter, *Which Way for the Socialist Party?* (Milwaukee, 1937), pp. 5–47; *ASM* (June, 1936), pp. 27–32; Max Delson and Herbert Zam, "For a Clean Socialist Campaign," *SR* (September, 1937), pp. 18–20; Gus Tyler, "For a United Revolutionary Party," *ASM* (May, 1937), pp. 18–22; Max Schactman, "Towards a Revolutionary Socialist Party," *ASM* (May, 1937), pp. 13–18; Carl Pemble, "Correction to the Porter Pamphlet," February 28, 1937; Pemble to Thomas, March 6, 1937 (in NT Papers); Schactman, "Prospects for a Labor Party," *SA* (January, 1937), pp. 15–16; Glen Trimble, "Should Socialists Build a Farmer-Labor Party?" *SA* (January, 1937), pp. 17–19; Tyler, "For a Labor Party," *SA* (August, 1936), pp. 4–5; James Burnham, "For a Revolutionary Socialist Party," *SA* (September, 1936), pp. 5–8; Pemble, "On the Labor Party," *SA* (November 1, 1936), pp. 7–8.

25. *SA* (August 14, 1937), pp. 2–8; Glen Trimble, "NEC Suspends California Charter," *SA* (August 21, 1937), pp. 1, 7; Max Schactman, "The Politics of Gus Tyler," *SA* (August 28, 1937), pp. 6–8; *SC* (August 21, 1937), p. 3; *SC* (August 21, 1937), p. 4; *SC* (September 11, 1937), p. 4; Al Hamilton, "Trotskyites Set Out on Sectarian Po-

litical Line," *SC* (September 11, 1937), p. 7; Trimble to All Revolutionary Socialists, July 8, 1937; Lillian Symes to Thomas, August 16, 1937; Frank Trager to Thomas, February 23, 1937; Senior to Thomas, March 19, 1937; Mary Fox to Senior, March 22, 1937; Symes to Thomas, March, 1937; Alfred Baker Lewis to Thomas, July 21, 1937; Referendum to Be Proposed to Local New York for Submission to the Whole Party, 1937; Decision of City Executive Committee of Local New York, July 26, 1937; Trager to Thomas, December 15, 1936; Paul Porter to Thomas, January 27, 1937; Trager to Thomas, March 14, 1937; John Hall to Thomas, July 15, 1937; J. Clark Waldron to Thomas, July, 1937; Thomas to Max Delson, Murray Gross, Murray Baron, Hal Siegel, and Jack Altman, August 7, 1936, to Trimble, November 24, 1936, to Altman, December 5, 1936, to Trimble, January 21, 1937, to David Lasser, January 21, 1937, to Symes, February 3, 1937; Symes to Thomas, February 6, 1937; Thomas to the Party Meeting, February 19, 1937, to Dear Comrades, June 22, 1937; Thomas, "The Party Situation," June, 1937; Thomas to Senior, July 19, 1937, to John Hall, July 21, 1937, to the St. Louis Local, July 27, 1937, to Senior, August 19, 1937, to Devere Allen, Jack Altman, and Gus Tyler, October 6, 1937; Thomas, Memorandum for Altman, Baron, 1937; Symes to Thomas, July 10, 1937; Porter to Thomas, July 14, 1937; Thomas to N.E.C., July 21, 1937; Porter to Thomas, February 3, 1937; Frank McClelland, Mark Lehner, and Everett Washburn to Thomas, August 26, 1937; Jack Altman to New York Membership, August 26, 1937; Robert Delson to Dear Comrade, August, 1937 (in NT Papers); Jack Altman, Murray Baron *et al.* to Dear Comrade, February 10, 1937; Charges of the Executive Committee of Local New York against Harold Draper and 69 others, 1937; Statement of Jack Altman, 1937; James Lipsig and Jack Altman to Roy Burt, 1937; Gus Tyler and Max Delson to Roy Burt, July, 1937; Robert Delson to Dear Comrade, 1937 (in SP Papers, Duke); Porter, *Which Way For the Socialist Party?*, pp. 40–41. Porter, who by early 1937 had become vocally anti-Trotskyist, had felt in 1936 that the new Trotskyist members would bring "vigor and enthusiasm" to the party. In Minnesota, he wrote Senior, most of the opposition to their admittance came from Communist Party "stooges" and "extremely muddled right wingers." See Porter to Senior, April 20, 1936 (in SP Papers, Duke). See also Aaron Levenstein, *A Letter to a Comrade* (New York, 1937), pp. 1–13 (in Tamiment).

26. Laidler, *Toward a Farmer-Labor Party*, pp. 38–39; Thomas, *SC*

(November 7, 1936), p. 12; Thomas, *SC* (November 14, 1936), p. 12; *SC* (November 21, 1936), p. 6; Thomas, *SC* (November 21, 1936), p. 12.

27. *SC* (December 12, 1936), p. 2. The intention of the resolution was to bring about more coordination and disciplined action in mass work. However, it made cooperation with farmer-labor parties easier by placing them on a par with other types of non-Socialist mass organizations.

28. Thomas, *SC* (December 12, 1936), p. 12.

29. Thomas to Maynard Krueger, November 1, 1936 (in NT Papers). In January, 1937, Thomas also wrote to Paul Porter that he found no evidence of a satisfactory farmer-labor movement on a national scale. See Thomas to Porter, January 21, 1937 (in NT Papers). This contrasted with Porter's more optimistic assessment of national trends. See Porter, *Which Way For the Socialist Party?*, pp. 14–16.

30. Porter to Thomas, February 3, 1937; Hoan to Thomas, March 22, 1937 (in NT Papers). For Thomas's fears of isolation resulting from sectarian attitudes, see Thomas to Irving Barshop, January 18, 1937; to Max Delson, Murray Gross, Murray Baron, Hal Siegel, and Jack Altman, August 7, 1936 (in NT Papers). In a letter to Glen Trimble in early 1937, Thomas wrote: "It is better under present conditions to sacrifice a certain theoretical precision and even a certain ability to lay down an emphatic Party line on practically every conceivable subject to a united front of Socialists in which a healthy educational process can be carried out and from which a sufficient unity of action can be got to make the Party effective." Thomas to Trimble, January 27, 1937 (in NT Papers).

31. Murray Gross, "A Labor Party," February 25, 1937 (in NT Papers).

32. Thomas, "To the Party Meeting," February 19, 1937 (in NT Papers); Thomas, *SC* (March 6, 1937), p. 12; *SC* (February 6, 1937), p. 6; *SC* (February 13, 1937), p. 6; *SC* (April 3, 1937), pp. 1–2.

33. *SC* (April 3, 1937), pp. 1–2; Thomas to the Editor, September 14, 1933 (in NT Papers).

34. *SC* (February 13, 1937), p. 8.

35. Thomas, Memorandum, November 6, 1936; Thomas to Laidler, March 31, 1937 (in NT Papers). Thomas's memorandum did not specifically indicate that discussions should begin, but his optimism about common A.L.P. and Socialist endorsement of future candidates obviously entailed the beginning of discussions.

36. *SC* (October 9, 1937), p. 3; *SC* (July 10, 1937), p. 4; George Baker, *SC* (July 17, 1937), p. 12; Baker, *SC* (July 24, 1937), p. 8; Baker, *SC* (July 31, 1937), p. 12; Baker, *SC* (August 7, 1937), p. 7; *SC* (July 17, 1937), p. 2; Thomas to Gus Tyler and Roy Burt, August 2, 1937 (in NT Papers); *SC* (August 7, 1937), p. 4. For the defense of Thomas's withdrawal, see Harry W. Laidler, "For a Party with Mass Contacts," *SR* (September, 1937), pp. 16–18. For Clarity's criticism, see Max Delson and Herbert Zam, "For a Clean Socialist Campaign," *SR* (September, 1937), pp. 18–20; Gus Tyler, "Socialist Discipline and Action," *SR* (September, 1937), pp. 23–25. For the Trotskyist criticism, see Max Schactman, "Against LaGuardia Socialism," *SR* (September, 1937), pp. 21–22; *SA* (August 14, 1937), pp. 1, 8; Schactman, "Supporting LaGuardia Betrays Socialism," *SA* (September 11, 1937), p. 3; Schactman, "Prospects for a Labor Party," *SA* (January, 1937), pp. 15–16; James Burnham, "For a Revolutionary Socialist Party," *SA* (September, 1936), pp. 5–8; *SA* (September 11, 1937), p. 1.

37. Gus Tyler, "The Labor Party Is Endangered as the Democratic Party Splits," *SC* (August 21, 1937), p. 8; Tyler, " 'Do-Nothing' Congress Ends," *SC* (August 28, 1937), p. 3; Tyler, "Labor Needs Its Own Political Party," *SC* (September 4, 1937), p. 8.

38. Symes to Thomas, July 10, 1937; Trager to Thomas, September 16, 1937; "The Struggle for Revolutionary Socialism Must Go On!," 1937 (in NT Papers).

39. *SC* (September 11, 1937), p. 1; *SC* (August 21, 1937), p. 3. For Trotskyist criticism of the Clarity group, see Max Schactman, "The Politics of Gus Tyler," *SA* (August 28, 1937), pp. 6–8; Schachtman, "Against LaGuardia Socialism," *SR* (September, 1937), pp. 21–22; *SA* (September 18, 1937), p. 8; *SA* (March 12, 1938), p. 1.

40. Thomas, "Draft Reply to Clarity," 1937; Thomas to Roy Burt, August 4, 1937; Thomas to Jack Altman and James Lipsig, August 4, 1937; Thomas, "The New York Municipal Campaign," August, 1937; Thomas to Senior, August 19, 1937; to Burt, July 19, 1937; to N.E.C., July 21, 1937; Thomas *et al.,* "Letter on the New York Municipal Campaign to Members of Local New York," August, 1937 (in NT Papers); Thomas, *SC* (October 9, 1937), p. 4.

41. Thomas, Memorandum for Laidler, Altman, Lipsig, September 3, 1937; Thomas to Dear Comrades, September, 1937 (in NT Papers). For Thomas's attempt to bring pressure on the A.L.P. in negotiations, see Thomas to Vladeck, July 13, 1937 (in BCV Papers). For Vladeck's reply, see Vladeck to Thomas, July 19, 1937 (in NT Papers).

42. *SC* (October 9, 1937), p. 3; Symes to Thomas, October 3,

1937; Ben Fischer to Thomas, October 5, 1937 (in NT Papers); Altman, "New York Socialists End Campaign with Rallies," *SC* (October 30, 1937), p. 6; Thomas, *SC* (November 13, 1937), p. 4; Altman, "N.Y. Elections Show Labor Is Ready for Independent Action," *SC* (November 6, 1937), p. 7; Murray Gross to Thomas, November 27, 1937 (in NT Papers).

43. Thomas, Reflections on 1937 Elections, November, 1937 (in NT Papers).

44. Altman to Dear Comrade, November 30, 1937 (in NT Papers).

45. According to Johnpoll, I.L.G.W.U. president David Dubinsky and the members of the Social Democratic Federation favored admitting the Socialist Party as a unit, but Chairman Alex Rose, in a fit of personal pique at a premature news story about the secret negotiations, refused to permit it and would only allow them to enter as individuals. See Johnpoll, p. 194. There is no doubt that Rose's anger broke off negotiations, and the evidence seems to indicate that the S.D.F. wished to admit the Socialist Party as a unit. See Roy Burt to N.E.C. (in SP Papers, Duke); *NL* (March 12, 1938), pp. 1, 7. However, the S.D.F. sometimes had a strange way of showing its support. Following the denial of the Socialist Party application, the S.D.F. issued an invitation to all "sincere" Socialists to resign from the Socialist Party and join the S.D.F. and thus be able to participate in the activities of the A.L.P. See *NL* (March 19, 1938), p. 2. On the Socialist negotiations with the A.L.P. and Thomas's shifting attitudes toward the A.L.P. in 1938, see Thomas to Laidler, February 9, 1938; Porter to Thomas, June 13, 1938; Thomas to Porter, June 17, 1938 (in NT Papers); Thomas, *SC* (January 1, 1938), p. 4; *SC* (February 5, 1938), p. 5; Thomas, *SC* (June 25, 1938), p. 5; *NL* (June 11, 1938), p. 3; *SC* (August 6, 1938), p. 1; Thomas, *SC* (August 13, 1938), p. 5; Thomas, *SC* (October 1, 1938), p. 5; Thomas, *Socialism on the Defensive* (New York, 1938), pp. 278–280, 291.

46. John [Newton Thurber] to Gus [Tyler], December, 1937 (in NT Papers); Tyler, "Labor Party Tactics," *SR* (January-February, 1938), pp. 17–18; Verne, "The Socialist Party and the American Labor Party," December 24, 1937; Becker, untitled, February 7, 1938 (in NT Papers).

47. Thomas to Laidler, February 9, 1938; "Labor Party Resolution," National Convention, Socialist Party, April 21–23, 1938; Thomas to Porter, June 17, 1938 (in NT Papers); *SC* (May 7, 1938), p. 9. A Thomas-Hoan resolution endorsing outright entry of the Socialist Party

into labor parties was defeated at the Convention by a narrow margin. See Bell, *Marxian Socialism in the United States,* p. 177.

48. Thomas to Porter, June 17, 1938 (in NT Papers); Arthur G. McDowell, "American Labor Party Relations," *SC* (June 18, 1936), p. 6; *SC* (August 6, 1938), p. 1; Thomas, *SC* (August 6, 1938), p. 4; Johnpoll, p. 195. The A.L.P. did provide Lehman with his margin of victory.

49. Delson, Horowitz, Trager, Zam, "Vote 'Yes' in the Referendum," 1938 (in NT Papers).

50. Altman, Laidler, Levenstein, Sexton, "Vote 'Yes' in the Referendum," 1938; Hughan to Thomas, December 12, 1938; Severn, "Vote 'No' in the Referendum," 1938 (in NT Papers).

51. "New York Socialists Vote to Join American Labor Party— Will Enter as Individuals," December 25, 1938 (in NT Papers); Thomas, "Our Party's Future," *SC* (December 24, 1938), p. 4.

52. For the Clarity conception of the Socialist Party, see Frank Trager, "Party Perspectives: Present and Future," *ASM* (June, 1936), pp. 23–27; Gus Tyler, "For a United Revolutionary Party," *ASM* (May, 1937), pp. 18–22.

53. Altman, Laidler, Levenstein, Sexton, "Vote 'Yes' in the Referendum," 1938; Delson, Horowitz, Trager, Zam, "Vote 'Yes' in the Referendum," 1938 (in NT Papers).

54. For Norman Thomas and the Communist issue in the A.L.P., see Thomas, "To Socialists in the A.L.P." December 20, 1939; to Comrade Lamont, March 2, 1940; to Gerry or Loren, January 31, 1940; to Irving Barshop, February 16, 1940; to Paul Allen, October 23, 1939; to Laidler, March 26, 1940 (in NT Papers). For Thomas's dissatisfaction with the A.L.P., see Thomas to A. J. Muste, January 26, 1940; to Walter O'Hagan, February 13, 1940; to Comrade Massey, April 24, 1940 (in NT Papers). For Thomas's separation from his old political allies, see Porter to Altman, June 17, 1940; Porter to Thomas, June 17, 1940; Thomas to Porter, June 21, 1940; Lazar Becker to Porter, June 27, 1940; Porter to Thomas, June 5, 1940 (in NT Papers). Altman's letter resigning from the Socialist-organized Keep America Out of War Congress was sent to the *New Leader.* See Altman to *NL* (June 1, 1940), p. 8. On the war issue blocking reunification talks between the S.D.F. and the Socialist Party, see National Office of the Socialist Party, "Full Account of Negotiations Between S.P. and S.D.F. for Organic Unity up to April 17, 1939," April 20, 1939 (in NT Papers); *SC* (April 29, 1939), p. 2; Thomas, untitled, January,

1940; Thomas, "Report on Unity Negotiations," April 1, 1940 (in NT Papers); *NL* (April 15, 1939), p. 8.

55. For the Altman Socialists' reservations about a 1940 Socialist campaign, see Murray Gross to Thomas, January 30, 1940; Altman to Thomas, February 13, 1940 (in NT Papers); Johnpoll, p. 215. For the problems of the Socialists in the A.L.P. and Thomas's attempt to deal with them, see Thomas to Laidler, January 26, 1940; Coleman Cheney to Thomas, January 26, 1940; Warren Atkinson to Thomas, January 28, 1940. Walter O'Hagan to Thomas, February 11, 1940; Thomas to O'Hagan, February 13, 1940; to Laidler, March 26, 1940; Harold Massey to Thomas, April 22, 1940; Thomas to Comrade Massey, April 24, 1940; George Dimmick, Harold Massey, and Albert Tully to Thomas, May 11, 1940; Laidler to Thomas, October 1, 1940; Thomas to Cheney, August 14, 1940 (in NT Papers); Ben Horowitz, "A.L.P. Committee Meeting," June 25, 1940; "Perspectives on American Labor Party Activity," June, 1940 (in SP Papers, Duke).

56. Laidler, *Toward a Farmer-Labor Party,* pp. 30–33; *SC* (September 18, 1937), p. 2; Ben Fischer, "Back Detroit Labor," *SC* (September 18, 1937), p. 2; Thomas to Central Committee of Wayne County, September 21, 1937; Fischer to Thomas, October 5, 1937 (in NT Papers); Fischer, "The Lesson of Detroit's Labor Campaign," *SR* (January-February, 1938), pp. 15–17.

57. For the dilemmas facing the Socialist Party and Reuther, see Bell, *Marxian Socialism in the United States,* pp. 178–179; Irving Howe and B. J. Widick, *The U.A.W. and Walter Reuther* (New York, 1949), pp. 194–195; George Edwards to Thomas, September 24, 1938 (in NT Papers).

58. When Reuther decided to support Murphy, he submitted his resignation, but was persuaded to withdraw it. See Thomas to Ben Fischer and Tucker Smith, August 19, 1938 (in NT Papers). Ben Fischer, Roy Reuther, and Hy Fish were originally censured by the National Office for introducing into their unions resolutions calling for the election of Murphy in Michigan and Sawyer in Ohio. See Roy Burt to N.E.C., September 3, 1938 (in NT Papers). For Fish's explanation, see Hy Fish to Dear Comrades, August 29, 1938 (in NT Papers). In the campaign itself, Socialists who tacitly supported Murphy escaped censure. Thomas's criticisms were elicited by a letter from George Edwards suggesting that the Socialists withdraw their candidates. See Edwards to Thomas, September 24, 1938 (in NT Papers). For Thomas's criticism, see Thomas to Alan Strachan, January 3, 1938; to Leonard Woodcock, January 5, 1938 (in NT Papers).

These last two letters are dated 1938, but it is obvious that they were written in January, 1939.

59. In a recent interview, Brendan Sexton, a former Socialist and long-time U.A.W. official, describes how U.A.W. Socialists "drifted away" from the Party. He says that he would have stayed "if the Socialist party had not put . . . [him] in a position where . . . [he] had to oppose the union's political choices." He feels other Socialists would have also remained in the party, although their union obligations would likely have made them "nominal Socialists." See "The Tradition of Reutherism," *Dissent* (Winter, 1972), p. 57. This may be so, but it dodges the question of what happens to a *socialist* party which constantly supports capitalist politicians.

Chapter VI The Problem of Failure

1. Shannon, *The Socialist Party of America,* pp. 262–268.
2. Ibid., pp. 258–262.
3. Ibid., pp. 261–262.
4. Ibid., p. 260. In December, 1939, Morris Milgram resigned from the Socialist Party (he later withdrew his resignation) because he felt the necessary discipline was impossible in a situation where the Party was divided between antagonistic groups—prowar Socialists, pure pacifists, and revolutionaries. See Milgram to Thomas, December 30, 1939 (in NT Papers). The main debate among the factions after the outbreak of World War II centered on the Symes Amendment, which would have withheld "political support" from the war. The Amendment was supported by "revolutionary" Socialists and pacifists, and opposed by Thomas and the "critical" supporters of the war (although Thomas refrained from using the phrase "critical support" in the N.E.C. Resolution), as well as the few remaining prowar Socialists. The Symes Amendment was offered to the N.E.C. and defeated. The issue carried over into the Socialist Party's May, 1942 Convention, where a compromise was written. See Johnpoll, *Pacifist's Progress,* pp. 233–235. For statements of the "revolutionary" Socialist position, see Lillian Symes and Travers Clement, Dear Comrade, January 19, 1942; Roger Payne, "The Socialist Position on War," February, 1942; Robin Myers, "Report Committee, Y.P.S.L. to the National Executive," January 6, 1942 (in NT Papers); Payne, "Are We Quitters on the War Question?" *HT* (April, 1942), pp. 7–8. For the prowar Socialist position, see John Lester Lewine to Thomas, December 14, 1941; to Thomas, January 21, 1942; Lewine, "A Program for the Party in War," *HT* (April, 1942), pp. 6–7. For the Socialist pacifist position on war, see Pearl Weiner,

"Socialists and Pacifists," *HT* (June, 1940), pp. 1–3; David Berkingoff, "For Pacifism," *HT* (November, 1940), p. 11. For a revolutionary position that opposed both Thomas and the Symes Amendment, see Dan Roberts, "Resolution on War," May 23, 1942 (in SP Papers, Duke). For a general discussion of the various positions, see "Socialist Convention States Position on War and Fascism," *SC* (June 12, 1942), pp. 1, 7; Hyman Bookbinder to *SC* (June 26, 1942), p. 6. For Thomas's position, see Thomas, "Memorandum for the N.E.C.," December 9, 1941; Thomas to Maynard Krueger, December 11, 1941; Thomas, "A Short Personal Statement on the War," January 2, 1942; Thomas to Ken Cuthbertson, January 2, 1942; Thomas, "Statement against the Symes Amendment," January, 1942; Thomas to Roger Payne, February 4, 1942; Thomas to Harold Flincken and George Kingsley, January 21, 1942 (in NT Papers).

5. Thomas to Porter, June 6, 1940, to Porter, June 21, 1940 (in NT Papers); *NL* (June 8, 1940), p. 2.

6. Porter to Thomas, June 17, 1934; Most to J. B. Matthews, September 21, 1933; Most to Thomas, September 30, 1933; Biemiller to Thomas, September 12, 1933; Thomas to Most, October 5, 1933; to Biemiller, September 14, 1933; to Senior, November 14, 1933; to Members of the National Executive Committee, November, 1934; to Board of the *New Leader,* June 6, 1934; Doris Preisler to National Executive Committee, June 6, 1934; Thomas, Memorandum on the Release Concerning the Visit of Lasser and Others to the Mayor in Behalf of the Unemployed, 1934; Thomas to Louis Waldman, January 16, 1934; to Julius Gerber, January 4, 1934; to Jack Altman, January 4, 1934; to City Executive Committee, January 16, 1934; to Waldman, January 25, 1934; John Brooks Wheelwright to Thomas, June 5, 1934; Mary Duemlee to Senior, June 26, 1934; Altman to Dear Comrades, December 2, 1935; Haim Kantorovitch to Senior, June 18, 1934; Oneal to Senior, June 23, 1934; George H. Goebel to Thomas, October 25, 1935; Maurice Goldsmith to Thomas, March 24, 1936 (in NT Papers). Thomas was also upset by the Old Guard's threat to split from the Socialist Party over the Declaration of Principles because he felt it was a tactic whereby a minority could "bludgeon" a majority into line. See Thomas to Samuel Friedman, June 15, 1934; to Biemiller, June 22, 1934 (in NT Papers).

7. Arthur G. McDowell, untitled (first page missing), January 12, 1938; Roy Burt to N.E.C., February 1, 1938; to N.E.C., February 5, 1938; to N.E.C., March 3, 1938 (in SP Papers, Duke); to Comrade Lasser, March 2, 1938 (in NT Papers); *SC* (October 30, 1937), p. 6;

Thomas to Members of the Grievance Committee, November 25, 1938; to Burt, November 29, 1938; Irving Barshop to Thomas, August 6, 1940; Thomas to Barshop, August 7, 1940; Trager, "Perspectives: 1937," 1937; Trager to the Members of the Socialist Party, February 24, 1941 (in NT Papers).

8. The Party's antiwar Committee endorsed strict neutrality. However, because the Party as a whole had not acted on strict neutrality and because many Socialists did not believe rigid neutrality was necessary, Thomas suggested, in May, 1939, that the Party not impose discipline on the matter. See Thomas to Arthur McDowell, May 5, 1939 (in NT Papers). At this stage, he urged a lenient policy toward those who, like Alfred Baker Lewis, disagreed with the Party's position on neutrality. See Thomas to National Office, May 18, 1939 (in NT Papers). The Party did take a clear stand against repeal of the neutrality legislation in the fall of 1939. Thomas, however, was still anxious not to make support for repeal of the embargo a matter subject to discipline, except where Socialists made extreme public attacks on the Party's position. See Thomas to Travers Clement, September 21, 1939 (in NT Papers). During the 1940 campaign, he wrote Jack Altman that he did not want to take disciplinary action over different opinions, but that he expected prowar Socialists to give the Party at least qualified support (as Albert Sprague Coolidge was doing) and not support Roosevelt. See Thomas to Altman, June 13, 1940 (in NT Papers). As the war crisis developed, Thomas came increasingly to feel that one was either working to get the United States into the war or to keep her out. There was no "middle ground." He still warned against a "monolithic" party. See Thomas to Marion Severn, February 26, 1941 (in NT Papers). In February, 1941, the N.E.C. was still wrestling with the problem of discipline. In a statement on discipline, it declared that loyalty to democratic socialism was required, but that persons were free to state disagreements with the Party's foreign policy publicly as long as they made it clear they were speaking for themselves and that they did not make them in publications or meetings of organizations who were actively opposing the Socialist Party. See Minutes of N.E.C. Meeting, February 7–9, 1941; Minutes of National Action Committee, February 15, 1941 (in SP Papers, Duke). But by early 1941, those who opposed the Party's foreign policy position wanted to be able to speak on the issues of aid to the Allies without any restrictions. See Paul Porter and Frank Trager, "A Statement Accompanying Resignation from the National Executive Committee of the Socialist Party," February, 1941 (in SP Papers, Duke).

9. Shannon, p. 235; Bell, *Marxian Socialism in the United States,* p. 9.

10. Shannon, pp. 258–260.

11. Bell, *Marxian Socialism in the United States,* pp. viii–ix.

12. Ibid.; Johnpoll, pp. 175–176, 289–290.

13. The clearest statement of this Trotskyist position can be found in James Cannon, "American Radicalism: Yesterday, Today and Tomorrow," *International Socialist Review* (Winter, 1960), pp. 9–16. Here, Cannon writes: "Then the situation changed, almost overnight. The terrible financial and social crisis really shook up this country —and the workers. The radicalism produced by this shake-up was far stronger than the radicalism of the two previous decades. It had a firmer social composition of invincible power. It had the advantage of a more advanced ideology. The inspiration and ideas of the Russian Revolution permeated the Communist movement of that time and gave it a tremendous advantage over all other tendencies. And then in the changed situation in the thirties the impossible was accomplished [the organization of the mass production industries]. . . . Along with that there was a growing sentiment for a Labor Party which under proper leadership could have brought this whole new movement of labor radicalism toward a glorious new epoch of independent class action in this country. But that didn't happen. And the main reason it didn't was that the Communist party, which was the main leader of this new movement of labor radicalism, failed in its mission, even more shamefully, even more disgracefully than the Socialist party of the two previous decades. And more catastrophically, because it was not defeated in battle; it was corrupted from within. . . . They [the Stalinists] looked upon the great movement of American radicalism as something to be expended cheaply. They diverted it, through the leadership of the Communist party, into the Roosevelt camp. They steered it away from the movement for an independent labor party, which was called for by the conditions of the time and the sentiments of hundreds of thousands of workers. . . . The first part of Trotsky's prediction about the military eruption of American capitalism has been confirmed to the letter. The second part was only partly carried out; the revolutionary prospects of the upsurge of the thirties were not realized. But even there, Trotsky had qualified his prediction. He said, the American workers could possess a scientific guide in the form of communism provided its representatives had 'a correct policy.' The American Communist party failed to provide that correct policy. Trotsky saw both the transformation of American capitalism into a world-embracing

imperialist power on the one hand, and a revolutionary proletariat on the other, as a possible outcome of the thirties. And it really was possible. For the reasons we have cited, that possible outcome was lost the first time. We owe that failure, above all, to Stalinism" (pp. 13–16). Cannon's viewpoint is also implicit in George Novack's "Can American Workers Make a Socialist Revolution?," *International Socialist Review* (January-February, 1969), p. 62.

14. On the student movement, see Hal Draper, "The Student Movement of the Thirties: A Political History," in Rita Simon, ed., *As We Saw the Thirties* (Urbana, Ill., 1967), pp. 151–189. In a recent article, B. J. Widick, one of the leaders of the Flint sitdown strikes, has written: "The sitdowns of the 1930's turned out to be a demand for a voice and a share in the system rather than a prelude to revolution—as antagonists feared and some proponents hoped." See B. J. Widick, "Black City, Black Unions?," *Dissent* (Winter, 1972), p. 145.

15. Melvyn Dubofsky, *We Shall Be All: A History of the IWW* (Chicago, 1969), p. 481.

Chapter VII Socialists and the New Deal

1. Carl N. Degler, *Out of Our Past* (New York, 1959), pp. 379–416; Edgar E. Robinson, *The Roosevelt Leadership* (Philadelphia, 1955), *passim*. Examples of New Left criticism are Barton J. Bernstein, "The New Deal: The Conservative Achievements of Liberal Reform," in Bernstein, ed., *Towards a New Past* (New York, 1968); Howard Zinn, Introduction to *New Deal Thought* (Indianapolis, 1966); Brad Wiley, *Historians and the New Deal* (n.d.).

2. Johnpoll, *Pacifist's Progress,* pp. 101–105; Thomas to Filene, November 23, 1933 (in NT Papers); Thomas, *The Choice Before Us* (New York, 1934), pp. 92–94. For Thomas's early, more favorable, writings on the New Deal, see Thomas, "New Deal or New Day," *WT* (August 31, 1933), pp. 488–489; Thomas, "Along the Class Struggle Front," *WT* (September 28, 1933), pp. 537–538. Even these articles revealed no great faith in the New Deal; what positive accomplishments Thomas found in it in no way negated his belief that a new political alignment was necessary.

3. Thomas, *The Choice Before Us,* pp. 7, 98–101, 139, 141–142; Thomas, *After the New Deal, What?* (New York, 1936), pp. 16–55; Thomas, "Timely Topics," *NL* 1934–1935 *passim;* Thomas, *Why Did NRA Go Wrong?* (Chicago, n.d.), pp. 1–3; Thomas, "Draft of Statement," December, 1934; Thomas, "Statement on the President's

Security Program," 1934; Thomas to Members of the Public Affairs Committee, 1935; Thomas, "The Story of High Point: What Some Employers Are Doing to N.R.A.," August 9, 1933; Thomas to General Hugh Johnson, December 20, 1933; to General Hugh Johnson, September 15, 1934; to Editor of the *New York Times,* November 23, 1936; to Senate Committee on Agriculture, May 1, 1935; to Rhoda E. McCulloch, January 11, 1934; to Robert Bruere, January 15, 1934; to *Christian Science Monitor* Editorial Board, June 13, 1934; to Fred Blacker, August 17, 1934; to Alton Lawrence, November 17, 1933; to Dr. Henry Goddard Leach, December 16, 1933; to Mr. Joseph Woolf, Janary 3, 1934; Thomas, untitled (answers to questions 1, 2, 3, 4), 1935 (in NT Papers).

4. For the Socialist critique of the New Deal, see *NL* 1933–1935 *passim; SC* 1935–1941 *passim.* On Thomas and the Southern Tenant Farmers Union, see, e.g., Thomas to Henry Wallace, February 22, 1934; to Oscar Johnson, March 3, 1934; to Wallace, May 9, 1934; to Rexford Tugwell, March 6, 1935; to Felix Frankfurter, March 2, 1935; "The Social and Economic Consequences of the Cotton Acreage Reduction Program," 1934; Thomas to Tugwell, March 21, 1935; to Chester Davis, March 22, 1935; to Franklin D. Roosevelt, April 9, 1935; to Roosevelt, April 23, 1935; Wallace to Thomas, March 8, 1934; to Thomas, May 14, 1934; Joe T. Robinson to Thomas, April 3, 1935; Roosevelt to Thomas, April 22, 1935 (in NT Papers); M. S. Venkataramani, "Norman Thomas, Arkansas Sharecroppers, and the Roosevelt Agricultural Policies, 1933–1937," *Mississippi Valley Historical Review* (September, 1960), pp. 225–246.

5. For the need for workers to take advantage of labor's right to organize and bargain collectively under N.R.A., but for their own ends, see Thomas, "New Deal or New Day," *WT* (August 31, 1933), pp. 488–489; Thomas to Joseph Woolf, January 3, 1934 (in NT Papers); Morris Hillquit, "The Significance of This Campaign," in Henry J. Rosner and Louis E. Yavner, eds., *A Socialist Plan for New York* (New York, 1933), p. 47; National Executive Committee of the Socialist Party. *The National Recovery Act* (July 4, 1933), pp. 1–2; John F. Sullivan, Andrew J. Biemiller, Maynard C. Krueger, *The National Industrial Recovery Act* (Chicago, 1933), pp. 3–16; Will Herberg, "The N.R.A. and American Labor," *MM* (October, 1933), pp. 519–524. For the dangers of unions becoming "docile partners" in the governmental structure, see, e.g., Thomas to Rhoda McCulloch, January 25, 1934; *SC* (April 6, 1935), p. 4. On the Colt strike, see Thomas, *After the New Deal, What?,* pp. 29–30; Thomas, *SC* (May

4, 1935), p. 8; *SC* (May 25, 1935), p. 3. On the New Deal Social Security measures, see Thomas, *NL* (February 9, 1935), p. 8; *NL* (February 9, 1935), p. 4–L; Dr. Eveline Burns, "Sham Unemployment Insurance," *NL* (February 16, 1935), p. 6; Thomas, *NL* (February 23, 1935), pp. 3, 6; *NL* (February 23, 1935), p. 10; Thomas, *SC* (June 29, 1935), pp. 1, 10; Thomas to Editor of the *New York Times,* November 23, 1936 (in NT Papers); Thomas, *After the New Deal, What?* pp. 19–21. For post-1936 Socialist criticism of the New Deal, see *SC* 1936–1941 *passim.*

6. David Berenberg, "Roosevelt," *ASQ* (Summer, 1933), pp. 45–52; *ASM* (June, 1935), pp. 3–7; Berenberg, "The Roosevelt Honeymoon Is Over," *SR* (October-November, 1937), pp. 1–3; Algernon Lee, "Bourgeois 'Planning' and Antidemocracy," *ASQ* (Summer, 1932), pp. 22–27.

7. Henry J. Rosner, "The Economic Policies of Roosevelt," *ASQ* (Autumn, 1933), pp. 3–12; Harry W. Laidler, "The N.R.A. in American Economic Development," *ASQ* (December, 1934), pp. 26–37; Thomas, *After the New Deal, What?* p. 16; Thomas, *The Choice Before Us,* pp. 89, 92, 124. For Thomas's definition of state capitalism, see Thomas to Dennis Brane, December 5, 1936 (in NT Papers). For the Socialists' stress on labor not tying its fate to the Democratic Party, see Thomas and Max Delson, "Call for an Offensive against Reaction," *SC* (June 1, 1935), p. 3; *SC* (May 25, 1935), p. 6; Sidney Hertzberg, Campaign Caravan," *SC* (September 12, 1936), p. 5; Frank N. Trager, "Labor Perspectives for the Convention," *ASM* (February, 1937), pp. 2–11.

8. Thomas, *After the New Deal, What?* pp. 54–55. Johnpoll places great stress on the New Deal taking over the Socialists' "immediate demands." See Johnpoll, pp. 102–103, 176–177, 289–290. Gus Tyler also stresses this in the Oral History Socialist Movement Project (at Columbia University), May 28, 1965. However, Thomas's recognition in the 1930's that the New Deal never "took" the "fundamental idea" of Socialism and that it unsatisfactorily and inadequately implemented some immediate demands remains a just evaluation of the problem. See Thomas to Robert Allen, December 20, 1935 (in NT Papers). In *After the New Deal, What?,* Thomas wrote of the relationship between Socialist ideas and Roosevelt: "The trouble is not that he took some of them, but that he took so few and carried them out so unsatisfactorily. The moral of the tale is that if you want a child brought up right you better leave him with his parents, not turn him over to unsympathetic strangers" (p. 21).

9. Sidney Fine, *The Automobile under the Blue Eagle* (Ann Arbor, Mich., 1963), *passim;* David Conrad, *The Forgotten Farmers* (Urbana, Ill., 1965), *passim;* M. S. Venkataramani, "Norman Thomas, Arkansas Sharecroppers, and the Roosevelt Agricultural Policies, 1933–1937," pp. 225–246; Fred Greenbaum, "The Anti-Lynching Bill of 1935," *Journal of Human Relations* (Third Quarter, 1967), pp. 72–85; Raymond Wolters, *Negroes and the Great Depression* (Westport, Conn., 1970), *passim;* David Shannon, "FDR and Congress at a Turning Point of the New Deal" (talk delivered at the Columbia University Seminar on American Civilization), December 19, 1968; Ellis Hawley, *The New Deal and the Problem of Monopoly* (Princeton, N.J., 1966), *passim;* Gabriel Kolko, *Wealth and Power in America* (New York, 1962), *passim.* On the New Deal and the Negro, see also Christopher G. Wye, "The New Deal and the Negro Community: Toward a Broader Conceptualization," *Journal of American History* (December, 1972), pp. 621–639.

10. On the origins of the N.R.A., see William Leuchtenburg, *Franklin D. Roosevelt and the New Deal* (New York, 1963), pp. 55–58. On Johnson's attitudes toward labor, see Leuchtenburg, pp. 107–108.

11. Ronald Radosh, "The White Liberal's Crisis," *Studies on the Left* (Summer, 1964), pp. 118–119. The Wagner Act was not originally a New Deal measure. See Leuchtenburg, *Franklin D. Roosevelt and the New Deal,* pp. 150–152.

Chapter VIII Socialists and Communism

1. Frank A. Warren, *Liberals and Communism* (Bloomington, Ind., 1966), pp. 63–88, 163–192.

2. James Weinstein, *The Decline of Socialism in America 1912–1925* (New York, 1967), *passim;* Johnpoll, pp. 53–54; Howe and Coser, *The American Communist Party,* pp. 245–251.

3. Paul Porter to *NL* (January 3, 1931), p. 5; *NL* (February 7, 1931), pp. 1–2; Oneal, *Socialism versus Bolshevism* (New York, 1935), pp. 5–27; Algernon Lee to *NL* (February 21, 1931), p. 8; *NL* (February 4, 1928), p. 2; Johnpoll, p. 53; Harry Fleischman, *Norman Thomas,* p. 112; Thomas, *NL* (December 5, 1925), pp. 1–2; James Maurer, *It Can be Done* (New York, 1938), pp. 290–292. Thomas was a member of the International Committee for Political Prisoners, which protested political persecution in foreign countries. See its publication, *Political Persecution Today* (New York, 1925), pp. 4–48, and

a statement of its aims, "The International Committee for Political Prisoners," June 25, 1938 (in Tamiment). In 1925, the Communists broke up a meeting of the International Committee for Political Prisoners that was protesting the lack of civil liberties in Russia. See *NL* (March 14, 1925), pp. 1, 11; Roger Baldwin, "The Bolshevik Gag on Free Speech," *NL* (March 21, 1925), p. 2.

4. Oneal, *Socialism versus Bolshevism,* pp. 3–19; Hillquit to *NL* (December 6, 1930), p. 8; *NL* (March 21, 1931), p. 4; *NL* (February 7, 1931), pp. 1–2.

5. Oneal, "The Socialist Party Attitude toward Soviet Russia," *NL* (January 10, 1931), p. 4; *NL* 1937–1941 *passim.* In December, 1938, Oneal said Dies "confused" the fight against the Communist Party. See Oneal, *NL* (December 10, 1938), p. 7. The next year, the *New Leader* argued that the Committee had gathered valuable information, but that Dies should resign because his methods aped the Bolsheviks. See *NL* (December 30, 1939), p. 8. In February, 1940, Victor Riesel, a regular contributor, was advising Dies where to look for Communists. See Riesel, "Heard on the Left," *NL* (February 24, 1940), p. 3. In September, 1940 a story in the *New Leader* said that Californians were surprised at Dies's "whitewash" of Hollywood's "Caviar Comrades." See Dorothy Tait, *NL* (September 14, 1940), p. 5. Subsequent stories treated Dies's investigations favorably. See, e.g., Sidney Hamlin, "Dies Promises Startling Exposes of Intensified Fascist Work in America," *NL* (November 9, 1940), pp. 1, 7; V. Rogers, "Dies Reveals Nazis Exploit Many U.S. Isolationist Groups," *NL* (November 23, 1940), pp. 1, 7.

6. Paul Porter to *NL* (February 21, 1931), p. 8; Alfred Baker Lewis to *NL* (April 2, 1932), p. 6; Johnpoll, *Pacifist's Progress,* p. 79; Richard Briggs, "A Socialist Defense of the Soviet Union," *NL* (February 28, 1931), p. 4; *NL* (February 7, 1931), pp. 1–2; *SC* (May 18, 1935), p. 6.

7. Porter to *NL* (February 21, 1931), p. 8; *RSR* (February, 1935), pp. 3–5; Haim Kantorovitch, "Is This Militancy?" *ASQ* (April, 1932), pp. 37–43; David Berenberg, Review of William Z. Foster, *Toward Soviet America, ASQ* (Summer, 1932), pp. 56–63.

8. Thomas to William Raoul, January 1, 1935; to Robert O. Spivak, February 2, 1937 (in NT Papers); David Felix, "A Basis for a Proposed Program for Revolutionary Socialism," *ASQ* (Autumn, 1934), pp. 20–34; Berenberg, review of William Z. Foster, *Toward Soviet America,* pp. 56–63; Haim Kantorovitch, "Towards Reorientation," *ASQ* (Autumn, 1933), pp. 13–19.

9. Murray Baron to *NL* (November 29, 1930), p. 8; McAlister Coleman to *NL* (December 27, 1930), p. 5; Porter to *NL* (January 3, 1931), p. 5; Lewis to *NL* (January 31, 1931), p. 8; Porter to *NL* (February 21, 1931), p. 8; McDowell to *NL* (March 7, 1931), p. 4; *NL* (December 27, 1930), p. 5; Lee to *NL* (February 21, 1931), p. 8. The compromise resolution at the Milwaukee Convention read: "Whereas: The Socialist party recognizes that the Soviet experiment is being watched closely and with intense interest by the workers; that its success in the economic field will give an immense impetus to the acceptance of Socialism by the workers, while its failure will discredit an economy based upon planned production and the abolition of capitalism: be it Resolved: That the Socialist party, while not endorsing all policies of the Soviet government, and while emphatically urging the release of political prisoners and the restoration of civil liberties, endorses the efforts being made in Russia to create the economic foundations of a Socialist society and calls on the workers to guard against capitalist attacks on Soviet Russia. We believe that economic and political conditions in each counrty should determine the revolutionary tactics adopted in that country, and that the Russian experiment is a natural outgrowth of the conditions peculiar to that country." See Notes for Speakers, February, 1934, p. 6 (in SP Papers, Tamiment).

10. Porter to Thomas, January 28, 1934; Lewis to *NL* (January 31, 1931), p. 8; Paul Blanshard to *NL* (September 19, 1935), p. 4; Murray Baron to *NL* (November 29, 1930), p. 8; *NL* (February 7, 1931), pp. 1–2. For Hillquit's view that the Russian regime was irrelevant to Socialism in the United States, see Hillquit to W. W. Passage, July 25, 1932 (in MH Papers, Tamiment). This judgment stands in sharp contrast to Hillquit's views in 1923. Then he wrote: "In the more advanced countries of Europe the new economic and political conditions have created a potential 'revolutionary situation'; the direct object of the next Socialist attack in any of them may be the immediate conquest of the powers of government. The spirit and tempo of such renewed movements and their eventual success or failure will inevitably be influenced to a large extent by developments in Soviet Russia. For no matter how justly the conditions of Russia and the special kind of Socialism produced by them may be differentiated from the conditions in the West and the type of Socialism which is expected to be reared on their foundations, the world at large will invaribly and summarily sweep aside all such distinctions. To the masses of workers and non-workers Soviet Russia is and always will

be a practical demonstration of Socialism at work, and the prototype of all Socialist governments. The successes of the Russian struggle will inspire and stimulate the Socialist movement of all countries. Her failures will be direct set-backs to the whole of international Socialism." See Hillquit, *From Marx to Lenin* (New York, 1923), p. 141. For Hillquit's reply to Baron, see *NL* (December 6, 1930), p. 8.

11. Porter to Thomas, January 28, 1934 (in NT Papers); David Felix, "A Basis for a Proposed Program for Revolutionary Socialism," *ASQ* (Autumn, 1934), pp. 20–34; *NL* (February 7, 1931), pp. 1–2. For the Militant Socialists' views on democratic rights, see Andrew Biemiller, "Socialism and Democracy," *ASQ* (Spring, 1934), pp. 20–28; Alfred Baker Lewis, "Political Democracy—Blind Alley or Road to Power?" *ASQ* (June, 1935), pp. 40–47. References to Thomas's views on Russia may be found in note 4 of Chapter Three. In addition, see Thomas, "Timely Topics," *NL* (1929–1935), *passim;* Thomas to Senior, November 24, 1933; to Editor of *The Enterprise,* August 27, 1934 (in NT Papers). See note 9 above for the 1932 Party Resolution on Russia.

12. Bell, *The End of Ideology,* pp. 403–407; Lewis Coser and Irving Howe, "Authoritarians of the 'Left,' " *Dissent* (Winter, 1955), pp. 40–50; David Berenberg, "Moscow Trial," *ASM* (December, 1936), p. 33. For the debate over whether the Soviet system was state capitalist or state socialist, see *MM* (March, 1938), pp. 2–3; Liston M. Oak, "Is Stalinism—Bolshevism?" *MM* (March, 1938), pp. 8–10; R. L. Worrall, "U.S.S.R.: Proletarian or Capitalist State?," *MQ* (Winter, 1938), pp. 5–19; Lillian Symes, "Bolshevism—What Is It?," *SC* (October 21, 1939), p. 4; Rudolf Hilferding, "State Capitalism or Totalitarian State Economy," *PQ* (May-June, 1940), pp. 1–5; Max Nomad, "Scholar and Politician," *PO* (May-June, 1940), pp. 6–9; Integer, "Revisionism—1940," *SC* (April 6, 1940), p. 2; Max Nomad, "The Tyranny of Marxist Orthodoxy," *SC* (April 13, 1940), p. 2; Nomad, "The Great Confusion," *NL* (November 30, 1940), pp. 5–6; *ICC* (January, 1937), pp. 8–16. Norman Thomas believed that Russia had adopted the economics of state capitalism. See Thomas to Harold Spivak, March 1, 1941 (in NT Papers). But for the most part Thomas, who was hardly a theoretician, did not participate in these debates. However, he accepted one very important aspect of the anti-Stalinist, non-Trotskyist critique—that the Soviet Union was not a true socialist state. In 1938, he wrote: "Various socialist and revolutionary groups are still debating whether Russia can still be called a proletarian state. It now seems to me a verbal exercise of no great importance. Certainly

Russia is not a socialist state. It is a totalitarian state under a monolithic party which through the state apparatus appropriates the surplus
value of labor as it wills and for its own ends. In no sense important to
masses of human beings does the state become a working class institution simply by reason of the absence of private capitalism or by the
constant assertion that all its deeds, good and bad alike, are done in
the name and for the sake of the workers." See Thomas, "The Moscow
Trials," *MM* (March, 1938), p. 4. See also Thomas, *SC* (March 19,
1938), p. 5; Thomas to Dear Comrade, September 9, 1938 (in NT
Papers). At the same time that there was a radical debate over the
nature of the Soviet system, there was also a reexamination of "revolutionary socialism" and "revolutionary morality." See, e.g., Lillian
Symes, "Towards a New Beginning," *MQ* (Fall, 1938), pp. 29–37;
Liston M. Oak, "Bourgeois and Revolutionary Morals," *SR* (March-
April, 1939), pp. 7–9, 17.

13. In September, 1936, Thomas wrote that although he was not an
"uncritical admirer" of Russia, he felt that "Russia rather than Germany sets the type of society which has promise for the future." See
Thomas to Editor of the *St. Louis Post-Dispatch,* September 9, 1936
(in NT Papers). In January, 1937, Senior wrote that despite its mistakes Russia was "the only country in the world making any serious
attempt to lay the foundation for Socialism." See Senior, "Memorandum on Trotskyites in the S.P.," January 25, 1937 (in NT Papers).
For Thomas's views on the Moscow Trials in 1936–1937, see note 5
in Chapter Three. Thomas's struggle over evaluating developments in
Russia can be seen in an exchange of letters with the novelist James
Farrell. See Farrell to Thomas, January 26, 1937; Thomas to Farrell,
January 27, 1937 (in NT Papers). Even though he did not want to
have the issue divide the Party, Thomas could not keep silent. He
wrote to Alfred Baker Lewis, who had advised a playing down of the
issue: "I do not agree the Party can ignore the whole matter to the
extent that you seem to suggest. . . . It is too vital; it goes deep; and
it plays too terrible a role now in dividing the working class and in
discrediting Socialist idealism." See Thomas to Lewis, January 29,
1937 (in NT Papers). Thomas's views after early 1937 were stronger;
he did not express certainty that the trials were complete frame-ups, but
his condemnation of Stalin's "reign of terror" had none of the earlier
ambiguity, where he had seemed as angry at Zinoviev and Kamenev as
at Stalin. See Thomas, *SC* (March 12, 1938), p. 5; Thomas, *SC* (March
19, 1938), p. 5. Thomas also was coming increasingly to feel that
Trotsky, because of the intolerant core in Bolshevik ideology, would

probably have acted like Stalin if he had won power. And he was beginning to extend this into a generalized critique of the Communist dictatorship. Finally, he was coming to feel that the "important differences" between Communism and fascism were increasingly diminishing. See Thomas, *SC* (June 5, 1937), p. 3; Thomas, *SC* (June 26, 1937), p. 12; Thomas, *SC* (November 6, 1937), p. 4; Thomas, *Socialism on the Defensive,* pp. 52–69; Thomas, "The Moscow Trials," *MM* (March, 1938), pp. 4, 13; Thomas, *Democracy versus Dictatorship* (New York, 1937), pp. 3–33; Thomas and Joel Seidman, *Russia—Democracy or Dictatorship?* (New York, 1939), pp. 3–66.

14. On the anti-Stalinist Left and the trials, see Friedrich Adler, *The Witchcraft Trial in Moscow* (Chicago, 1937); Max Schactman, *Behind the Moscow Trial* (New York, 1936); John Dewey, *Truth Is on the March* (New York, 1937); John Dewey et al., *The Case of Leon Trotsky: Report on the Charges against Him in the Moscow Trials* (New York, 1937). For Lewis's advice, see Lewis to Thomas, January 27, 1937; to Thomas, 1937 (in NT Papers). For Adamic's initial response, see Louis Adamic, *My America* (New York, 1938), p. 82. On Roosevelt, Dies, and Hague, see James MacGregor Burns, *The Lion and the Fox* (New York, 1956), pp. 369, 379, 424.

15. Thomas to Dear Comrades, September 9, 1938 (in NT Papers); Lillian Symes, "Towards a New Beginning," *MQ* (Fall, 1938), pp. 29–37; *SC* (March 19, 1938), p. 4; Alfred Baker Lewis, "Dictatorship vs. Democracy," *SC* (September 3, 1938), p. 6.

16. Schlesinger, *The Vital Center,* pp. 142–143; David Berenberg, review of William Z. Foster, *Toward a Soviet America, ASQ* (Summer, 1932), pp. 56–63; Haim Kantorovitch, "Is This Militancy?," *ASQ* (April, 1932), pp. 37–43; Kantorovitch, "Towards Reorientation" *ASQ* (Autumn, 1933), pp. 13–19; Warren, *Liberals and Communism,* pp. 83–87; Randolph Bourne, "The Twilight of Idols," in Carl Resek, ed., *War and the Intellectuals* (New York, 1964), pp. 53–64.

17. Schlesinger, *The Vital Center,* p. 147; Waldo Frank to *NR* (May 12, 1937), pp. 19–20. Frank wrote that an investigating body should "be formed of jurists and lawyers remote from revolutionary politics and of unimpeached professional honor." But he then went on to suggest that these "technically equipped" men should be formed by the "constituted executive organs of Socialists and Communists in the United States and Great Britain." See also Reinhold Niebuhr to *NR* (June 9, 1937), p. 132. Niebuhr wrote: "It is just barely possible that the rulers of Russia, forced by the world situation to opportunistic statesmanship, foolishly thought it necessary to tar the more intran-

sigent Marxist foes with the taint of fascism in order to neutralize the charges of these foes against them." Berenberg, "The Moscow Trial," *ASM* (December, 1936), pp. 26–33.

18. Warren, *Liberals and Communism*, pp. 105–107; Schlesinger, *The Vital Center*, p. 148; Gus Tyler, "People's Front Government vs. Proletarian Dictatorship," *ASM* (March, 1936), pp. 20–23; Henry Haskell, "Popular Front—Middle Class Weapon," *SR* (July-August, 1938), pp. 8–11; Porter, *Which Way for the Socialist Party?*, pp. 23–30, 35–47. Porter considered himself a Marxist, but in terms of urging closer cooperation with bourgeois parties in certain instances, his approach was clearly more "flexible" than Tyler's or Haskell's.

19. Willie Sue Blagden to Thomas, August 26, 1934; Powers Hapgood to Maynard Krueger, July 3, 1934 (in NT Papers); Thomas, *The Choice Before Us*, pp. 78–81. There was, it is true, much confusion on the Left about what a "united front" was. In a call for a united front, V. F. Calverton criticized the Communist line of a "united front from below." But his own positive contribution did not spell out whether a true united front would be on specific actions or whether it would be a general fusion of organizations. See *MM* (April, 1933), pp. 133–134. Haim Kantorovitch distinguished between "joint action" and a "united front"—the former of which he favored. But this left confusion as to what a "united front" would entail, since what Kantorovitch called "joint action" Thomas usually referred to as a united front for immediate ends. See Kantorovitch, "Notes on the United Front Problem," *ASM* (May, 1936), pp. 7–11. B. J. Field, then an orthodox Trotskyist, defined the united front as "joint action on limited and specified aims" with the right of "mutual criticism." "March separately, strike unitedly," he wrote. See B. J. Field, "The Viewpoint of the Left (Trotsky) Opposition," *MM* (June, 1933), p. 280.

20. For the Old Guard objections to the United Front, see Oneal, *Some Pages of Party History* (New York, 1934), pp. 22–23; Oneal, *Socialism versus Bolshevism*, pp. 20–27; Oneal to Harold Kelso, July 7, 1934 (in NT Papers); *NL* 1933–1935, *passim*. Dan Hoan shared the Old Guard opposition. See Hoan to Kelso, July 9, 1934 (in NT Papers). One of the Old Guard's chief tactical objections was that a united front would hurt Socialist influence in the trade unions. See Oneal to the Secretariat of the L.S.I., July 31, 1935 (in NT Papers). For Tyler's views, see Gus Tyler, *The United Front* (New York, 1933), pp. 3–19; Tyler, "The United Front," in Abraham Cahan, ed., *Hear the Other Side* (New York, 1934), pp. 44–49. For Thomas's position on a united front, see Thomas, *The Choice Before Us*, pp. 78–81,

147–155; Thomas, "Timely Topics," *NL* (1933–1935), *passim;*
Thomas to Senior, December 8, 1933; to Editor of *The Enterprise,*
August 27, 1934; to Leon Resner, April 12, 1934; to Milton Harvey,
April 12, 1934; to Herbert Solow, May 5, 1934; to Roger Baldwin,
July 26, 1934; to Earl Browder, August 21, 1934; to Browder, August
28, 1934; to W. Sherman, December 3, 1934; to J. Dombrowski,
January 30, 1935; to Messrs. Mitchell, Kester, Carpenter, January,
1935; to Henry Black, February 4, 1935 (in NT Papers). For Militant
criticism of the Communist attitude toward a united front, see also
Haim Kantorovitch, "The United Front," *ASQ* (December, 1934),
pp. 16–25. For a cautious Militant approval of united-front activities,
see Devere Allen to Thomas, October 13, 1933 (in NT Papers). For
support by Socialists in the League for Industrial Democracy for
united-front activities, see Mary Hillyer to Ethel Davis, November 1,
1933; Mary [Hunter] to Senior, November 22, 1933 (in SP Papers,
Duke). For enthusiastic support from a young Militant, see Paul A.
Rasmussen to Thomas, August 13, 1934 (in NT Papers). Rasmussen
urged the N.E.C. to reverse its position on a united front with the
Communists and to take an "aggressive stand." Sentiments like Rasmussen's concerned Thomas enough to want not to "ignore" the
Communist invitation for a united front or to answer it with a "blunt
dismissal." He liked the answer Leo Krzycki, the Party's chairman,
gave to the Communist invitation. Krzycki spelled out the problem and
kept the door open for cooperation. See Thomas to Senior, August 16,
1934; Leo Krzycki to Browder, July 29, 1934 (in NT Papers). By
November, however, Thomas was willing to drop all united-front
negotiations between the two parties and have a general rule covering
joint demonstrations. See Thomas to James Maurer, November 15,
1934 (in NT Papers). In November, the Socialist Party ended all
united-front negotiations with the Communist Party until the question
could be decided at the 1936 National Convention of the Party. At
its November meeting, the National Executive Committee made all
"sporadic and spontaneous local united front agreements" subject to
approval by state and national executive committees. See Hoan to
Edwin L. James, Managing Editor of the *New York Times,* December
5, 1934 (in NT Papers). See also Darlington Hoopes to State Executive
Committee of the Socialist Party of New York, December 8, 1934;
Thomas to J. T. Landis, December 17, 1934; Senior to N.E.C.,
December 18, 1934 (in NT Papers). Many members of the Old Guard,
however, interpreted the N.E.C.'s action not as a restriction on united-
front activities, but as a way to "open the door to local negotiations."

This would make local organizations "subject to Communist intrigue." See Sarah Limbach to Thomas, December 8, 1934 (in NT Papers).

21. For Thomas's and other Militants' criticism of Communist united-front practices, see preceding note. In *After the New Deal, What?*, Thomas wrote: "I am anxious on the one hand to cooperate where cooperation can be effective, and on the other to maintain that I am a Socialist and not a Communist, and that the two are different" (p. 220). The temporary "peace pact" between the Militants and the Old Guard in New York in the summer of 1935 was chiefly broken by the announcement of a debate between Browder and Thomas—a debate sponsored by the Militants' newspaper, the *Socialist Call*. The Old Guard interpreted the debate as a "united front" activity. See Julius Gerber to Thomas, October 4, 1935; Herbert Merrill to Thomas, October 5, 1935; Matthew Levy to Thomas, October 9, 1935; Robert A. Hoffmann to Thomas, October 10, 1935; (in NT Papers). At least one Militant, Alfred Baker Lewis, was also afraid that the debate meant Thomas was lining up for a united front. Lewis believed that the necessity of building a farmer-labor party in which organized labor would join required not participating with Communists in a united front. See Lewis to Jack Altman, December 5, 1935 (in NT Papers). For Thomas's defense of his participation in the debate and his explanation of the debate, see Thomas to Comrade Fruchter, October 14, 1935; to Margaret Gage, November 3, 1935; "Statement on the Thomas-Browder Debate," November 28, 1935; Andrew Biemiller to Thomas, November 28, 1935; Thomas to Biemiller, December 3, 1935, to Woodburn Harris, January 20, 1936 (in NT Papers).

22. For the Communist switch and the Popular Front line, see Howe and Coser, *The American Communist Party*, pp. 319–386. Thomas recognized that the new Communist line was attractive to many of the younger Socialists. This was one reason why he wished to debate Browder: to set forth clearly the *Socialist* position. See Thomas to Joseph J. O'Brocta, November 13, 1935 (in NT Papers). On the difficulties for the Socialists in the Communists' new position on war, see Norman Thomas vs. Earl Browder, *Which Way for American Workers, Socialist or Communist?* (New York, 1936), pp. 14–16, 36–37; Thomas, *After the New Deal, What?*, pp. 216–217; Thomas to Woodburn Harris, January 20, 1936 (in NT Papers); Herbert Zam, "World Socialism," *SC* (1935–1936), *passim;* Thomas, *SC* (December 7, 1935), p. 12; *SC* (April 25, 1936), p. 7; Thomas, *SC* (June 13, 1936), p. 12.

23. For the tacit Communist support of Roosevelt in the 1936

election, see Senior to Thomas, October 6, 1936 (in NT Papers); Howe and Coser, *The American Communist Party,* pp. 329–331. For Socialist criticism of the Communist campaign and stress on running a *socialist* campaign, see David Berenberg, "Ferment in Politics," *ASM* (August, 1936), pp. 2–7; Gus Tyler, "Two Conventions—With One Line," *ASM* (August, 1936), pp. 7–10; Tyler, "How Shall We Conduct Our Election Campaign?" *ASM* (October, 1936), pp. 13–19. Johnpoll's comment is in *Pacifist's Progress,* p. 173. For Thomas's connecting the building of a farmer-labor party with a national *socialist* campaign, see Thomas, "Why Labor Should Support the Socialist Party," *ASM* (July, 1936), pp. 2–7; Thomas, "May Day, 1936," *SC* (May 2, 1936), p. 24. For the Socialist campaign in general, see Thomas, *SC* (April 8, 1936), p. 12; Thomas, *SC* (June 6, 1936), p. 12; Thomas, *SC* (October 3, 1936), p. 12; *SC* (1936), *passim.* After the election, Thomas insisted that there was a need to continue to contrast the Socialist position of socialism versus capitalism with the Communist position of bourgeois democracy versus fascism. See Thomas to Glen Trimble, January 27, 1937 (in NT Papers). In rejecting the Popular Front, Thomas said that it was a "defensive tactic" that was justified only in an emergency. This did not exist in the United States. The issue was still "Socialism versus Capitalism," and the defeat of fascism depended on "the success of the struggle for Socialism." See Thomas to William Floyd, July 6, 1938 (in NT Papers). See also Thomas, *Socialism on the Defensive,* pp. 143–145.

24. On the Lash case, see Ben Fischer, "N.E.C. Motion," 1936; "Statement of NOC on Candidacy of Joe Lash as National Secretary of ASU," December 29, 1936; Roy Burt to Thomas, December 30, 1936; Frank Trager to Thomas, December 30, 1936; Lash to Thomas, January 5, 1937; Lash, Report, January 5, 1937; Al Hamilton and Alvaine Hollister to Dear Comrade, January 6, 1937; National Organization Committee, Y.P.S.L., "Report on the National Convention of the American Student Union," January 12, 1937 (in NT Papers); *SC* (October 30, 1937), p. 6; *SC* (December 25, 1937), p. 8. On the Lasser case, see to Dear Comrade, December 23, 1936; Trager to Brendan Sexton, January 29, 1937; to Glen Trimble, June 29, 1937; Burt to Thomas, September 21, 1937; Lasser to Thomas, December 29, 1937; Arthur G. McDowell to Thomas, January 12, 1938; Burt to N.E.C., February 1, 1938; to N.E.C., February 8, 1938; to Lasser, March 2, 1938 (in NT Papers); *SC* (January 14, 1939), p. 2. For Clarity's anti-Popular Front beliefs, see, e.g., Gus Tyler, "People's Government vs. Proletarian Dictatorship," *ASM* (March, 1936), pp.

20–23; Tyler, "People's Front Prepares War," *ASM* (February, 1937), pp. 38–43; Herbert Zam, "May Day and International Labor," *SR* (May-June, 1938), pp. 1–3; Zam, "World Socialism," *SC* (1936–1937), *passim; SC* (October 9, 1937), p. 4.

25. For Lewis's critique of Clarity and his urging that the *Socialist Call* boost the achievements of foreign Popular Front governments, see Lewis to Devere Allen, November 12, 1937 (in NT Papers). For Porter's views, see Porter, *Which Way for the Socialist Party?,* pp. 5–47; Porter to Thomas, January 27, 1937; to Thomas, June 5, 1936 (in NT Papers). Clarence Senior also hoped for better working relations with the Communists and was highly critical of the Trotskyists. See Senior to Devere Allen, February 3, 1937 (in NT Papers). The Trotskyists labeled Porter's pamphlet "liquidationist." It was representative, they said, of those who were liquidating the Socialist Party ideologically and organizationally. See, e.g., Carl Pemble, "A Correction to the Porter Pamphlet," February 28, 1937 (in NT Papers).

26. Porter, *Which Way for the Socialist Party?,* pp. 13–47. For Porter's critique of "sectarianism"—especially Trotskyist sectarianism —see Porter to Thomas, January 27, 1937 (in NT Papers).

27. Thomas to Porter, February 4, 1937; to Porter, February 4, 1937 (two different letters—in NT Papers).

28. Thomas, *Socialism on the Defensive,* pp. 105–145; Thomas, *SC* (1936–1938), *passim.* For the Clarity critique of Thomas for his position of criticizing the French People's Front government as opportunist at the same time that he endorsed it, see Ben Fischer to Thomas, October 3, 1936 (in NT Papers). For the Trotskyists' critique of the Popular Front, see Max Schactman, "Towards a Revolutionary Socialist Party," *ASM* (May, 1937), pp. 13–18; Ernest Erber, "Spain: New Outpost of World Revolution," *ASM* (December, 1936), pp. 17–20, James Burnham, *The People's Front* (New York, 1937).

29. Bell, *The End of Ideology,* p. 288. On the Socialist criticism of the embargo and demand to lift it, see Roy Burt, Statement on Neutrality Legislation, January 8, 1937 (in SP Papers, Duke); *SC* (January 2, 1937), pp. 1, 6; Burt, "Ban of Arms to Spain by Administration Is Pro-Fascist Step," *SC* (January 16, 1937), p. 2; *SC* (March 13, 1937), p. 3; Burt, "Socialists Must Push Campaign against War; Increase Aid to Spain," *SC* (June 12, 1937), p. 5; *SC* (April 23, 1938), p. 1; "Resolution on Spain," National Convention Socialist Party, U.S.A., April 23, 1938 (in SP Papers, Tamiment); *SC* (May 14, 1938), p. 1; Thomas, *SC* (May 21, 1938), p. 5; Thomas, *SC* (May 28, 1938), p. 5; *SC* (July 16, 1938), p. 4; Thomas to Max Raskin,

December 4, 1936; Release of the National Action Committee of the Socialist Party, January 6, 1937; Burt, Statement on Neutrality Legislation before House of Representatives Foreign Affairs Committee, February 19, 1937; Thomas, Statement on Neturality Legislation Presented to House of Representatives Foreign Affairs Committee, February 20, 1937; "On Spanish Neutrality Legislation," 1937; Thomas to Burt, November 25, 1938 (in NT Papers); Thomas, *Socialism on the Defensive,* pp. 131–132; Sam Romer, "Personal Notes from Spain," *SR* (September-October, 1938), pp. 4, 6; Thomas and Devere Allen, *Justice Triumphs in Spain,* December 15, 1938 (in Tamiment). Point Three of a Program for Action in the Resolution on War at the 1938 Socialist Party Convention read: "The immediate lifting of the embargo now directed against the democratically elected Loyalist government of Spain. Generous aid by the American people to the Spanish Loyalists in their fight against the international forces of fascism and to the workers in the underground movements abroad in an heroic struggle against fascist oppressors." See "Resolution on War," p. 6 (in SP Papers, Tamiment). Certainly—and with good reason—the Socialists did not place their faith in capitalist governments and certainly they claimed that only workers' aid would save Spain. See *SC* (July 3, 1937), p. 4; Herbert Zam, *SC* (July 10, 1937), p. 5; Gus Tyler, "Democracy and War," *SC* (December 25, 1937), p. 5; Zam, *SC* (March 27, 1937), p. 5. But this ideological argument existed in conjunction with the Party's demand to repeal the embargo. On Thomas's fears that Baron's testimony would kill the last hopes for repealing the embargo, see Thomas, *SC* (December 3, 1938), p. 4; Thomas to Burt, November 25, 1938 (in NT Papers). When James Loeb resigned from the editorial board of the *Socialist Review,* he wrote that Baron's article contradicted a previous article by Sam Romer. Romer's article, he said, reflected the views of the Spanish comrades: they wanted American Socialists to "Lift the Embargo." See Loeb to Zam, November 8, 1938 (in NT Papers).

30. *SC* (1936–1939), *passim.*

31. Thomas's views on the French and Spanish Popular Front can be found in "At the Front," *SC* (1936–1939), *passim;* Thomas, *Socialism on the Defensive,* pp. 105–145; Thomas to Hon. Leon Blum, June 3, 1936 (in NT Papers). Thomas said that it should be possible to criticize the Popular Front government in Spain without "bitterly attacking" it. See Thomas to Glen Trimble, January 27, 1937 (in NT Papers). For the Trotskyist position on Spain and the Popular Front, see Ernest Erber, "Spain: New Outpost of World Revolution," *ASM*

(December, 1936), pp. 17–20; Felix Morrow, *Revolution and Counter-Revolution in Spain* (New York, 1938), *passim;* Glen Trimble to All Revolutionary Socialists, July 8, 1937; George M. Whiteside to Thomas, September 16, 1936 (in NT Papers). A referendum proposal in Local New York singled out the denunciation by "certain groups" of the Party's position on Spain. The denunciation, it said, was "scurrilous and abusive." This reference was to the Trotskyists' attacks on the Party's position on Spain. See "Referendum to be proposed to Local New York for submission to the whole Party, 1937" (in NT Papers). Thomas's sharp displeasure at the Trotskyists' charges (where those who did not agree with them on the Barcelona uprising were labeled "butchers") can be seen in Thomas to Senior, July 19, 1937 (in NT Papers). For the Clarity position on Spain and the foreign Popular Fronts, see Al Hamilton to the Editor of the *Daily Worker,* July 30, 1936 (in NT Papers); Herbert Zam, *SC* (February 22, 1936), p. 4; Zam, *SC* (April 11, 1936), p. 8; Zam, *SC* (May 16, 1936), p. 8; Zam, *SC* (July 18, 1936), p. 8; Zam, *SC* (December 12, 1936), p. 5; Zam, *SC* (July 3, 1937), p. 5; Gus Tyler, "The People's Front in France," *SC* (May 16, 1936), p. 6; John Newton Thurber, "People's Front Tried and Found Wanting," *ASM* (October, 1936), pp. 19–23; *ASM* (May, 1937), p. 2; Zam, "Notes on International Events," *SR* (October-November, 1937), pp. 13–14; Zam, "May Day and International Labor," *SR* (May-June, 1938), pp. 1–3.

32. On the National Office difficulties, see Roy Burt to N.E.C., January 6, 1937; Thomas, Memorandum on the Spanish Situation, January 11, 1937; National Action Committee, Socialist Party. Statement on Present Confusion in Party on Spanish Question, January 11, 1937; Burt to Thomas, January 20, 1937; Frank Trager to Jack Altman, January 27, 1937 (in NT Papers). For Thomas's response to the news release on the Debs Column, see Thomas to Altman, December 24, 1936 (in NT Papers). For Thomas's general defense of the Debs Column, see Thomas, Memorandum on the Socialist Party and the Debs Column, December, 1936; Thomas to Devere Allen, Roy Burt, and the Staff, December 24, 1936; Thomas, Memorandum on the Spanish Situation in the Socialist Party, January 11, 1937 (in NT Papers). For the pacifists' protests, see, e.g., John Haynes Holmes to Thomas, December 23, 1936; Elizabeth Gilman to Thomas, December 24, 1936; Holmes to Thomas, December 28, 1936; to Thomas, January 7, 1937 (in NT Papers); Winston Dancis, Jessie Wallace Hughan, and A. J. Muste to *SC* (January 23, 1937), p. 7. For Thomas's replies to the pacifists, see Thomas to Holmes, December 24, 1936; to Hughan,

December 30, 1936, to John Nevin Sayre, December 30, 1936; to Holmes, January 6, 1937, to Holmes, January 19, 1937; to Mrs. Horace Eaton, January 21, 1937, to K. Brooke Anderson, January 26, 1937 (in NT Papers). Thomas was aided in keeping the pacifists in the Party by his close pacifist friend, Devere Allen, who had reservations about the Debs Column, but urged pacifists to remain loyal to the Socialist Party. See Allen to Abraham Kaufman, December 30, 1936 (in NT Papers). For the pacifists' decision to remain in the party, see Hughan to Thomas, January 4, 1937 (in NT Papers). Some pacifists, however, did resign. See the report of Jean Maxwell's resignation in Louis Mann to Thomas, January 21, 1937, and also Maxwell to Laidler, January 21, 1937 (in NT Papers). For Clarity's criticism of the pacifists, see *SC* (December 26, 1936), p. 4; Gus Tyler, "Violence in the Class Struggle," *SC* (January 9, 1937), p. 8; Tyler, "Pacifism—or Class Struggle," *SC* (January 23, 1937), p. 7; Trager to Allen, January 15, 1937 (in NT Papers). Trager favored the "arms to Spain" slogan, but Thomas was able to eliminate it. See Thomas to Allen, December 19, 1936 (in NT Papers). Thomas also had earlier opposed a plan to send a shipload of arms to Spain. See Glen Trimble to N.E.C., August 22, 1936; Thomas to Trimble, August 25, 1936 (in NT Papers). For criticism of Clarity's attack on the pacifists, see Allen to National Action Committee, January 13, 1937 (in NT Papers). On Allen's plea for toleration within the Party on differences of opinion on the Debs Column, see Allen to Thomas, January 5, 1937; untitled memorandum, 1937 (in NT Papers).

33. For support of the Debs Brigade, see *SC,* 1937, *passim.* For the Clarity's position, see Herbert Zam, "What Next in Spain?" *SC* (August 1, 1936), p. 10; John Newton Thurber, "People's Front Tried and Found Wanting, Spain 1936," *ASM* (October, 1936), pp. 19–23. For Trotskyist criticism, see George M. Whiteside to Thomas, September 16, 1936 (in NT Papers). For Thomas, see Thomas to Editor of *St. Louis Post-Dispatch,* September 9, 1936 (in NT Papers); Thomas, *SC* (January 23, 1937), p. 12; Thomas, *SC* (February 27, 1937), p. 12; *SC* (June 12, 1937), p. 3. Jack Altman, who was closely aligned with Thomas on domestic issues, was somewhat harsher on foreign Popular Front governments; see Altman, "People's Front and Moscow Trials," *SC* (January 30, 1937), p. 4. Thomas believed the Trotskyist position could jeopardize the Loyalist cause. See Thomas to Glen Trimble, November 24, 1936 (in NT Papers).

34. Thomas, *SC* (June 19, 1937), p. 8; Thomas, "Spain: A Socialist View," *N* (June 19, 1937), pp. 698–700; Thomas, *Socialism on the*

Defensive, pp. 136–142; Herbert Zam, *SC* (June 12, 1937), p. 5; Sam Baron and Liston Oak, "Stalinist 'Cheka' Method in Spain Destroys Unity of Anti-Fascist Struggle," *SC* (July 3, 1937), p. 3; Felix Morrow, *Revolution and Counter-Revolution in Spain* (New York, 1938), *passim.* See also the series of articles on Spain by Baron and Oak in *SC,* 1937, *passim.*

35. On May 15, 1937, the *New Leader* wrote that if the Fascists succeeded, the Barcelona Anarchists would "have a heavy share of the responsibility." See *NL* (May 15, 1937), p. 8. The new Prieto government was reported in highly favorable terms. See *NL* (May 22, 1937), pp. 1, 3; Victor Schiff, "A New Partnership Arises," *NL* (June 5, 1937), p. 4. On August 7, 1937, the *New Leader* reported that "Communist vituperation" was being turned against Caballero. See *NL* (August 7, 1937), pp. 1, 5. But the next week the paper headed its story on Spain, "Caballero Unites with Gov't Enemies, Attack Loyalists," *NL* (August 14, 1937), p. 1. Little or nothing was said about the anti-Stalinist purges in Spain until the war was lost. Only then did the *New Leader* editorialize on the "GPU in Spain" and print articles by the former Loyalist ambassador to France, Luis Ariquistain, criticizing the role of the Communists in Spain. See *NL* (April 22, 1939), p. 8; Ariquistain, *NL* (June 3, 1939), p. 4; Ariquistain, *NL* (June 10, 1939), p. 6; Ariquistain, *NL* (June 17, 1939), p. 4. See also Sam Baron to *NL* (July 8, 1939), p. 8; *NL* (July 15, 1939), pp. 3, 6.

36. Thomas to Hon. Fernando de los Rios, November 8, 1937; to Oswald Garrison Villard, December 22, 1937; to Friedrich Adler, November 29, 1937; to Juan Negrin, July 26, 1938; to de los Rios, October, 1938; to de los Rios, October 9, 1938; to de los Rios, November 18, 1937; to Dear Comrade, June 28, 1937; Thomas, Memorandum to the Sub-Committee on Spain, July 2, 1937 (in NT Papers); Thomas, *SC* (November 26, 1937), p. 4; Thomas, *Socialism on the Defensive,* pp. 138–139. The party was opposed to "insurrection" against the Spanish government, but believed the Negrin government's policy of excluding the "so-called 'left' elements" was ineffective in the struggle against Franco. It also felt that the new government's failure to carry out "social change" until the end of the war was damaging to the war effort and to the triumph of socialism. See N.E.C. Sub-Committee on Spain, Suggested Additional Party Statement on Spain, June 14, 1937 (in SP Papers, Duke). On Baron's testimony, see Thomas to Roy Burt, November 29, 1938 (in NT Papers). For Thomas's belief that the Barcelona Trial of late 1938 was "pretty well-handled," see Thomas to Burt, November 26, 1938 (in NT Papers). See also Thomas to

Charles C. Schleicher, November 30, 1938; to Schleicher, December 13, 1938 (in NT Papers); Thomas and Devere Allen, *Justice Triumphs in Spain,* December 15, 1938 (in SP Papers, Tamiment). James Loeb did not seek to cover up the purges. See Loeb, "Two May Days in Spain," *SC* (April 30, 1938), p. 4. However, strategically he felt it bad to accent the negative aspects in the manner that Baron did. See Loeb to Herbert Zam, November 8, 1938 (in NT Papers). A year earlier, after receiving a sharply worded cable from Spain that rebuked those "disguised" antifascists who favored the rebels and fascists, Loeb advised Thomas that the Party should "lay off for a while" until "some specific incident presents itself." He suggested that "for the sake of our relations with Negrin" a reply pledging continued support be sent. See Loeb to Thomas, December 3, 1937 (in NT Papers). For Clarity's position on Baron's testimony, see Travers Clement to N.E.C., December 2, 1938 (in NT Papers).

37. Thomas, *SC* (February 4, 1939), p. 1; Devere Allen to Thomas, April 13, 1939; Hal Siegel to Thomas, April 17, 1939; Thomas to Irving Barshop, May 19, 1939; to Herman Reissig, May 20, 1939; to Mrs. America Gonzalez, July 21, 1939 (in NT Papers). In *My Mission to Spain* (New York, 1954), Bowers quoted Roosevelt as telling him: "We have made a mistake; you have been right all along" (p. 418).

Chapter IX Socialists and World War II

1. Johnpoll, p. 249.

2. For the Socialist Party's antiwar activities, see *SC* (1938–1941), *passim.* The Party's 1940 Resolution on War and the minority position can be found in the *SC* (April 20, 1940), pp. 2–3. For Lewis, see Lewis to Thomas, December 16, 1938; to Thomas, February 17, 1939; to Thomas, February 21, 1939; to Thomas, April 26, 1939; to Thomas, May 2, 1939; to Thomas, September 30, 1939; to Fellowship of Reconciliation, October 7, 1939; to Thomas, November 29, 1939; to Thomas, July 22, 1940; to Frank Trager, July 19, 1940 (in NT Papers); Lewis, "Axis Victory Would Hem in U.S. for Fascist Push," *NL* (October 26, 1940), pp. 4, 7; Lewis, "The Implications of Socialist Policy," July 17, 1940 (in SP Papers, Duke). On Porter, see Porter, "The Struggle of the Empires," *SC* (September 23, 1939), p. 2; Porter to Thomas, June 5, 1940 (in NT Papers); Arthur G. McDowell to National Executive Committee, June 27, 1940; Porter to National Executive Committee, December 24, 1940 (in SP Papers, Duke). On Altman, see Altman to *NL* (June 1, 1940), p. 8; Irving Barshop to

Thomas, August 6, 1940; Thomas to Barshop, August 7, 1940; Lazar Becker to Porter, June 27, 1940 (in NT Papers). See also Johnpoll, *Pacifist's Progress*, pp. 220–226. In January, 1941, Jack Altman, Reinhold Niebuhr, Murray Gross, Frank Crosswaith, Lazar Becker, Gus Tyler, Alfred Baker Lewis, and other Socialists issued a statement opposing Thomas's views on Lend-Lease. See *NL* (January 25, 1941), p. 7. The *SC* replied that only Becker and Gross were still in the Socialist Party and charges were pending against them. See *SC* (February 8, 1941), p. 3. For Trager, see Trager to the Members of the Socialist Party, February 24, 1941; to Thomas, June 17, 1941 (in NT Papers); Porter and Trager, A Statement Accompanying Resignation from the National Executive Committee of the Socialist Party, February, 1941 (in SP Papers, Duke). For McDowell, see McDowell to the National Executive Committee, June 25, 1940 (in SP Papers, Duke); McDowell, "Questions to Socialist Pacifists," *HT* (July-August, 1940), pp. 22–24; Kellam Foster, John Mill, Arthur G. McDowell, Mordecai Shulman, "For Aid to Britain," *HT* (February-March, 1941), pp. 7–11; McDowell, "A Personal Political Communication to Active Members of the Socialist Party," January 17, 1941; Kellam Foster, Arthur G. McDowell, John Mill, Mordecai Shulman, "A Letter to the National Executive Committee," January 15, 1941 (in SP Papers, Tamiment). Albert Sprague Coolidge had also broken with the Party's war policy and become inactive in the Party. See Coolidge and Lewis, "Imperialist War?" *HT* (March, 1940), pp. 10–13; Coolidge to Thomas, June 4, 1939; to Thomas, October 1, 1939; to Trager, March 1, 1941 (in NT Papers); Coolidge to *SC* (June 22, 1940), p. 3. See also Lazar Becker, "The War: Another View," *HT* (March, 1940), pp. 14–21; Minutes of the National Action Committee, Socialist Party, U.S.A., December 19, 1940 (in SP Papers, Duke). Many of these same people had previously shared the Party's position on war. Alfred Baker Lewis had opposed any new "war for democracy" and had ridiculed sanctions and the Old Guard's support of them. See Lewis to Thomas, November 29, 1935 (in NT Papers). See also Lewis, "Socialists and Sanctions," *SC* (February 1, 1936), p. 10. Here he wrote that sanctions meant war, that reliance on the League of Nations would be a mistake, that the neutrality legislation should be strengthened, and that labor could stop war by a labor embargo. In August, 1938, Lewis said that Socialists shouldn't oppose "collective security" by labor and Socialist governments, but should oppose "collective security action when carried out by a capitalist government." See Lewis to *SC* (August 6, 1938), p. 4. On Altman's earlier opposition to collective security, see Altman,

"What Happened in London," *SC* (March 27, 1937), p. 6. Here he wrote that "only working class action can help Spain and prevent war."

3. The Party's basic statements on war were the 1936 and 1938 Resolutions on War adopted by the National Conventions. See *ASM* (July, 1936), pp. 15–17; "Resolution on War," Kenosha Convention (in SP Papers, Tamiment). For Zam's position, see Zam, "Ask Workers Sanctions Against Japan," *SC* (October 9, 1937), p. 5; Zam, "A War for Profits," *SC* (September 23, 1939), p. 2; Zam, "War Policies, Sanctions, and Socialism," *ASM* (May, 1936), pp. 17–21; Zam, "May Day 1886–1937," *ASM* (May, 1937), pp. 3–8; Zam, "No Support to Imperialism," *SR* (September, 1937), pp. 13–15, 25; Zam, "Notes on International Events," *SR* (October-November, 1937), pp. 13–14; Zam, "May Day and International Labor," *SR* (May-June, 1938), pp. 1–3; Zam, "Munich—and After," *SR* (September-October, 1938), pp. 1–3; Zam, "Notes on Current Events," *SR* (January-February, 1939), pp. 16–18; Zam, "Notes on Current Events," *SR* (March-April, 1936), pp. 14–16. For Tyler, see Tyler, "Democracy and War," *SC* (December 25, 1937), p. 5; Tyler, "Europe Rushes toward War," *SC* (August 1, 1936), p. 7; Tyler, "Should U.S. Labor Back a War Against Hitler?," *SC* (November 13, 1937), p. 8; Tyler, "Collective Security With Imperialists Doesn't Aid Labor," *SC* (May 14, 1938), p. 5; Tyler, "People's Front Prepares War," *ASM* (February, 1937), pp. 38–43. See also Henry Haskell, *SC* (1938–1939), *passim;* Haskell, "Popular Front—Middle Class Weapon," *SR* (July-August, 1938), pp. 8–11; *SC* (August 28, 1937), p. 8; *SC* (September 25, 1937), p. 4; *SC* (October 16, 1937), p. 4; *SC* (November 13, 1937), p. 2; *SC* (February 5, 1938), p. 4; *SC* (May 27, 1939), p. 4. The Clarity had no faith in neutrality laws—something Thomas favored strengthening. See *SC* (August 7, 1937), p. 1; Tyler, "Can the Neutrality Law Keep U.S.A. Out of War?," *SC* (May 8, 1937), p. 6; Tyler, "What Has Happened to the Neutrality Law," *SC* (July 24, 1937), p. 7; *SC* (January 16, 1937), p. 6. Tyler was willing to concede that neutrality legislation could be useful in hampering American entrance into a war. But, at the same time, it was necessary to warn workers not to rely on neutrality legislation to prevent war. See Tyler to Devere Allen, March 6, 1937 (in NT Papers). For the Socialist Party's reaction to the beginning of World War II, see *SC* (September 23, 1939), pp. 1–2; *SC* (September 16, 1939), p. 1; Zam, "A War for Profit," *SC* (September 23, 1939), p. 2; Henry Haskell, *SC* (September-October, 1939), *passim;* Devere Allen, "Who Is Responsible for the War?," *SC* (October 14, 1939), p. 1; Thomas, "It's Still an

Imperialist War," *MQ* (Fall, 1939), pp. 7–17; Zam, "The New Imperialist War," *SR* (September-October, 1939), pp. 3–4. When Russia invaded Finland, Gerry Allard, the editor of the *Socialist Call,* called for the Socialist Party to aid Finland. See *SC* (December 9, 1939), p. 4. Under criticism from those who said that his position would lead to a new crusade and that Socialists could not rely on capitalist governments for aid, Allard retreated to say that he had meant that Socialists should support *workers'* aid. This still left it un-clear where the aid would be going—to the Finnish government or to the Finnish workers' organizations. The Party was willing to help the latter—i.e., willing for Socialists to send help to Finnish working-class organizations. Beyond that it would not go. On the controversy over aid to Finland, see Raymond Hofses, "Reflections on Finland," *SC* (De-cember 23, 1939), p. 2; *SC* (December 23, 1939), p. 4; Henry Haskell, "The Soviet Onslaught on World Socialism," *SC* (December 23, 1939), p. 1; Lillian Symes, *SC* (December 16, 1939), p. 4; Symes, *SC* (January 13, 1940), p. 4; *SC* (December 9, 1939), p. 1; Thomas, "Finland's Fight," *SC* (December 16, 1939), pp. 1–2; *SC* (December 16, 1939), p. 4; *SC* (February 3, 1940), p. 4; Alfred Baker Lewis to *SC* (January 6, 1940), p. 3. Herbert Zam was the only prominent Socialist calling for a strategy of "revolutionary defeatism" by the Finnish workers. See Zam, "The Russo-Finnish Struggle," *SR* (Novem-ber-December, 1939), pp. 8–9. For a criticism of Zam from the view-point of the Party's official position, see Frank Trager and Lillian Symes, "The Finnish Problem," *SR* (November-December, 1939), pp. 6–8.

4. On European "collective security" against Germany, see, e.g., Gus Tyler, "How the Democratic States Aided the Fascist Powers," *SC* (May 1, 1937), p. 14; Thomas, "Collective Security and Socialism," *SR* (May-June, 1938), pp. 4–5, 15. On the fears that the sanctions called for under collective security would not work, see "Do Sanc-tions Mean War?" in *World Events* (November 15, 1934), edited by Devere Allen (in NT Papers); John Dewey, "Are Sanctions Necessary to International Organization? No," *Foreign Policy Association Pamphlets,* No. 83 (June, 1932), pp. 26–28; Charles Beard, "Collec-tive Security—a Debate: II A Reply to Mr. Browder," *NR* (February 2, 1938), p. 357; Joel Seidman, "Socialism, Sanctions, and War," *SC* (October 26, 1935), p. 12. On the remembrances of World War I, see, e.g., Tyler, "Democracy and War," *SC* (December 25, 1937), p. 5; *SC* (August 19, 1937), p. 4; Lillian Symes, "Then and Now," *SC* (October 14, 1939), p. 4; Tyler, "Should U.S. Labor Back a War

Notes for page 161 251

Against Hitler?," *SC* (November 13, 1937), p. 8; Tyler, "Democracy and War," *SC* (December 18, 1937), p. 5; Thomas, "Dangerous Illusions About the Next War," *SR* (March-April, 1939), pp. 1–4, 12. For the imprisonment of Evan Thomas during World War I, see Fleischman, *Norman Thomas,* pp. 72–75. On the earlier fears of the United States going fascist in wartime by a later prowar radical, see Sidney Hook, "Against Sanctions," *MM* (April, 1936), pp. 14–17. For Hook's later support of aid to the Allies, see Hook, "Socialism, Common Sense and the War," *NL* (August 31, 1940), p. 7. See also the symposium "When America Goes to War," *MM* (June, 1935), pp. 199–204; *MM* (September, 1935), pp. 264–273; *MM* (December, 1935), pp. 382–383. For the desire to aid the Allies and still stay out of war, see Paul Porter, "The Struggle for Empire," *SC* (September 23, 1939), p. 2; Alfred Baker Lewis to Thomas, February 21, 1939 (in NT Papers). Thomas was anxious not to make support of repeal of the embargo a matter of party discipline. What worried him, however, was that those who, in the fall of 1939, were pushing for repeal as a way to keep the United States out of war would really support American entrance into the war. See, e.g., Thomas to Travers Clement, October 3, 1939; to Mary Felton, October 12, 1939; to Clement, October 27, 1939 (in NT Papers).

5. Thomas's views can be found in *SC* (1936–1941) *passim;* Thomas, "Collective Security and Socialism," *SC* (May-June, 1938), pp. 4–5, 15; Thomas, "Dangerous Illusions about the Next War," *SR* (March-April, 1939), pp. 1–4, 12; Thomas, "The New Deal Faces the Election," *SR* (Spring, 1940), pp. 4–8; Thomas, "It's Still an Imperialist War," *MQ* (Fall, 1939), pp. 7–17; Thomas, "We Needn't Go to War," *H* (November, 1938), pp. 657–664; Thomas, *Socialism on the Defensive* (New York, 1938), pp. 165–209; Thomas and Bertram D. Wolfe, *Keep America Out of War* (New York, 1939), *passim;* Thomas to Lewis, February 20, 1939; to Lewis, February 23, 1939; to Lewis, August 29, 1939; to Lewis, October 3, 1939; to Lewis, October 1939; to Lewis, July 23, 1940; to Albert Sprague Coolidge, June 2, 1939; to Coolidge, June 5, 1939; to Editor of the *Swarthmore Review,* February 13, 1940; to Henry Pinski, April 8, 1941; to Jerry Voorhis, November 14, 1941; to Louis Sadoff, March 5, 1941; to M. Matlin, May 10, 1940; to Comrade Levine, December, 1940; to Ralph Harlow, June 5, 1940 (in NT Papers). In *Isolationism in America* (New York, 1966), pp. 32–99, Manfred Jonas distinguishes between "timid" and "belligerent" isolationists and between liberal, radical, and conservative isolationism.

6. For Thomas's desire for a negotiated peace, see Thomas, "It's Still an Imperialist War," *MQ* (Fall, 1939), p. 16; Thomas to Lewis, June 20, 1940 (in NT Papers); Thomas, *SC* (November 18, 1939), p. 2. For the idea of workers making the peace, see *SC* (November 4, 1939), p. 4; Lillian Symes, "Then and Now," *SC* (October 14, 1939), p. 4. On Thomas's warning to place no trust in the "old" imperialism, even if it was preferable to the "new" imperialism, see, e.g., Thomas to Henry Pinski, April 8, 1941 (in NT Papers); Thomas and Bertram D. Wolfe, *Keep America Out of War*, pp. 150–151. German imperialism, he wrote in 1939, was worse, but preservation of the British Empire was "not equivalent to the preservation of democracy." See Thomas to the Editor of the *New York Times*, August 10, 1939 (in NT Papers). For views of the American Far East policy, see, e.g., Thomas to Henry Sloan Coffin, August 6, 1940 (in NT Papers); Thomas, "It's Still an Imperialist War," pp. 13–14; Thomas, *Socialism on the Defensive*, p. 195.

7. Lillian Symes to Norman Thomas, September 23, 1939 (in NT Papers); Symes, "Peace—But How?" *SC* (September 30, 1939), p. 4.

8. The pessimism of the revolutionary Socialists concerning a workers' revolution can be clearly seen in their comments on the Russo-Finnish war. See Lillian Symes, *SC* (January 13, 1940), p. 4; Trager and Symes, "The Finnish Problem," *SR* (November-December, 1939), pp. 6–8. Even when they discussed the possibilities of revolution emerging from a war-weary Europe, they did so in more modulated tones than those used in the mid-1930's. See Travers Clement to Alfred Baker Lewis, October 14, 1939; Symes to Oskar Lange, November 7, 1939 (in NT Papers). Lange saw revolution being quickened by an Allied victory. See Lange, "The Socialist Attitude toward the War," *MQ* (Summer, 1940), pp. 11–22. For Lewis's comment, see Lewis to Thomas, June 5, 1940 (in NT Papers). Lewis wrote: "I guess my feeling at bottom is a very simple one. The labor movement will be destroyed in Europe if Hitler wins and won't if he is defeated."

9. Wayne Cole, *America First* (Madison, 1953), *passim;* Chadwin, *The Hawks of World War II* (Chapel Hill, 1968), pp. 43–73. For Thomas's criticism of Henry Luce, see Thomas to Leslie Seviringhous, July 16, 1941; to Dorothy Thompson, February 24, 1941 (in NT Papers). For Thomas's view of Roosevelt and Willkie as candidates of Wall Street and other interventionists, see Thomas to Peter Sargent, September, 1940 (in NT Papers). On Thomas's criticism of the values of the leading interventionists, see Thomas to Robert Alexander, June

Notes for pages 163–166

253

19, 1941; to Jimmie [Loeb], September 24, 1941 (in NT Papers). See also *SC* (August 3, 1940), p. 4.

10. For Thomas's refusal to become a member of the America First Committee, see Thomas to R. E. Wood, May 2, 1941 (in NT Papers). On Thomas's comparison of his relationship with the America First Committee to Socialist work in mass organizations, see Thomas to Grace Milgram, July 28, 1941; to Louis Gottesman, November 19, 1941 (in NT Papers). For Thomas's "gentle prodding," see Thomas to Sen. Burton K. Wheeler, March 5, 1941; to R. Douglas Stuart, Jr., May 1, 1941; to John T. Flynn and Stuart, June 25, 1941 (in NT Papers). On the Lindbergh controversy, see *SC* (September 27, 1941), p. 4; *SC* (October 4, 1941), p. 3; Socialist Party Release, September 23, 1941 (in SP Papers, Duke); Thomas to Stuart, September 10, 1941; to Lawrence Stiller, September 16, 1941; to Mrs. Kellog Fairbanks, September 12, 1941; to Stuart, September 16, 1941; to Gen. R. E. Wood, September 17, 1941; to Ralph Oscar Robinson, September 22, 1941; to Stuart, September 23, 1941; to Colonel Charles A. Lindbergh, September 24, 1941; to Rev. Hugh C. Barr, September 24, 1941; to Mrs. Janet Ayre Fairbank, September 27, 1941; to Stuart, September 29, 1941 (in NT Papers).

11. Sidney Hook, "Against Sanctions," *MQ* (April, 1936), p. 15. For Thomas's fears that the United States would turn fascist if it went to war, see *SC* (June 15, 1940), p. 1; Thomas, "What War Would Mean for America," *SC* (February 15, 1941), p. 5; Thomas, *SC* (August 23, 1941), pp. 5, 8; Thomas to Meyer Rabinowitz, December, 1940; to Mr. Dewirtz, January 24, 1941; to Charles Schwager, February 26, 1941; to Arnold Hoffman, June 4, 1941 (in NT Papers).

12. *NL* (May 11, 1940), p. 8; *NL* (May 31, 1941), p. 8; Algernon Lee, *NL* (September 16, 1939), p. 8; *NL* (February 22, 1941), p. 8; Francis Loewenheim, review of Saul Friedlander, *Prelude to Downfall, New York Times Book Review* (February 4, 1968), p. 12.

13. Charles Alexander, "Leftist Critics of the American Left, 1938–1942" (paper presented at the 1968 Meeting of the Organization of American Historians). Professor Alexander is less critical of the interventionist argument in his subsequent book, *Nationalism in American Thought, 1930–1945* (Chicago, 1969). But he still finds it often "vague and cryptic" (p. 185). Archibald MacLeish, "Post-War Writers and Pre-War Readers," *NR* (June 10, 1940), pp. 789–790. In speaking of Hemingway, DosPassos, and the post-world war writers MacLeish wrote: "Those writers must face the fact that the books they wrote in

the years just after the war have done more to disarm democracy in the face of fascism than any other single influence. . . . I do undertake to maintain that what they wrote, however true as a summary of their personal experience, was disastrous as education for a generation which would be obliged to face the threat of fascism in its adult years" (p. 790). See also MacLeish, *The Irresponsibles* (New York, 1940), pp. 3–34. The phrase "age of conformity" is taken from Irving Howe, "This Age of Conformity," *Partisan Review* (January-February, 1954), pp. 7–33.

14. Lewis Mumford, *Men Must Act* (New York, 1939), pp. 96–131; Mumford, *Faith for Living* (New York, 1940), pp. 305–333; Mumford, "United States Attack Axis Armies Now," *NL* (June 7, 1941), p. 5; Mumford, "FDR Loses First Pacific Battle," *NL* (September 6, 1941), p. 3; Mumford, "Reply to Gen. Rivers," *NL* (October 4, 1941), p. 4; Mumford, "Mumford Calls for Housecleaning," *NL* (December 13, 1941), p. 5; Waldo Frank, *A Chart for Rough Waters* (New York, 1940), *passim;* Reinhold Niebuhr, review of *Faith for Living, N* (September 14, 1940), pp. 221–222; Niebuhr, review of *Chart for Rough Waters, N* (May 11, 1940), pp. 600–601.

15. Mumford, *Men Must Act, passim;* Mumford, *Faith for Living, passim;* Frank, *Chart for Rough Waters, passim.*

16. Mumford, *Men Must Act,* pp. 86–87, 98–99; Frank, *Chart for Rough Waters,* pp. 52–56, 160–176. The quote is from a radio address that Mumford delivered in December, 1940 for the Canadian Broadcasting Corporation. See Mumford, *Values for Survival* (New York, 1946), pp. 53–54.

17. On the Luce publications' desire for "affirmative" literature, see "Wanted: An American Novel," *Life* (September 12, 1955), p. 48; "Advice from and to Writers," *Life* (June 11, 1956), p. 40.

18. *NL* (October 25, 1941), p. 1; *NL* (January 4, 1941), p. 8. In April, 1941, the *New Leader* blasted the A.C.L.U. for criticizing appropriations to the F.B.I. to investigate government employees. It said that the A.C.L.U. should think of the rights of the majority instead of defending Nazis and Communists. This is not the "theoretics of peace, but the logistics of a military situation," the editorial declared. See *NL* (April 26, 1941), p. 8.

19. *NL* (July 19, 1941), p. 8. This editorial was not so much an attack on the prosecution of the Minneapolis Trotskyists as an inquiry into why there was not a crackdown on the Stalinists. The Trotskyists, it said, "merely yearn for power," but the Stalinists "have power and . . . have used it again and again for seditious and subversive ends."

See also *NL* (December 6, 1941), p. 8. The quote about loyally supporting elected leaders is from *NL* (December 28, 1940), p. 8.

20. In an essay written in March 1941, Mumford wrote: "Perhaps
the greatest catastrophe of the war was that those who emerged from
it accepted, consciously or unconsciously, the romantic defeatism that
Bourne had preached in 1917." See Mumford, *Values for Survival*, p.
63.

21. Thomas, *SC* (January 21, 1939), p. 2; Thomas, *SC* (February
4, 1939), p. 1; Thomas, *SC* (March 25, 1939), p. 2; Thomas, *SC*
(September 2, 1939), p. 2; Arthur McDowell, "The New Deal Fails,"
SC (February 10, 1940), p. 2; Thomas to Ralph Harlow, June 5, 1940;
to Gerry [Allard], June 3, 1940; to J. M. Baumgartner, August 29,
1940; to Grant Knight, October 2, 1940; "Proposed Platform of the
Keep America Out of War Congress," May, 1938 (in NT Papers);
Herbert Zam, "Roosevelt's Pro-War Economy," SR (March-April,
1938), pp. 4–6; Travers Clement, "The Challenge of 1940," *SR*
(September-October, 1939), pp. 9–10; *SC* (May 4, 1940), p. 8;
Thomas, *SC* (September 2, 1939), p. 2; Thomas, *SC* (1940–1941),
passim; SC (May 24, 1941), p. 4.

22. Arthur G. McDowell, "How Draft Threatens Labor," *SC*
(October 5, 1940), p. 3; Albert Hamilton, "Democracy and Militariza-
tion," *SC* (December 28, 1940), p. 2; *SC* (April 19, 1941), p. 6; *SC*
(August 3, 1940), p. 1; Thomas, *SC* (August 10, 1940), pp. 1–2;
Thomas, *SC* (September 7, 1940), p. 5; Thomas, *SC* (September 14,
1940), p. 5; Thomas, *SC* (September 21, 1940), p. 5; Thomas, *SC*
(August 9, 1941), pp. 5, 8; *SC* (September 28, 1940), p. 1; *SC* (August
10, 1940), pp. 1, 3; *SC* (July 6, 1941), p. 4; *SC* (July 20, 1941), p. 1;
Thomas to Burton Wheeler, July 31, 1940; to Maynard Krueger, July
10, 1940; to Oswald Garrison Villard, July 11, 1940; to Franklin
Delano Roosevelt, July 24, 1940; to Members of the House Military
Affairs Committee, July 30, 1940; to Roosevelt, August 5, 1940; to
Editor of the *Des Moines Evening Tribune*, August 16, 1940 (in NT
Papers); *Mr. Jones Becomes Private Jones*, pamphlet (in SP Papers,
Tamiment).

23. On the reliance on one man in foreign policy, see *SC* (June 1,
1940), p. 4; *SC* (June 7, 1941), p. 1; *SC* (September 14, 1940), p.
1; *SC* (June 7, 1941), pp. 1, 4; Thomas to Margaret Lamont, November 2, 1936; to Howard Lee, February 8, 1937 (in NT Papers). The
Socialists supported the Ludlow Amendment, although the *Socialist
Call* said it was "far from a surefire way of keeping us out of war." See
SC (December 25, 1937), p. 1; *SC* (January 15, 1938), p. 1; *SC*

(March 26, 1938), p. 4. Norman Thomas felt it was no "panacea," but could be helpful. He warned that war was "inherent in the nature of the institutions and loyalties of capitalism, nationalism and militarism." See Thomas to Fred Emerson, November 2, 1937 (in NT Papers). See also Thomas, *SC* (December 25, 1937), p. 4; Statement (untitled), December, 1937; Thomas to Senator Robert LaFollette, March 7, 1939; to Frances B. Shepherd, May 17, 1939; "Local Wayne County Bulletin against War," January 6, 1938 (in NT Papers). In early 1941, Thomas, believing that war was imminent and that there was not enough time to mount a full-scale drive for the Ludlow Amendment, urged an "advisory war referendum." See Thomas to John T. Flynn, March 15, 1941; to Mr. Boscaino, March 18, 1941 (in NT Papers). The historian Selig Adler has labeled the Ludlow Amendment the product of "American schizoid thinking." See Selig Adler, *The Uncertain Giant 1921–1941* (London, 1965), p. 42. It is interesting that Sidney Hook, in entertaining the possibility of modifying the Neutrality Act in the fall of 1939, also urged the inclusion of the Ludlow Clause as in "keeping with democratic processes." See Sidney Hook to *NL* (November 4, 1939), p. 8. On the people's general right to decide on war, see Thomas, *SC* (January 21, 1939), p. 2; Thomas, "Let the People Speak on War!," *SC* (October 21, 1939), pp. 1–2; *SC* (October 14, 1939), p. 4; Thomas, *SC* (March 8, 1941), p. 5.

24. Israel Knox to Thomas, December 8, 1942 (in NT Papers); David S. Wyman, *Paper Walls: America and the Refugee Crisis 1938–1941* (Amherst, Mass., 1968); Arthur D. Morse, *While Six Million Died: A Chronicle of American Apathy* (New York, 1967). On Thomas's and the Socialist Party's attempts to aid refugees, see Johnpoll, *Pacifist's Progress,* pp. 218–220; Heinrich Erlich, "The Evian Conference," *SC* (July 30, 1938), p. 2; Thomas to Franklin Delano Roosevelt, October 21, 1938; Roy Burt to Dear Comrades, November 4, 1938; Thomas to Paul Allen, Ocotber 17, 1939; to Travers Clement, October 10, 1939; Thomas, "Memorandum for Committee on International Labor Solidarity," 1938; Devere Allen to Thomas, January 30, 1940; Frank Trager to Albert Sprague Coolidge, June 6, 1940; Thomas to Roosevelt, June 11, 1940; Travers Clement to Thomas, June 25, 1940; Thomas to A. A. Berle, July 9, 1940 (in NT Papers); *SC* (July 5, 1941), p. 2. The Old Guard Socialist B. C. Vladeck replied to Thomas's suggestion of a campaign to relax immigration quotas by saying that the strong resentment against admitting more immigrants made it unwise. Roosevelt, Vladeck said, was acting privately on a "lot of things" and it would be harmful to have them publicized. See

Vladeck to Thomas, October 10, 1938 (in BCV Papers). The *New Leader* had an editorial in November, 1938, urging help for the refugees, and, in the same month, it urged a relaxation of immigration quotas. See *NL* (November 5, 1938), p. 8; *NL* (November 26, 1938), p. 1. Apparently its pro-New Deal orientation, however, prevented any further public campaign, since there was little subsequent follow-up. The *New Leader*'s apologetics concerning the New Deal and the refugees eventually led Dwight MacDonald to attack its portrayal of Secreatry of State Hull. See Dwight MacDonald, "The Jews, 'The New Leader,' and Old Judge Hull," *Politics* (January, 1945), pp. 23–25. The pro-New Deal *Nation* and *New Republic* were much more critical of the New Deal's handling of the refugee problem than was the *New Leader*. See Freda Kirchwey, *N* (July 6, 1940), pp. 4–5; Kirchwey, *N* (August 17, 1940), p. 124–125; Kirchwey, *N* (August 31, 1940), pp. 163–164; Kirchwey, *N* (December 28, 1940), pp. 648–649; *N* (August 3, 1940), p. 83; Kirchwey, *N* (July 19, 1941), pp. 45–46; Kirchwey, *N* (June 5, 1943), pp. 796–797; I. F. Stone, "For the Jews—Life or Death?" *N* (June 10, 1944), pp. 670–671; Kirchwey, *N* (August 26, 1944), p. 229; *NR* (July 5, 1939), pp. 234–235; *NR* (June 10, 1940), p. 776; *NR* (January 20, 1941), p. 72; *NR* (July 28, 1941), pp. 105–106; *NR* (August 18, 1941), p. 208; *NR* (January 12, 1942), pp. 37–38; *NR* (March 9, 1942), pp. 316–317; *NR* (July 13, 1942), p. 37; *NR* (August 31, 1942), p. 244; Varian Frey, "The Massacre of the Jews," *NR* (December 21, 1942), pp. 816–819; Special Supplement, *NR* (August 30, 1943), pp. 299–316; *NR* (September 6, 1943), p. 319; *NR* (December 6, 1943), p. 797; *NR* (December 20, 1943), pp. 867–868; *NR* (April 3, 1944), p. 452; *NR* (December 31, 1945), p. 885.

25. On the Socialists' fear that war would end reform and threaten democracy, see *SC* (April 29, 1939), p. 12; Thomas, "Labor and War," *SC* (April 29, 1939), p. 4; Henry Haskell, "Peace for America," *SC* (July 8, 1939), p. 4; Thomas to Anton Garden, May 29, 1940; to Frank Zeidler, July 15, 1940 (in NT Papers); *SC* (March 29, 1941), p. 5; *SC* (June 21, 1941), p. 4; *SC* (June 28, 1941), p. 3; *SC* (July 12, 1941), p. 4; *SC* (December 6, 1941), p. 1. On the dismantling of the more liberal New Deal agencies, the struggle over the National Service Act, and the internment of Japanese-Americans, see Richard Polenberg, *War and Society* (Philadelphia, 1972), pp. 60–89, 177–183. The *New Leader* was editorially silent on the internment of the Japanese-Americans; its silence can only be interpreted as meaning it did not consider the action an outrage. It printed a couple of articles that

spoke of West Coast hysteria, but it also printed one that seemed to justify the action and one that concluded that the scarcity of necessary material made it "difficult to form an intelligent opinion." See Robert Henderson, "West Coast Hysteria Hits Japs," *NL* (December 20, 1941), p. 1; *NL* (January 10, 1942), p. 2; George Short, "Coast Panic Lumps 'Good and Bad' Aliens in Drive to Clear Pacific Area," *NL* (February 7, 1942), p. 2; Harvey Wolf, "West Coasters Fear of Sabotage Rises," *NL* (February 21, 1942), p. 5; *NL* (March 7, 1942), pp. 1, 7; Robert Plank, "Coast Hysteria," *NL* (March 21, 1942), p. 5. The type of articles the *New Leader* published on the "Japanese mind" were hardly designed to make its readers worry much about the rights of those of Japanese ancestry. See Edward Hunter, "Scratch a Jap, and You'll Find a Fanatical Shinto Priest—An Essay in Nipponese Psychology," *NL* (May 2, 1942), pp. 5, 7. The *Nation* and the *New Republic* printed a number of articles and editorials highly critical of the methods used in evacuation, the hysteria surrounding it, and the conditions in the camps. But they never challenged the right of the government to take such actions as a wartime measure. Thus they skirted the basic civil liberties question. See Robert Bendiner, "Cool Heads or Martial Law," *N* (February 14, 1942), pp. 183–184; *N* (February 21, 1942), p. 206; *N* (June 6, 1942), p. 643; Charles Inglehart, "Citizens Behind Barbed Wire," *N* (June 6, 1942), pp. 649–651; Marvin Randall Parsons to *N* (June 6, 1942), p. 666; Rockwell D. Hunt to *N* (June 20, 1942), p. 722; M. S. Heinemann to *N* (June 20, 1942), p. 722; John Larison, " 'Jap Crow' Experiment," *N* (April 10, 1943), pp. 517–519; *N* (March 4, 1944), p. 261; *N* (May 6, 1944), p. 527; *NR* (December 15, 1941), p. 814; Carey McWilliams, "California and the Japanese," *NR* (March 2, 1942), pp. 295–297; McWilliams, "Japanese Out of California," *NR* (April 6, 1942), pp. 456–457; Richard Lee Strout, "The War and Civil Liberties," *NR* (March 16, 1942), p. 355; *NR* (May 25, 1942), p. 716; *NR* (June 15, 1942), pp. 815–816; Ted Nakashima, "Concentration Camp: U.S. Style," *NR* (June 15, 1942), pp. 822–823; *NR* (June 22, 1942), pp. 848–849; *NR* (August 10, 1942), p. 158. In addition to his comments on the disloyal "Japs," Oneal wrote: "The sappy Civil Liberties crowd is giving comfort to the most dangerous fifth column in the United States by its action in this matter." See Oneal to Algernon Lee, March 6, 1942 (in JO Papers). If Oneal was thinking of the American Civil Liberties Union in particular, his remarks were even more scandalous, since that organization was lax in its protest about the civil liberties issues involved. See Thomas to John Haynes Holmes, March 9, 1942;

Holmes to Thomas, March 12, 1942; Thomas to Roger Baldwin, September 1, 1942; Holmes to Thomas, November 13, 1942; Thomas to Holmes, November 14, 1942; Arthur G. Hays to Thomas, November 16, 1942; Baldwin to Holmes, November 18, 1942; Thomas to Baldwin, November 20, 1942 (in NT Papers); *SC* (November 27, 1942), p. 8. For Thomas's and the Socialist Party's criticism of the internment of Japanese-Americans and the rationalizations for it, see Thomas, *Democracy and Japanese Americans* (New York, 1942); Thomas to Hon. Francis Biddle, February 13, 1942 (in NT Papers); *SC* (February 21, 1942), p. 4; Travers Clement, "The Re-Winning of the West," *SC* (February 21, 1942), p. 1; Thomas, *SC* (March 7, 1942), p. 5; *SC* (March 14, 1942), p. 4; Lillian Symes, *SC* (March 28, 1942), p. 2; Thomas, *SC* (March 28, 1942), p. 3; Clement, " 'Git Movin'—A Shameful Chapter in Our History," *SC* (April 4, 1942), pp. 1, 7; *SC* (April 18, 1942), pp. 1, 4; *SC* (May 1, 1942), p. 16; *SC* (May 8, 1942), pp. 1, 8; Thomas, *SC* (May 22, 1942), pp. 1, 3; Clement, "Our First Official Internment Camps," *SC* (May 22, 1942), p. 5; *SC* (August 7, 1942), p. 4; Thomas, *SC* (August 21, 1942), pp. 3, 5; *SC* (September 4, 1942), pp. 1, 4; Thomas, *SC* (December 25, 1942), pp. 1, 8; Maynard Krueger, Memo to the National Action Committee, 1942 (in SP Papers, Duke).

26. Richard Polenberg acknowledges the mixed record of World War II civil liberties and feels that it is incorrect to compare the situation to World War I. See Polenberg, *War and Society,* pp. 37–72. A survey of a number of standard college textbooks reveals that the authors often cite the greater support for World War II than World War I, but then go on to write complacently of civil liberties in World War II, with the exception of the internment of Japanese-Americans. In *America and World Leadership 1940–1965* (New York, 1965), Dumas Malone and Basil Rauch write that the removal of Japanese-Americans was "the only important flaw in the governmental record" (p. 46). In *A History of the United States since 1865* (New York, 1959), T. Harry Williams, Richard N. Current, and Frank Freidel say that "the persecution of Japanese-Americans was the only major blemish in the wartime civil liberties record" (p. 571). In *American Epoch,* vol. 3, *1938–1966* (New York, 1966), Arthur S. Link writes: "The one great blot on the administration's otherwise excellent civil liberties record during the war was the detention and forced removal of Japanese Americans from the West Coast to internment camps in the interior" (p. 539). In *The Growth of the American Republic,* vol. 2 (New York, 1962), Samuel Eliot Morison and Henry Steele Com-

mager call the internment "the major exception to a clean record on civil liberties in this war" (p. 787). For Socialist and liberal protest of the prosecution of the Minneapolis Trotskyists, see *SC* (December 13, 1941), p. 4; James T. Farrell, "The Minneapolis Case and the Bill of Rights," *SC* (January 10, 1942), p. 8; *SC* (May 29, 1942), p. 8; Samuel H. Friedman, "High Court Must Reconsider Its Refusal to Hear Case of 18 Minneapolis Defendants!" *SC* (January 7, 1944), p. 1; *N* (January 8, 1944), p. 30; *N* (January 15, 1944), pp. 60–61; Thomas to Fay Campbell, November 2, 1941; to Charles R. Walker et al., October 6, 1941 (in NT Papers). The response to the government's prosecution of the Bundists or its ban on Father Coughlin's *Social Justice* was related to one's position on the limits of civil liberties in wartime. The prowar liberals were more apt to demand the curbing of the fascist press, support the sedition trial of the American fascists, and justify their position on the basis of the wartime struggle between democracy and fascism. Reinhold Niebuhr provided a theoretical rationalization for limiting civil liberties in wartime by arguing that certain periods required "closer social cohesion." The Socialists and the American Civil Liberties Union were more inclined to worry about the implications of limiting civil liberties, even those of the fascists in wartime. In late 1942, the A.C.L.U. decided not to take cases where the defendants either cooperated or acted on behalf of the enemy. On the issue of civil liberties during World War II, see Freda Kirchwey, "Curb the Fascist Press!," *N* (March 28, 1942), pp. 357–358; *N* (April 11, 1942), p. 412; Roger Baldwin to *N* (April 11, 1942), p. 444; *N* (April 25, 1942), p. 474; *N* (May 16, 1942), p. 558; Baldwin to *N* (April 25, 1942), p. 499; Alan Brown to *N* (May 16, 1942), p. 582; Reinhold Niebuhr, "The Limits of Liberty," *N* (January 24, 1942), pp. 86–88; Baldwin to *N* (February 7, 1942), p. 175; James N. Rosenberg, "Words Are Triggers," *N* (May 2, 1942), pp. 511–512; Arthur G. Hays, "Indictments Pull the Triggers," *N* (May 9, 1942), pp. 543–545; Rosenberg to *N* (May 9, 1942), p. 555; John Haynes Holmes to *N* (May 23, 1942), p. 611; *N* (January 2, 1943), pp. 2–3; *N* (December 9, 1944), p. 702; *NR* (December 15, 1941), pp. 812–813; *NR* (April 6, 1942), p. 446; Michael Straight, "Hitler's Guerillas Over Here," *NR* (April 13, 1942), pp. 481–483; *NR* (April 27, 1942), pp. 559–560; *NR* (July 20, 1942), p. 69; *NR* (February 7, 1944), p. 166; Edwin A. Lahey, "Fascism's Day in Court," *NR* (June 5, 1944), pp. 759–760; *NR* (January 15, 1945), p. 69; *NL* (April 18, 1942), p. 8; Morris Ernst, *NL* (May 9, 1942), p. 5; Albert Sprague Coolidge, " 'Clear and Present Danger' Clause," *NL* (May 23, 1942), p. 4; Baldwin, "What

Liberties in Wartime?" *NL* (December 5, 1942), p. 4; Daniel Bell, "Sedition on Trial," *NL* (June 3, 1944), p. 5; SC (April 25, 1942), p. 8; *SC* (September 25, 1942), p. 8; Thomas, *SC* (September 25, 1942), p. 3; Thomas, *SC* (October 16, 1942), p. 3; *SC* (November 27, 1942), p. 8; *SC* (December 4, 1942), p. 8; Thomas, "The State of Wartime Civil Liberties," *SC* (November 17, 1944), p. 6; Thomas to Kirchwey, March 5, 1942; Kirchwey to Thomas, March 9, 1942; Thomas to Kirchwey, April 3, 1942; Kirchwey to Thomas, April 9, 1942; Thomas to Helen Phelps Stokes, April 28, 1942; to Paul Hutchinson, June 23, 1942; to Baldwin, September 1, 1942; to Albert Hamilton, October 7, 1942 (in NT Papers). On the New Deal and interracial violence during World War II, see Harvard Sitkoff, "Radical Militancy and Interracial Violence in the Second World War," *Journal of American History* (December, 1971), pp. 661–681.

27. On the United States and British imperialism, see Thomas to Comrade Levine, December, 1940; to Ralph Harlow, October 4, 1940; to Harold E. Gibson, October 8, 1940; to Mrs. Fred Becker, May 14, 1941; to Mina Lewis, March 5, 1941; to the Editors of *Common Sense,* September 3, 1942 (in NT Papers). On fears that the end result of the war would not be democracy, but rather imperialism and/or totalitarianism, see, e.g., *SC* (July 5, 1941), p. 8; Thomas, *SC* (July 5, 1941), p. 5; Thomas, *SC* (July 19, 1941), p. 5. On Far Eastern imperialism, see Thomas to Ralph Harlow, June 5, 1940; Thomas, "Outline of Town Hall Talk," December 8, 1941 (in NT Papers); *SC* (August 23, 1941), p. 2; *SC* (September 13, 1941), p. 1. On imperialism in South America, see Thomas to Alice Dodge, July 8, 1940; to Ralph Harlow, June 5, 1940; to Gerry [Allard], June 3, 1940; to Paul [Porter], June 6, 1940; to Harlow, October 4, 1940 (in NT Papers); S. Fanny Simon, "U.S., Latin America and Fascism," *SR* (March-April, 1939), pp. 5–6, 17; Simon, "Roosevelt and Latin America," *SR* (September-October, 1939), pp. 14–16; Simon, "Roosevelt, Latin America and the War," *SR* (November-December, 1939), pp. 9–12; Sidney Steinman, " 'South of Border' U.S. Theme Song," *SC* (September 14, 1940), p. 2.

28. For the response of the *Nation* and *New Republic* to the dropping of the atom bomb, see Freda Kirchwey, *N* (August 18, 1945), pp. 150–151; Kirchwey, *N* (August 25, 1945), pp. 170–171; J. D. Bernal, "Everybody's Atom," *N* (September 1, 1945), pp. 201–204; *N* (September 8, 1945), p. 213; *N* (October 13, 1945), pp. 355–356; *N* (November 17, 1945), p. 509; Kirchwey, *N* (November 17, 1945), pp. 511–512; Richard Schlegel, "Scientists of the World, Unite!" *N*

(November 17, 1945), pp. 515–516; King Gordon "The Bomb Is a World Affair," *N* (November 24, 1945), pp. 541–543; *N* (December 1, 1945), pp. 568–569; Special Supplement, *N* (December 22, 1945), pp. 701–720; *NR* (August 13, 1945), pp. 173–174; Bruce Bliven, "The Bomb and the Future," *NR* (August 20, 1945), pp. 210–212; *NR* (October 8, 1945), pp. 451–453; *NR* (November 5, 1945), pp. 587–589; *NR* (November 19, 1945), pp. 659–660; Raymond Blackburn, "A British Appeal on Atomic Energy," *NR* (November 19, 1945), p. 663; *NR* (November 26, 1945), pp. 691–692; Louis Falstein, "The Men Who Made the A-Bomb," *NR* (November 26, 1945), pp. 707–709; *NR* (December 31, 1945), p. 885. For the *New Leader*'s response, see Leo Comorau, "Atom Smashing Can Smash the World," *NL* (August 11, 1945), pp. 1, 16; Liston M. Oak, "The Atomic Age," *NL* (August 11, 1945), p. 16; William Bohn, *NL* (August 11, 1945), p. 10; Bohn, *NL* (September 8, 1945), p. 11; Eduard C. Lindeman, "Morality for an Atomic Age," *NL* (September 8, 1945), p. 4; William Green, "Labor and the Atomic Bomb," *NL* (September 8, 1945), p. 6; James Rorty, "The Atomic Apocalypse," *NL* (September 15, 1945), pp. 8–9. For the response of Norman Thomas and the Socialist Party, see *SC* (August 13, 1945), p. 1; *SC* (August 13, 1945), p. 5; Thomas, *SC* (August 20, 1945), p. 8; Thomas, *SC* (August 27, 1945), p. 8. For the response of one antiwar radical, see Dwight MacDonald, *Politics* (August, 1945), p. 225; MacDonald, "The Bomb," *Politics* (September, 1945), pp. 257–260.

29. Dwight MacDonald, "Notes on the Truman Doctrine," *Politics* (May, 1947), p. 86.

Chapter X Socialists and "Utopian" Politics

1. Devere Allen, "The Conquest of Industry," *ASQ* (March, 1935), p. 12.

2. Seidler, p. 217; Johnpoll, p. 247; Thomas, "An Open Letter to Prof. Reinhold Niebuhr," *SC* (August 4, 1944), pp. 1–2; *SC* (September 8, 1944), p. 5.

3. Hal Draper, "The Ultra Right and the Liberals," *New Politics* (Spring, 1962), p. 81.

4. Louis Hartz, *The Liberal Tradition in America* (New York, 1955), pp. 259–283; James MacGregor Burns, *Roosevelt: The Lion and The Fox* (New York, 1956), pp. 225–226. On the inadequacies of the Bankhead Bill, see Thomas to Senate Committee on Agriculture, May 7, 1935 (in NT Papers). On the overall inadequacies of the New

Deal's program for tenant farmers and sharecroppers, see M. S. Venkataramani, "Norman Thomas, Arkansas Sharecroppers, and the Roosevelt Agricultural Policies, 1933–1937," *Mississippi Valley Historical Review* (September, 1960), pp. 225–246.

5. Randolph Bourne, "The Twilight of Idols," in Carl Resek, ed., *War and the Intellectuals* (New York, 1964), pp. 61–62.

6. Leszek Kolakowski, *Toward a Marxist Humanism* (New York, 1968), pp. 70–71.

7. John Kenneth Galbraith, *The New Industrial State* (Boston, 1968).

8. Ray Ginger, *The Bending Cross* (New Brunswick, 1949), pp. 116–120.

9. Ibid., p. 119.

10. Johnpoll, pp. 292–293.

11. Schlesinger, *The Vital Center,* p. 56; Bell, *The End of Ideology,* p. 407.

Index

Abraham Lincoln Brigade, 155
Adamic, Louis, 143
Agricultural Adjustment Act (A.A.A.), 125, 128, 132, 184
Alexander, Charles, 253n13
Allard, Gerry, 250n3
Allen, Devere, ix, 176, 213n1, 216n12, 245n32
Altman, Jack, 84, 111, 114; and American Labor Party, 84, 85, 88, 90, 95–103 passim, 107; and Trotskyists, 85, 103, 104; and Norman Thomas, 87, 88, 107; and 1937 mayoralty campaign, 90, 95, 96, 102; and Clarity, 4, 93, 102; and foreign policy, 103, 104, 114, 159, 248–249n2; and 1940 presidential campaign, 104; and Union for Democratic Action, 211n1
America First Committee, 163
American Civil Liberties Union, 169, 258n25, 260n26
American Committee to Defend Leon Trotsky, 38, 143
American Federation of Labor (A. F. of L.), 21–36 passim, 52, 110, 111
American Guardian, 75
American Labor Party, 10, 77, 78, 92; and Socialist Party, 81–108 passim, 120, 150
American League Against War and Fascism, 113
American Railway Union, 187, 188
American Socialist Monthly, 141
American Socialist Quarterly, 29
Americans for Democratic Action, 50
American Student Union, 114, 149, 150, 154
Ameringer, Oscar, 76. *See also American Guardian*

Ameringer, Siegfried, 76, 216n12
Atom bomb, 173, 174

Bakunin, Michael, 139, 164
Ball, John, 82
Barcelona uprising, 41, 154, 155
Baron, Sam, 41, 42, 152–153, 156, 243n29, 247n36
Becker, Carl, 134
Becker, Lazar, 98–99, 248n2
Bell, Daniel, x, xi, xii, 50, 125, 141, 189; and "realist" critique, 4–7 passim, 200n2, 200n3; and "in-of" world, 43, 44, 45, 49; and Socialist Party failures, 116–120 passim; and Spanish Civil War, 152, 153, 157; and Union for Democratic Action, 211n1
Berenberg, David, 141–145 passim
Berger, Victor, 10
Berle, A.A., 92
Biemiller, Andrew, 11, 14, 71, 72, 113, 211n1
Bingham, Alfred, 52–54, 62–68 passim, 69, 73, 108, 120. *See also Common Sense*
Blanshard, Paul, 73, 74, 89, 108
Blum, Leon, 153
Bourne, Randolph, 145, 170, 185, 186, 255n20
Bowers, Claude, 157
British Labor Party, 50
Brookwood Labor College, 23
Browder, Earl, 147, 148. *See also* Browder-Thomas debate
Browder-Thomas debate, 13, 148, 240n21, 240n22
Burns, James MacGregor, 184

Caballero Largo, 153, 156
California Socialists, 37, 74, 75, 76
Calverton, V.F., 135, 212n7, 238n19